Contents

English for Specific Purposes in Theory and Practice

EDITED BY DIANE BELCHER

Ann Arbor
University of Michigan Press

Copyright © by the University of Michigan 2009
All rights reserved
Published in the United States of America
The University of Michigan Press
Manufactured in the United States of America

∞ Printed on acid-free paper

ISBN-13: 978-0-472-03384-3

2012   2011   2010   2009   4   3   2   1

What ESP Is and Can Be: An Introduction

DIANE BELCHER
Georgia State University

> *General (language for no purpose) courses at any proficiency level almost always teach too much, e.g., vocabulary, skills, registers or styles some learners do not need, and too little, e.g., omitting lexis and genres that they do. Instead of a one-size-fits-all approach, it is more defensible to view every course as involving specific purposes. . . . (Long, 2005, p. 19)*

Ideally, as Michael Long suggests, English, or any language, is taught with specific purposes explicitly in mind. The reality, of course, is that the purposes served in language instruction are not always those of the language learners, so the instruction may look to learners like "language for no purpose," to borrow Long's words, or more troubling, like language for other people's purposes (i.e., individuals or even national entities in positions of power; see Morgan & Fleming, this volume). Commitment to the goal of providing language instruction that addresses students' own specific language learning purposes is what those who take an English for Specific Purposes (ESP)[1] approach see as distinguishing it from other approaches to English Language Teaching (ELT) (Hyland, 2002). However, while the

---

[1] We should note that the specific-purposes approach is not exclusive to the teaching of English; it can be used to teach any language, hence the broader term *Language for Specific Purposes (LSP)* also exists. Since this volume focuses primarily on the teaching of English, the term *ESP* will be used throughout.

goal of ESP—specific-learner-centered language instruction—may appear straightforward enough, how best to meet the goal may be less obvious. At the very least, the ESP approach requires a willingness on the part of the language educator to enter (not unlike ESP students themselves) as a stranger into strange domains—academic and occupational areas that may feel quite unfamiliar—and to engage in a degree of reflection that attempts to sort out the extent to which learners' purposes are actually served when the language practices of any target discourse community are taught (Belcher, 2006). For many involved in ESP, these intellectual and, some would add, ethical challenges (Hyland, 2006; Pennycook, 1997) are among the main reasons why they find ESP exciting, intellectually stimulating, and professionally and personally gratifying.

One gets a sense of the enormous range of domains that ESP specialists enter into by noting just some of the seemingly endless acronyms generated by the various branches of ESP. There are, and no doubt will be, as many types of ESP as there are specific learner needs and target communities that learners wish to thrive in. Perhaps the best known of these (especially among language educators who are themselves most often situated in academia) is EAP, or English for Academic Purposes, tailored to the needs of learners at various, usually higher, educational levels (see Hyland, 2006, for an excellent overview of EAP issues and practices). Less well known (to many academics) and potentially more diversified, given the breadth and variety of the worlds of work, is EOP, or English for Occupational Purposes. The fastest growing branches of EOP are those associated with professions that are themselves constantly expanding and generating offshoots, such as EBP, English for Business Purposes; ELP, English for Legal Purposes; and EMP, English for Medical Purposes. There are also numerous other less well known but equally intriguing varieties of EOP, such as English for Air Traffic Controllers, English for Tourist Guides, English for Horse Breeders, and English for Brewers.[2] The ESP picture is further complicated by numerous hybrid permutations of EOP and EAP, combining elements of both, such as EAMP, English for Academic Medical Purposes (for health science students); EABP, English for Academic Business Purposes (for students majoring in business), and EALP, English for Academic Legal Purposes (for law students). EAP, EOP, and still further combinations of both are not the whole story either, as socially conscious ESP specialists have begun to consider highly specialized sociocultural purposes too (hence, English for Socio-

---

[2]For more extensive lists of ESP varieties see Dudley-Evans & St. John (1998), Hutchinson & Waters (1987), and Orr (2002).

cultural Purposes, or ESCP; see Master, 2000, and de Silva Joyce & Hood, this volume) by addressing such needs as those of language and literacy learners who are incarcerated, coping with physical disabilities, or seeking citizenship (Belcher, 2004, 2006; Morgan & Fleming, this volume). What Hyland (2006) has recently observed of EAP is arguably also an apt descriptor of ESP in general: its motivation to help those especially disadvantaged by their lack of language needed for the situations they find themselves in, hope to enter, or eventually rise above.

This commitment to the purposes of the learners themselves is, to reiterate, what unites all the various branches of ESP. What the commitment entails is (1) first and foremost (before, during, and even after instruction), finding out what learners' needs are, then (2) developing or adapting materials and methods to enable needs-responsive instruction while concurrently (3) acquiring the expertise to function as needs-knowledgeable instructors (Dudley-Evans & St. John, 1998; Robinson, 1991).

Needs First

As a learner needs–based approach, ESP practitioners are, not surprisingly, particularly interested in the gap between learners' current and target competencies. This may at first sight not seem so different from the interests of many other language educators, even those teaching language for general— or in Long's terms, "no"—purposes. It is probably safe to say that most language instruction attempts to address learners' present needs, having gauged current proficiency levels (e.g., elementary, intermediate, advanced) with the help of test scores or educational background information. Less common outside of ESP, however, is a determination to identify and explicitly address specific **target** needs—that is, not the needs of generalized language learners but those of specific learners eager to join the "literacy clubs" (Smith, 1988) or ongoing conversations of target discourse communities, or what Ann Johns (this volume) refers to as the "target situation." Far from assuming that they already know what their students at a certain proficiency level need, ESP specialists accept responsibility for finding out what their learners will likely need (and want) to be able to read, write, speak, and comprehend as listeners to achieve their goals.

Acceptance of this needs-identifying responsibility means that well before actual instruction begins, ESP course designers will have collected and examined data, usually in the form of sample texts and audio or video recordings, from the target community, often with guidance, via interviews, from community insiders (see Long, 2005, for much fuller discussion of needs analysis than possible here). Informed by recent developments in genre theory (Hyland, 2004; Paltridge, 2001; Swales, 1990, 2004), ESP specialists proceed with discourse-sample analysis, by considering, ideally, both macro- (rhetorical, whole-text) and micro- (lexicogrammatical) level characteristics of the written and spoken genres (i.e., routine communicative events) represented, such as memos, conference presentations, progress reports, job interviews, or whatever else seems salient. Of interest will be not just these genres in isolation, but the contexts in which they function and interact with other genres: how one genre responds to others (intertextuality or interdiscursivity), such as application letters in response to job ads, and how they, in turn, form large community-specific genre colonies or networks (Bhatia, 2004, this volume; Cheng & Mok, 2008). Attention is also ideally given to how target genres vary within and across communities, how they allow room for personal agency or "voice," as well as to how they change over time. Rapidly evolving cyber genres like videoconferences, blogs, and email as used in specific communities are conspicuous examples of the dynamism and variability of genres, as new media and rhetorical situations develop, that ESP needs analysts need to be mindful of (see Nickerson & Planken, this volume).

While advances in technology, with resulting increased instability and proliferation of genres, may make the aims of ESP needs analysis seem like a moving target (metaphorically and actually), technology now also offers the means of making such assessments easier, more efficient, and more thoroughly empirical, and therefore less dependent on analyst intuition about specific registers (i.e., the linguistic features characteristic of genres in specific domains; see de Silva Joyce & Hood, this volume). Corpus linguistics, or computer-assisted collection and analysis of massive amounts of language data, has given ESP specialists access to mega-databanks of authentic spoken and written discourse (for a broader overview of what corpora can offer ESP, see Gavioli, 2005). Probably the best known, and certainly the largest, of these is the more than 500 million word (and still growing) Bank of English, with samples of written and spoken English representing a huge range of sources, including newspapers, textbooks, websites, television and radio broadcasts, meetings, and conversations (see, for example, www.titania.bham. ac.uk). Of increasing interest to many in ESP, as a result of the global spread and use of English, is the new corpus VOICE, the Vienna-Oxford International Corpus of English (www.univie.ac.at/voice/index.php), focusing exclusively on spoken English as a Lingua Franca (or ELF, English as used by speakers whose first language is not English, such as Korean and

German business associates) (see Planken & Nickerson on BELF, Business English as a Lingua Franca, this volume). A somewhat different perspective on the global use of English is offered by ICE (International Corpus of English, see www.ucl.ac.uk/english-usage/ice), with both written and spoken material representing a growing number of national and regional varieties of English. Another more specialized corpus, especially useful for EAP, is MICASE, the Michigan Corpus of Academic Spoken English (www.hti.umich.edu/m/micase), with transcriptions and sound files of higher education speech events like dissertation defenses, large and small class lectures, seminar discussions, student advising sessions, and service encounters.

With the help of relatively accessible concordancing software, such as MonoConc Pro and Wordsmith Tools (for extremely teacher-friendly concordancing assistance, see The Compleat Lexical Tutor at http://132.208.224.131), ESP specialists can now even compile and analyze their own small, specialized corpora of expert and learner texts, and thus determine the distribution of specific lexical and grammatical features within and across texts (Coxhead & Byrd, 2007; Reppen, 2001). Frequency data obtained with such software also make it possible to identify differences (and parallels) between domain-specific genres and more everyday language use through comparison of self-compiled corpora with data from existing large general corpora such as the Bank of English (Flowerdew, 2005; Gavioli, 2005). Even ESP students themselves, when trained in corpus tool use, can contribute to needs analysis by mapping the distance between their own and their target community's communicative performances (see Lee & Swales, 2006). As Lee and Swales remark, such tools have the added benefit of empowering learners to determine their own target needs, or goals, without reliance on "native speaker" (or even teacher) judgments of appropriateness.

Other recent developments in both qualitative and quantitative data collection have greatly increased the ability of ESP specialists to collect both "subjective" and "objective" needs data, or newcomer perceptions and old-timer expectations (Hyland, 2006; Lave & Wenger, 1991).[3] Scientific survey methods, for example, can tap into the varied, not-infrequently conflicting

---

[3]Long (2005) urges us not to over-privilege learners, or "newcomers," as informants on present and, especially, future needs. Morgan and Fleming (this volume), however, worry that too often not enough attention is given to learner concerns. Both views serve to underscore the value of multiple perspectives for needs analysis (i.e., triangulation, or better yet, analytic induction, on which see Silverman, 2006), as any single perspective is inevitably partial.

perspectives of large numbers of stakeholders, as Chia, Johnson, Chia, and Olive (1999) found in their survey of more than 300 Taiwanese medical students' and their professors' differing views of the main English language competencies needed by the students. Still more fine-tuned target needs data can be collected through ethnographic methods, as Bosher & Smalkoski (2002) discovered in their on-site observation and interviews of faculty and immigrant students in a U.S. nursing program. Journal entries from the student nurses augmented the ethnographic needs assessment by opening a window on culture and gender-related issues and revealing a need for assertiveness training that might not have otherwise surfaced. Another ethnographic technique, prolonged participant engagement, which Jasso-Aguilar (1999) very actively accomplished by working alongside hotel housekeeper language learners, can provide a deeply emic (insider) perspective on the actual day-to-day language needs and desires of learners, and may uncover, as it did for Jasso-Aguilar, the limitations (and possible motivations) of top-down managerial views of what learners need. Analysis of ethnographic data itself can be greatly facilitated by concordancing technology. Concordanced transcriptions of recorded data from Shi, Corcos, & Storey's (2001) months-long study of Hong Kong hospital ward teaching sessions helped reveal to researchers the common topics, types of interactions, and interlocutor roles, but also the importance of bilingual competence, in colloquial Cantonese and technical English, for successful patient/student/preceptor communication.

As valuable as recent theoretical, technological, or methodological advancements have been for needs analysis, an equally if not more significant contribution to the efficacy of needs analysis is the seemingly simple realization that needs assessment is best when ongoing. Learners themselves, especially when already in the target setting, can provide crucial data on the effectiveness of concurrent ESP instruction and identify new target needs that emerge as their community immersion deepens. Even after an ESP course ends, there is good reason for needs analysis to continue. Eggly's (2002) use of extended post-course videotaping of international medical residents interacting with their patients in a U.S. clinic not only provided information on any additional individualized ESP support needed but, at the same time, served as a means of helping the residents monitor and consider how to address their own ongoing needs (see Hussin, 2002, p. 35, on developing a "reflective practice model").

If needs analysis is now seen as previously too narrowly procedurally conceived as a one-time-only, pre-instruction investigation, it is now also seen as having been too ideologically narrow (Benesch, 2001; Pennycook, 1997;

see also Basturkmen, 2006, on ESP's need for more widely encompassing social theory). Key to this critical-theory-informed reconceptualization is recognition that any target discourse community is situated in other, still larger socioeconomic and political realities, and any community member, or would-be member, holds numerous subject positions, as citizen/non-citizen, insured/uninsured, steadily employed/transiently employed, or minority/majority race/ethnic group member, etc. (Morgan & Fleming, this volume; Vandrick, forthcoming). Too narrowly defining the target discourse community or the goals of those on the periphery of it can lead to too pragmatically identifying learners' target needs as what is necessary for assimilation in and accommodation to an existing hierarchy, which in turn could limit future options (on the need for **critical** pragmatism, see Pennycook, 1997). In her own broadly conceived needs analysis of immigrant factory workers in Chicago, Garcia (2002) found that while they certainly needed language to successfully function in the workplace, they had other goals and interests that extended well beyond their immediate factory floor needs, such as learning to use computers.

Target discourse communities may themselves too narrowly define what they are, as, for instance, in the case of academic communities viewed by domain experts as places where students should cover a certain amount of subject-area material in a certain amount of time no matter what their educational/linguistic/cultural backgrounds. Re-visioning needs analysis as **rights** analysis, Benesch (2001) has argued, can enable ESP practitioners and their students to see target communities of practice as not solely defined by those in power, but as places where newcomers have rights too—to be included and accommodated—hence as interactive social systems that can, and should, change as new members join (see also Casanave, 2002). Cadman's (2002) redefinition of EAP as "English for academic possibilities" captures this broader way of defining any target discourse community and related "needs" of learners.

Needs-Responsive Materials and Methods

It would make little sense to seek needs assessment data as input for ESP courses if those who develop and teach them were then to choose generic, ready-made commercial materials unresponsive to the specific target needs so carefully identified. In addition to the input that needs analysis provides for course design, another noteworthy advantage to performing it is that the very materials collected can also serve as authentic, needs-specific course materials and task stimuli. Hussin (2002) notes how effectively materials "produced for purposes other than to teach language" (p. 27)—such as audiotaped phone messages, videotaped interactions, and written documents gathered on-site—can function as language teaching tools. Viewing needs analysis as ongoing, as recommended, has an added course materials benefit as well. Students' written and spoken texts analyzed as an ESP course progresses, and any additional expert texts collected, can inform the design of "data-driven" materials, derived from instructor-compiled learner/expert corpora (T. Johns, 1994; T. Johns & King, 1991). Technology facilitates not just the archiving and analysis of such data, but also relatively easy creation of tailor-made materials (see Jabbour, 2001, for examples; Coxhead & Byrd, 2007, on "gap-maker" software) and direct, anytime/anyplace access for students.

While tailor-made ESP materials have clear advantages in terms of authenticity and specificity, discerning ESP practitioners can make effective use of carefully chosen commercial materials, especially those produced by other ESP specialists knowledgeable about relevant discourse/genre research and theory as well as target-domain data. One such off-the-shelf resource for business English purposes, Nickerson and Planken (this volume) tell us, is Koester's (2004) *The Language of Work*, a textbook unusually well grounded in recent research and replete with authentic workplace data. For wider-angle approaches, as often needed in EAP classes with students studying a variety of subject areas, somewhat less specialized texts can be useful. Swales and Feak's (2000, 2004) textbooks for graduate students and junior-level professional academics are excellent examples of texts based on authentic academic materials for use with disciplinarily heterogeneous learners. The Swales and Feak texts actually offer the best of both wide and narrow angle approaches, by encouraging learners to move from more general observations about academic discourse to ethnographic analysis of data in their own fields.

Students can, indeed, provide significant course materials themselves when taught to function as ethnographers, that is, to find and learn from data in their own areas of interest, and hence promote their own academic (or occupational) literacy (awareness of a community's usual communicative practices; see Ann Johns, 1997, and this volume, on this "socioliterate" approach). The products of such ethnographic work, student-generated portfolios—which may include genre samples from student-selected subject areas in the form of hard copies or digitized versions of expert and student texts, recordings of lectures, or notes on informant interviews—greatly increase the likelihood of individual students' access to authentic materials truly relevant to their needs (on portfolio use for EAP undergraduates, again see Ann Johns, 1997; for graduate-level EAP students, see Hirvela, 1997; Lee & Swales, 2006).

At this point, it should be noted that the presence of authentic materials in a classroom is no automatic guarantee of authenticity. Some have even suggested that once removed from the contexts where they naturally occur, authentic materials are anything but that (see Widdowson, 1979). One approach to enhancing authenticity is the use of simulation, or tasks inspired by real-life communicative activities. For instance, to use EMP again as an example, students can engage in role plays as patients and medical practitioners after watching videos of experienced medical professionals (see Bosher & Smalkoski, 2002; Eggly, 2002; Hussin, 2002). Problem-based learning (PBL) is an increasingly popular type of simulation in various EOP and EAP contexts. PBL activities are designed to engage students in collaborative solving of typical field-specific problems, simulated or actually occurring, using as resources materials that the learners themselves find and critically analyze (see Belcher, this volume; Shi, this volume; Wood & Head, 2004). As with all ESP instruction, the goal of such authentic-as-possible tasks is not just to serve as vehicles for developing communicative competencies but to equip students with language learning and personal problem-solving strategies (i.e., increased metacognitive awareness) that they can carry with them into their target communities.

Of course, it would be impossible to fully prepare learners for all the routine (and less routine) communicative events they will eventually need to engage in, all the spoken and written genres they will want to be functionally competent with. Even if all the crucial target situations could be anticipated and delineated, classroom time constraints would force instructors to make difficult choices. Another type of strategy training beyond simulation and PBL that can help address this pedagogical challenge is rhetorical and lexicogrammatical consciousness raising, or, increasing awareness of how written or spoken texts accomplish what they aim for. Genre awareness, Devitt (2004; see also Ann Johns, this volume) argues, is a much more realistic goal than actual acquisition of a wide array of target genres, and it is a goal best met by first teaching students to analyze more familiar "antecedent" genres, such as personal narratives. With genre-analytical tools in hand and an awareness of discourse as discourse—capable of being deconstructed and demystified (Hyland, 2006)—learners can move on to analyze and eventually produce more sophisticated genres with, and later without, instructor guidance. Another scaffolded approach, aiming not just at genre awareness but also acquisition of a sequence of progressively more challenging genres (see de Silva Joyce & Hood, this volume) involves a careful cline of instructor support: first immersing students in genre samples, thus providing a text and context-rich environment, followed by teacher modeling of text construction, collaborative text construction, independent generation of texts, and finally critical reflection on what has been learned about the genre itself (as well as related domain knowledge)—both how it enables and how it constrains (Feez, 2002; Macken-Horarik, 2002; see also Cruickshank and de Silva Joyce & Hood, both this volume).

While learner autonomy may be the ultimate goal of any ESP course, or of any type of instruction at all, success in ever more demanding environments may be still more likely if learners are supported by further scaffolding in their new settings. ESP instruction, like needs analysis, is now seen as ideally extending beyond the classroom through support of more experienced others that newcomers will likely come in contact with (and may need to please). With such support in mind, Hussin (2002) has offered nursing preceptor workshops aimed at boosting mentoring skills, with advice on communication strategies and guidelines for giving constructive performance feedback. In academic contexts, subject-area faculty have been helped by EAP specialists to make their classrooms more language-learner friendly through such scaffolding strategies as vocabulary glosses, previews of complex lecture content, peer collaboration opportunities, and more frequent and incremental feedback on student writing—types of support helpful, certainly, to all students (see Snow, 1997). ESP specialists may not be able to radically transform target environments into more tolerant, accepting places for all language learners (but see Cruikshank, this volume, on collective contextual change efforts) or to significantly alter performance expectations, but they can work as change agents by contributing to heightened understanding of how to help learners meet academic, workplace, and their own expectations (see Hafernik, Messerschmitt, & Vandrick, 2002) As more diverse learner populations succeed in more fully participating in their target discourse communities, the learners themselves, through their presence and involvement, will alter not just the composition of those communities but very likely the tenor of interactions in them (on "tenor" and power relationships, see de Silva Joyce & Hood, this volume; for more on transformative pedagogies, see Morgan & Fleming, this volume).

Needs-Knowledgeable Instructors

Being an ESP instructor may now look like an even taller order than might first have been envisioned, calling for knowledge of genre theory, corpus tools, scaffolding techniques, as well as metacognitive and metadiscoursal awareness-building strategies. Yet all of these are areas clearly connected with language teaching and are more and more likely to be included in the ELT training that pre-service teachers receive (though instruction on application of ELT methods to ESP goals may be far less common). What ELT teacher training programs do not understandably usually aim to provide, however, is the specialist-area knowledge that ESP instructional methods often require. It is not usually a comforting thought, to say the least, for any teachers, novice or experienced, to realize that their students may know more about a crucial subject area (or the "carrier content") of a language course than they, the teachers, do. This for many may be the single most daunting aspect of the ESP approach to language teaching. The question that remains to be, addressed here is, How can ESP instructors meet their own teacher knowledge needs? Considered in a possibly more helpful light, it might be, How have ESP practitioners succeeded in gaining control of the knowledge they need to address their students' needs?

Some have suggested that ESP practitioners may not really need as much specialist (or target situation) knowledge as has been assumed. According to Ferguson (1997), what ESP practitioners actually need is knowledge **about** an area—that is, its values (e.g., what counts as support for arguments) and preferred genres, rather than in-depth knowledge of an area. Dudley-Evans and St. John (1998) similarly remark, "Business people do not expect a Business English teacher to know how to run a business; they expect knowledge of how language is used in business" (p. 188). In many EAP situations, such as those involving first- and second-year tertiary students not yet in a major field of study, knowing about academic literacies in general may serve instructors well, especially with respect to equipping students with rhetorical flexibility, ability to move with relative ease from the literacy demands of one subject area to another (Ann Johns, this volume). Even when teaching a more disciplinarily homogeneous group, such as engineering students, a very narrow-angled approach may not be essential. Miller (2001) has pointed out his own successful use of more generally accessible topics from popular engineering periodicals, which kept him and his students confident in his expertise vis-à-vis the material.

Another means of keeping the subject matter at manageable levels, for both students and instructors, is the sustained content-based approach to instruction (SCBI), or, essentially, subject-area course simulation. SCBI classes focus on a limited range of closely related topics for an entire term, with materials taken from actual subject-area textbooks, such as introductory biology or world history, but usually at a lower grade level than that of the students, such as elementary or secondary school books for a class of tertiary language students. In this way, specialist knowledge demands on the instructor and language demands on the students are kept at less than overwhelming levels (Weigle & Nelson, 2001).

There are times, however, when a more narrow-angled approach would seem to serve students best, as when they are already immersed in a workplace or in advanced study of a discipline, such as dissertation writers or law students (Northcott, this volume). In such cases, increasing one's own content-area knowledge may be essential (not to mention invigorating), and dipping into actual texts that one's students are coping with may be helpful (see Bruce, 2002, on the value of tort textbooks and Northcott, this volume, on other resources for ELP; see Eggly, 2002, on medical journals and textbooks for EMP). ESP practitioners should remember, though, that they need not see themselves as working in complete isolation (though physically they may be) and that others may have faced similar content-area challenges and shared solutions in the ESP research literature, in such journals as *English for Specific Purposes*, the *Journal of English for Academic Purposes*, and the *ESPecialist*. Other professional resources include such medical English websites as www.englishmed.com and www.hospitalenglish.com and conferences, such as those held by BALEAP, the British Association of Lecturers in English for Academic Purposes.

Content-area specialists can also serve as significant resources for more narrow-angled approaches. The same specialist informants consulted for needs analysis can function as continuing sources of support, lending sample documents and recommending authentic communicative tasks (see Dudley-Evans & St. John, 1998). Some subject-area specialists are even willing to act as specialist mentors while students in their discipline take EAP classes, providing feedback on student performance to complement (and often reinforce) that of the EAP teacher (see Cavusgil, 2007). Other subject-area specialists collaborate even more extensively by team-teaching courses with ESP specialists, thus giving students access to subject and language experts simultaneously (Cruickshank, this volume; Dudley-Evans, 1995; Shi, this volume). Another more common type of subject-area and

ESP specialist collaboration is in the form of linked ESP and subject-area classes, or "learning communities" (Ann Johns, this volume). Members of a learning community take the same cluster of classes—for example, the same EAP and introductory psychology and geology classes. Subject matter in the shared subject areas can then become a source of materials and tasks for the EAP class, and instructors of the clustered classes can easily consult with each other on the needs of the language learners (for EAP, see Ann Johns, 1997; for an EMP example, see Johnson, 2000). Ideally, students in learning communities also become sources of content knowledge, linguistic knowledge, and emotional support for each other (Benesch, 2001).

Students are, in fact, probably the most readily available sources of specialist knowledge in any ESP classroom. Dudley-Evans (1997) has observed that what may be most crucial to the success of any ESP practitioner is willingness to learn from and with one's own students. Student-compiled portfolios and problem-based-learning presentations referred to earlier can be significant resources not only for students but for their instructor as well. Collaborating with students on investigations of disciplinary or workplace discourse and even on assessment of learner performance, acknowledging the students' content-area expertise while serving as the language specialist, not only scaffolds the specialist-knowledge learning curve for the instructor, but also gives the student a valuable confidence-boosting role to play (which may be especially helpful to adult language learners; see Orsi & Orsi, 2002, on their work with professional brewers).

While respect for students' subject-area knowledge, that of domain experts, and for the specialist area itself is vital to any ESP endeavor, it is possible to be overly respectful. As suggested earlier, domain specialists in particular, because of the tacitness and automaticity of their expert knowledge of discourse practices, limited understanding of language and literacy acquisition, and perhaps too distant memories of being novices, may not be especially sensitive to newcomers' needs or knowledgeable about how to meet them (Benesch, 2001). The traditional epistemologies and goals of their domain can keep insiders from recognizing the interests and needs of increasingly locally diverse and globally connected populations of students or workers (Jasso-Aguilar, 1999). As domain outsiders, discourse analysts, and language/literacy-learning specialists attuned to cultural diversity, ESP practitioners are especially well positioned to critically reflect on and help others consider how a community can promote more inclusive participation. ESP specialists have their own professional expertise to offer—to those who already belong to communities that can be enriched by greater inclusiveness and to those who hope to join them.

Overview of Contents

This volume is divided into three parts: English for Academic, English for Occupational, and English for Sociocultural Purposes. The EAP section considers academic contexts at progressively more advanced levels, from secondary school to the pursuit of a profession in tertiary-level academia. The EOP section, an immensely diverse branch of ESP, focuses on what are, to all appearances, the fastest growing EOP offshoots: English for Business, Legal, and Medical Purposes. There is invariably some overlap between EOP and EAP, as business, law, and medical schools fall under the "academic" umbrella, yet the interests of ESP specialists in these areas range well beyond learners' needs in school settings and indeed include the needs of those already at work in their professional communities. The ESCP section pushes the boundaries of ESP to encompass the needs of those who do not neatly fit into either academic or occupational categories but who definitely seek membership in communities new to them, communities anywhere from immediate neighborhood to nation-state levels. Throughout this volume, readers will find some recurring motifs, such as globalization, English as a Lingua Franca, and migrant populations, which, in effect, function as unifying strands across many of the chapters and reminders that despite the distinct purviews of EAP, EOP, and ESCP, there are many concerns that those committed to addressing learner-focused needs share.

Part 1 opens with Ken Cruickshank's chapter on secondary-level EAP. As Cruickshank notes, while EAP is most frequently associated with postsecondary settings, efforts to serve English language learners situated in any school context are, in fact, a type of EAP. Cruikshank's concerns lie primarily with the effects of increasing global migrations and the large numbers of students in English-dominant settings, many with interrupted educations, who must cope with learning a new language and learning academic subject matter alongside well-acclimated students. The challenges of transitioning from secondary to post-secondary school, especially for immigrant or Generation 1.5 students, have long been the concern of Ann Johns. In her chapter, Johns readily acknowledges and addresses the difficulties EAP practitioners face in attempting to meet the needs of this population, beginning undergraduates whose target situations are as diverse as are their own often undecided academic goals.

The last two chapters in Part 1 both consider the challenges of much more advanced, post-baccalaureate language use in academia. Although the goals of those already in a specific field of study may be more easily defined than those of many undergraduates, a disciplinarily heterogeneous class of graduate students is far from undemanding for EAP practitioners. In her chapter, Christine Feak identifies graduate-level learner needs that cut across disciplinary boundaries, needs that EAP specialists are well qualified to address. Interested in the high-stakes language-use challenges that confront those who complete their graduate degrees and pursue careers as professional academics, Ken Hyland highlights in his chapter strategies that are likely to be of value to academics writing for publication in any discipline.

Part 2 begins with Brigitte Planken and Catherine Nickerson's paired chapters on English for Business Purposes (EBP), the first focusing on spoken discourse, the second on written discourse. While other EOP branches can be described as rapidly growing, EBP's growth is actually explosive, as businesses continue to barrel ahead toward globalization and English is increasingly the preferred medium (at least for now). In their first chapter, Planken and Nickerson point to great strides in our understanding of BELF, or Business English as a Lingua Franca. In their second chapter, Nickerson and Planken call our attention to research on the types of multi-modal communication increasingly crucial to day-to-day operations in international business settings.

Jane Lockwood, Gail Forey, and Neil Elias focus on one very specific subarea of EBP in which the recent phenomena Nickerson and Planken discuss—the global spread of business, English, and technology—all come into play. Lockwood, Forey, and Elias consider the language training needs of outsourced call centers, needs not currently addressed by popular assessment strategies developed in English-dominant settings.

At first sight, law may seem an EOP area less likely to be greatly affected by globalization, as laws are quite specific to local contexts, yet, as Jill Northcott remarks in her chapter, globalization is expanding the demand for legal English instruction (or ELP). While legal English may well be the most challenging of all occupational varieties of English for outsiders to comprehend, Northcott assures us that there is a growing body of resources available to ELP instructors. Among these resources is the work of legal genre analyst Vijay Bhatia, whose chapter sheds light on one of the main contributors to the density and complexity of legal discourse, namely, intertextuality.

The impact of globalization on medicine in some respects parallels that on law, though professional mobility in the medical sciences may be even greater as English-speaking nations become increasingly dependent on immigrant health care personnel. In her chapter on medical English, Ling Shi reports that EMP specialists have been in the vanguard among ESP practitioners in investigating face-to-face communication, especially its cultural and sociopolitical dimensions. In my own chapter, I discuss the benefits that a recent development in medical education itself, problem-based learning, offers to EMP pedagogical practice.

The focal area of Part 3, English for Sociocultural Purposes (ESCP), can be defined, Helen de Silva Joyce and Susan Hood observe (this volume), as neither EAP nor EOP, or as inclusive of all subtypes of ESP, all of which serve both social and cultural purposes. In their chapter, de Silva Joyce and Hood address one of the great challenges of ESCP: how to help immigrant learners meet immediate survival needs yet be prepared for less easily defined future possibilities. Brian Morgan and Douglas Fleming argue for a critical approach to ESCP, focused on the actual needs and rights of immigrant learners "as workers, family members, participants in community activities." This last chapter of the volume makes abundantly clear what the learner focus of ESP can contribute in the service of these (and many other) learners: ability to empower them, in the words of Morgan and Fleming, "to act on the world *purposively* through language."

REFERENCES

Basturkmen, H. (2006). *Ideas and options in English for specific purposes*. Mahwah, NJ: Lawrence Erlbaum.

Belcher, D. (2004). Trends in teaching English for specific purposes. *Annual Review of Applied Linguistics, 24,* 165–186.

————. (2006). English for specific purposes: Teaching to perceived needs and imagined futures in worlds of work, study, and everyday life. *TESOL Quarterly, 40,* 133–156.

Benesch, S. (2001). *Critical English for academic purposes: Theory, politics, and practice*. Mahwah, NJ: Lawrence Erlbaum.

Bhatia, V. K. (2004). *Worlds of written discourse: A genre-based view*. London: Continuum.

Bosher, S., & Smalkoski, K. (2002). From needs analysis to curriculum development: Designing a course in health-care communication for immigrant students in the USA. *English for Specific Purposes, 21*(1), 59–79.

Bruce, N. (2002). Dovetailing language and content: Teaching balanced argument in legal problem answer writing. *English for Specific Purposes, 21,* 321–346.

Cadman, K. (2002). English for academic possibilities: The research proposal as a contested site in postgraduate genre pedagogy. *Journal of English for Academic Purposes, 1,* 85–104.

Casanave, C. P. (2002). *Writing games: Multicultural case studies of academic literacy practices in higher education.* Mahwah, NJ: Lawrence Erlbaum.

Cavusgil, S. (2007). Establishing effective graduate student writer/mentor relationships. *HEIS [TESOL Higher Education Interest Section] News, 26*(2). Retrieved from www.tesol.org//s_tesol/sec_issue.asp?nid=2746&iid=9183&sid=1#382

Cheng, W., & Mok, E. (2008). Discourse processes and products: Land surveyors in Hong Kong. *English for Specific Purposes, 27,* 57–73.

Chia, H.-U., Johnson, R., Chia, H.-L., & Olive, F. (1999). English for college students in Taiwan: A study of perceptions of English needs in a medical context. *English for Specific Purposes, 18,* 107–111.

Coxhead, A., & Byrd, P. (2007). Preparing writing teachers to teach the vocabulary and grammar of academic prose. *Journal of Second Language Writing, 16,* 129–147.

Devitt, A. (2004). *Writing genres.* Carbondale: Southern Illinois University Press.

Dudley-Evans, T. (1995). Common core and specific approaches to the teaching of academic writing. In D. Belcher & G. Braine (Eds.), *Academic writing in a second language* (pp. 293–312). Norwood, NJ: Ablex.

———. (1997). Five questions for LSP teacher training. In R. Howard & J. Brown (Eds.), *Teacher education for LSP* (pp. 58–67). Clevedon, UK: Multilingual Matters.

Dudley-Evans, T., & St. John, M. J. (1998). *Developments in English for specific purposes: A multi-disciplinary approach.* Cambridge, UK: Cambridge University Press.

Eggly, S. (2002). An ESP program for international medical graduates in residency. In T. Orr (Ed.), *English for specific purposes* (pp. 105–115). Alexandria, VA: TESOL.

Feez, S. (2002). Heritage and innovation in second language education. In A. Johns (Ed.), *Genre in the classroom: Multiple perspectives* (pp. 43–69). Mahwah, NJ: Lawrence Erlbaum.

Ferguson, G. (1997). Teacher education and LSP: The role of specialized knowledge. In R. Howard & J. Brown (Eds.), *Teacher education for LSP* (pp. 80–89). Clevedon, UK: Multilingual Matters.

Flowerdew, L. (2005). An integration of corpus-based and genre-based approaches to text analysis in EAP/ESP: Countering criticisms against corpus-based methodologies. *English for Specific Purposes, 24,* 321–332.

Garcia, P. (2002). An ESP program for entry-level manufacturing workers. In T. Orr (Ed.), *English for specific purposes* (pp. 161–174). Alexandria, VA: TESOL.

Gavioli, L. (2005). *Exploring corpora for ESP learning.* Amsterdam: John Benjamins.

Hafernik, J. J., Messerschmitt, D. S., & Vandrick, S. (2002). *Ethical issues for ESL faculty: Social justice in practice.* Mahwah, NJ: Lawrence Erlbaum.

Hirvela, A. (1997). "Disciplinary portfolios" and EAP writing instruction. *English for Specific Purposes, 16*(2), 83–100.

Hussin, V. (2002). An ESP program for students of nursing. In T. Orr (Ed.), *English for specific purposes* (pp. 25–39). Alexandria, VA: TESOL.

Hutchinson, T., & Waters, A. (1987). *English for specific purposes: A learning-centred approach.* Cambridge, UK: Cambridge University Press.

Hyland, K. (2002). Specificity revisited: How far should we go now? *English for Specific Purposes, 21,* 385–395.

———. (2004). *Genre and second language writing.* Ann Arbor: University of Michigan Press.

———. (2006). *English for academic purposes: An advanced resource book.* London: Routledge.

Jabbour, G. (2001). Lexis and grammar in second language reading and writing. In D. Belcher & A. Hirvela (Eds.), *Linking literacies: Perspectives on L2 reading-writing connections* (pp. 291–308). Ann Arbor: University of Michigan Press.

Jasso-Aguilar, R. (1999). Sources, methods and triangulation in needs analysis: A critical perspective in a case study of Waikiki hotel maids. *English for Specific Purposes, 18,* 27–46.

Johns, A. (1997). *Text, role and context: Developing academic literacies.* Cambridge, UK: Cambridge University Press.

Johns, T. (1994). From printout to handout: Grammar and vocabulary teaching in the context of data-driven learning. In T. Odlin (Ed.), *Perspectives on pedagogical grammar* (pp. 293–313). Cambridge, UK: Cambridge University Press.

Johns, T., & King, P. (Eds.). (1991). *Classroom concordancing.* Birmingham: Birmingham University.

Johnson, K. A. (2000). Communication skills for international pharmacy students. In P. Master (Ed.), *Responses to English for specific purposes* (pp. 138–141). Washington, DC: Bureau of Educational and Cultural Affairs.

Koester, A. (2004). *The language of work.* London: Routledge.

Lave, J., & Wenger, E. (1991). *Situated learning: Legitimate peripheral participation.* Cambridge, UK: Cambridge University Press.

Lee, D., & Swales, J. (2006). A corpus-based EAP course for NNS doctoral students: Moving from available specialized corpora to self-compiled corpora. *English for Specific Purposes, 25*(1), 56–75.

Long, M. (2005). *Second language needs analysis*. Cambridge, UK: Cambridge University Press.

Macken-Horarik, M. (2002). "Something to shoot for": A systemic functional approach to teaching genre in secondary school science. In A. Johns (Ed.), *Genre in the classroom: Multiple perspectives* (pp. 17–42). Mahwah, NJ: Lawrence Erlbaum.

Master, P. (Ed.). (2000). *Responses to English for specific purposes*. Washington, DC: Bureau of Educational and Cultural Affairs.

Miller, L. (2001). English for engineers in Hong Kong. In J. Murphy & P. Byrd (Eds.), *Understanding the courses we teach: Local perspectives on English language teaching* (pp. 236–255). Ann Arbor: University of Michigan Press.

Orr, T. (Ed.) (2002). *English for specific purposes*. Alexandria, VA: TESOL.

Orsi, L., & Orsi, P. (2002). An ESP program for brewers. In T. Orr (Ed.), *English for specific purposes* (pp. 175–188). Alexandria, VA: TESOL.

Paltridge, B. (2001). *Genre and the language learning classroom*. Ann Arbor: University of Michigan Press.

Pennycook, A. (1997). Vulgar pragmatism, critical pragmatism, and EAP. *English for Specific Purposes, 16*, 253–269.

Reppen, R. (2001). Review of *MonoConc Pro* and *WordSmith Tools*. *Language Learning and Technology, 5*(3), 32–36.

Robinson, P. (1991). *ESP today: A practitioner's guide*. New York: Prentice-Hall.

Shi, L., Corcos, R., & Storey, A. (2001). Using student performance data to develop an English course for clinical training. *English for Specific Purposes, 20*(3), 267–291.

Silverman, D. (2006). *Interpreting qualitative research*. London: Sage.

Smith, F. (1988). *Joining the literacy club: Further essays into education*. Portsmouth, NH: Heinemann.

Snow, M. A. (1997). Teaching academic literacy skills: Discipline faculty take responsibility. In M. A. Snow & D. Brinton (Eds.), *The content-based classroom* (pp. 290–304). White Plains, NY: Longman.

Swales, J. (1990). *Genre analysis*. Cambridge, UK: Cambridge University Press.

———. (2004). *Research genres: Exploration and applications*. Cambridge, UK: Cambridge University Press.

Swales, J., & Feak, C. (2000). *English in today's research world: A writing guide*. Ann Arbor: University of Michigan Press.

———. (2004). *Academic writing for graduate students: Essential tasks and skills*, 2nd. ed. Ann Arbor: University of Michigan Press.

Vandrick, S. (2009). *Interrogating privilege: Reflections of a second language educator.* Ann Arbor: University of Michigan Press.

Weigle, S. C., & Nelson, G. (2001). Academic writing for university examinations. In I. Leki (Ed.), *Academic writing programs* (pp. 121–136). Alexandria, VA: TESOL.

Widdowson, H. (1979). *Explorations in applied linguistics.* Oxford, UK: Oxford University Press.

Wood, A., & Head, M. (2004). "Just what the doctor ordered": The application of problem-based learning to EAP. *English for Specific Purposes, 23*(1), 3–17.

Part 1

ENGLISH FOR ACADEMIC PURPOSES

1

EAP in Secondary Schools

KEN CRUICKSHANK
University of Wollongong, Australia

Abstract

The term EAP is not commonly used for second language teaching in schools even though ESL and increasingly EFL programs focus on teaching the discourse and genres of a range of disciplines. This chapter gives an account of recent developments in secondary school EAP. The shift to "mainstreaming" provisions in secondary EAP at institutional and classroom levels has led to a range of teaching approaches and interesting developments in the theorization of these approaches. The chapter argues that the opening of a dialogue between secondary and post-secondary ESP would enrich research and teaching in both areas.

Worldwide migration patterns and the globalization of education in the past two decades have led to increasingly diverse student populations in most Western countries. In the United States, for example, 9.9 million children and youth come from homes where languages other than English are spoken (Anstrom & Kindler, 1996) with more than 4.5 million in need of

English language support (Kindler, 2002). There are now also increasing numbers of international students undertaking secondary education in the United States, United Kingdom, Canada, New Zealand, and Australia. The challenge for immigrant, refugee students, and international students is that they need to simultaneously learn English, learn in English, and learn about English in a limited time in order to achieve academic outcomes.

Although the term *EAP* has not been commonly used in the secondary and primary/elementary school contexts, it could be argued that all TESOL in school contexts falls under the umbrella of EAP. The aim of school programs is to support second language learners in their development of the discourses and genres of a range of disciplines. TESOL specialist teachers identify learners' needs and curriculum requirements, develop appropriate programs, and work collaboratively with grade and subject class teachers to provide access to these curriculum areas. The development in school TESOL has paralleled the shifts in EAP, moving from narrow focus on grammar and skills training through learner-centered, needs-based pedagogies to approaches relying on contextual frameworks.

The debates around genre, discourse, and learner needs have figured as much in school TESOL as in post-secondary EAP. The two main differences lie in the differences of the learners and the nature of the learning contexts. First, school-aged second language learners have particular needs in terms of their linguistic, cognitive, and social development as they are still maturing cognitively and socially. Second, school curriculum and organization tend to be premised on the development needs of native speakers where students are grouped and promoted according to age. Large education bureaucracies are, therefore, less flexible and less able to adapt quickly to changing second language learner needs.

There are, however, two areas in which school TESOL could contribute to our understanding of EAP in general. First, there has been a robust and long-standing debate around the theorization of genre, language, and content, challenging static notions of academic discipline knowledge and language (Davison & Williams, 2001; Macken-Horarik, 2002). The developments in content-based learning, the exploration of the roles of genre and register in language and literacy teaching/learning, and the work linking activity theory with notions of intellectual challenge in TESOL are examples of this research. The reason for this focus has been that the justification for school ESL programs has always been the improvement of second language learners' educational experiences and academic outcomes. There is, therefore, a body of research into second language learning and educational outcomes drawing on linguistics, sociology, education, and other disciplines, exploring interrelationships between language and learning.

The second contribution of secondary TESOL to EAP stems from the mainstreaming of TESOL provisions in the United Kingdom, United States, and Australia. Despite the real problems of marginalization and underfunding in this process, there have developed dialogues between language specialists and mainstream institutions and disciplines in terms of program organization, policy, and curriculum. Government and education system policy generally mandate school ESOL programs as being cross-institutional responsibilities, involving collaboration between TESOL specialists, classroom teachers, and school executives. In many countries, TESOL is linked with bilingual provisions developed within a multicultural policy framework (Cummins, 2000; Leung, 2003; Meltzer & Hamann, 2005; Mohan, Leung, & Davison, 2001). Programs, therefore, generally address learner needs at program and institutional levels.

Background to School Programs

It is difficult to provide a thumbnail sketch of school EAP organization, as the substantial and long-standing TESOL programs in the United States, Canada, United Kingdom, Australia, and New Zealand are organized at different levels of government and have been influenced by differing policies, reports, and historical developments. In general, support tends to be provided:

- through *intensive/transitional support* in English and learners' first language. In Australia, Canada, and the United States there are intensive language centers or schools where learners are taught in all academic areas by TESOL specialists before transition to mainstream schools.

- through *direct teaching* in secondary schools. In Canada, Australia, and the United States, there is provision of ESL instruction (and sometimes first language) to groups of ESL students separate from grade or class peers. This instruction focuses on teaching academic disciplines with language support. The names for this form of support vary: sheltered English instruction, pull-out classes, bilingual classes (U.S.), withdrawal, elective, or parallel classes (Australia).

- through *team teaching* in secondary schools where ESL students are taught in mixed groups with native speakers. ESL and subject specialists can share responsibility for planning, programming, teaching, assessment, and evaluation. This can also be called group teaching, ESL push-in, partnership, and collaborative teaching.

The most common pedagogical approaches in secondary EAP are those coming under the rubrics of content-based instruction, task-based learning or text-type/genre teaching/learning. All of these approaches have research evidence supporting their effectiveness (Thomas & Collier, 1997).

The development in pedagogical approaches in secondary has paralleled the changes in post-secondary EAP. In the 1980s there was a shift from structural and situational syllabuses to learner-centered needs-based approaches. By the end of the 1980s communicative language teaching formed the basis of many TESOL curricula. Programs focused on *language across the curriculum,* teaching the lexis, and *functions* and *notions* appropriate to discipline areas (Wilkins, 1976). These learner-centered approaches stemmed from several quarters: from the work of sociolinguists such as Hymes in the United States and the concept of *communicative competence* (Canale & Swain, 1980; Hymes, 1972; Krashen, 1988); from the work on language use in social contexts and frameworks from the Council of Europe (Halliday, 1975, 1976; Van Ek & Alexander, 1980) and from the changes in mainstream educational approaches to teaching literacy in the United Kingdom and from the American approaches of *process writing* and *whole language* (Barnes, 1976; Britton, 1979; Goodman,1986).

There was also a dramatic shift to *mainstreaming* in the United Kingdom, Australia, and New Zealand, as language support moved to being delivered through team teaching in discipline areas to mixed classes of native and second language learners. The situation in the United States was much more complex where, for various reasons, the main provision has been through separate *bilingual* or *sheltered English content* classes. In the United Kingdom, the Bullock (DES, 1975) and Swann Reports (DES, 1985) led to the disbanding of Intensive English Centers and separate TESOL classes and to the provision of support through team teaching in mainstream classes. In Australia, team teaching increased from 27 percent of classes in 1984 to 71 percent in 1995. The shifts to mainstreaming were due to several factors: the need to cater to ever increasing numbers of students with decreasing resources; the changing nature of the ESL student population (over 60 percent were now second generation); the findings in all major reports that provision of language support needed to be integrated and that separate classes tended to "ghettoize" second language learners.

These reforms were accompanied by the development of policy, syllabus, and curriculum documents that reflected the needs of second language learners. In the United Kingdom, there is an official ESL policy document (SCAA, 1996); in the United States there are the TESOL Standards (TESOL, 1997); and in Australia there are policy documents and curriculum, syllabus, and assessment frameworks (NSW Board of Studies, 2000; NSW DET, 2004; VCE 2006). In the early 1990s, literacy emerged as a key issue in education systems in the United States, United Kingdom, and elsewhere. In the literacy debates, the dominant concern was with the *English* literacy needs of native speakers, and the *second* language and literacy needs were bypassed as TESOL was subsumed into (English) literacy programs (Lo Bianco, 1998; Moore, 1995).

There has been almost a complete absence of any evaluation of "mainstreamed" TESOL provisions since the 1990s and of the implementation of the policy and curriculum documents (with a few notable exceptions). It has been claimed that the effects of these changes have been the masking of funding cuts to TESOL and that "ESL students have been marginalized . . . within a mainstreamed context" (Mohan et al., 2001, p. 215). Despite the history and scale of school TESOL programs, there is still strong evidence from every Western country of lower educational experiences and outcomes for second language learners and, in particular, of differential outcomes for specific sub-groups (Haque & Bell, 2001; Khoo, McDonald, Giorgas, & Birrell, 2002; Portes & Zhou, 1993; Ogbu & Simons, 1998). There is evidence of lower high school completion rates and less access to post-secondary education. Several studies have found that immigrant students who enter school systems in late primary or secondary schools (now called Generation 1.5) are performing less well in post-secondary education than those who received all of their education overseas (Schmid, 2001; Harklau, Losey, & Seigal, 1999). In both Australia and the United States, for example, TESOL programs have been estimated to meet only 50 to 60 percent of identified need (Cahill, 1996; Schmid, 2001). There is also strong evidence that TESOL remains very much marginalized. Government policy and the organization of support at school level are decided not on student needs but on pragmatic reasons. There is a lack of teacher education with 60 percent of U.S. teachers of ESL students reporting little or no training in ESL (James & Schecter, 2000; Mohan, Leung, & Davison, 2001).

Relevant Theory and Research

The research base for secondary EAP is broad, drawing on education, sociolinguistics, psycholinguistics, psychology, sociology, and anthropology. One of the key issues in secondary EAP has been the ways in which content/academic disciplines and language are theorized and integrated, an issue complicated by the differing ways diverse research traditions understand these terms. Language has predominantly been interpreted as *communicative competence* (Bachman, 1990; Canale & Swain, 1980; Hymes, 1972). But the dichotomy of language and content this implies is untenable in sociolinguistic grammars such as systemic functional linguistics (Halliday, 1976), which view language as inseparable from social functions and defined by its meaning potential. This approach aligns very much with notions of genre (Johns, 2002) that have been so influential in post-secondary EAP, where texts both construct and are constructed by context; what counts as language and what counts as content is dynamic and shifting. In practice, however, professionals see themselves as distinct language or discipline specialists.

Davison and Williams (2001) characterize the different approaches to language and content integration along a continuum. Secondary EAP approaches on the "content" end of the continuum include CALLA (Cognitive Academic Language Learning Approach) (Chamot & O'Malley, 1992, 1994), the Knowledge Framework (Mohan, 1986), and task-based approaches (Leung, 2003). One criticism of all three approaches is that they reify and do not sufficiently engage with or challenge discipline knowledge, with the result that language is constantly being tailored to curriculum concerns (Davison & Williams, 2001). The challenge has been how to effect the selection and sequencing of both *content* and language in principled ways that are coherent both in terms of discipline and second language development and contexts of use. The following section describes three recent answers to this question:

- genre-based approaches in which selection and sequencing of syllabus content is based on language criteria and content ideally is tailored toward these needs

- pedagogical approaches working from neo-Vygotskyan and activity theory concepts as organizational tools for the curriculum, building on notions of genre and register from systemic functional linguistics

- institutional strategies and program organization built around second language learner needs

Genre-Based Approaches: Exploring Text and Context

The necessity to meet ESL student needs within the mainstream has, paradoxically, generated educational innovations based on the understanding that both native speakers and second language learners are learning English for academic purposes, and both groups are using language to learn.

One example of this is the research project that began in the 1980s in inner city Sydney schools with mixed populations of ESL learners and native speakers. In the *Language and Social Power Project* researchers examined the range of genres in primary and secondary schools and the application of genre-based approaches to teaching literacy (Callaghan, Knapp, & Noble, 1993; Callaghan & Rothery, 1988). The subsequent project, *Write it Right*, incorporated register-sensitive accounts of secondary school literacy with workplace literacies (Christie & Martin, 1997). This research drew on a linguistic definition of genre as "staged, goal-oriented, social processes" (Martin, 1984) and a curriculum cycle of teaching/learning drawing on the work of Vygotsky (1986) and notions of scaffolding (Bruner, 1986). The curriculum cycle strategies of building background knowledge, modeling, joint construction, and independent construction were central to the approach. Programs and findings have been reported widely in EAP literature (Macken-Horarik, 2002). The work from these projects has informed the development of syllabus and curriculum frameworks in Australia, Hong Kong, the United Kingdom, and elsewhere.

Macken-Horarik (2002) provides a detailed account of this approach with a secondary Grade 9 science class of mixed second language learners and native speakers of English. The unit focused on students' developing the ability to explain natural and technological phenomena and the processes surrounding human reproduction. The initial classroom work supported all students' oral language development through typical TESOL activity sequences. Students were then introduced to prototypical examples of science explanations and information reports; the structure and purpose of written explanations were discussed, modeled, and analyzed. Students in small groups jointly constructed their own explanations. There was also a focus on critical literacy where students problematized specialized knowledge, working on and discussing videos and texts on sex determination, IVF, surrogacy, and motherhood. Students were guided in their apprenticeship in the discipline of science from common sense to specialized knowledge and then to *reflexive knowledge*. This critical literacy stage occurred at the interface between the scientific and the social, focusing on the effect of scientific developments on everyday life. Macken-Horarik argues for the explicit teaching of language and *rhetorical competence* within a flexible approach to the curriculum cycle.

Interesting developments continue to emerge from the "Sydney Genre School." Several researchers are exploring the developmental tasks in achieving control of literacy in the transition from primary to secondary schooling as an important rite of passage (Christie, 2002; Coffin, 2003; Derewianka, 2003; Martin, 2003). One recent study is focusing on the texts that adolescents read and produce in the different discipline areas in the secondary school (Christie, 2005). Using a framework of systemic functional grammar the researchers are documenting writers' developing control of resources such as grammatical metaphor in a range of text types. The key aspect of genre in the Sydney School has been its use as a tool for exploring the curriculum demands and learner development of both native and non-native speakers.

Intellectual Challenge: Negotiating the Academic Knowledge

The second area of development in EAP in the secondary schools has been the linking of work on genre from the Sydney School with conceptual tools drawn largely from sociocultural theory, providing a framework for negotiating discipline knowledge and goals. American research into school change has been linked with a sociolinguistic approach to language, systemic functional grammar, to address TESOL concerns.

The reforms in American education following the report *A Nation at Risk* (1983) led to many movements espousing excellence and school restructuring. The Accelerated Schools movement, established in 1986 in the United States, aimed for academic improvement through the use of pedagogy developed for the gifted and talented to replace remediation in urban working class schools (Levin, 1987, 1998). The pedagogical changes draw on constructivist approaches with an emphasis on problem-posing and solving (Lave & Wenger, 1991). The rationale of this movement has been one of providing enriched instruction to help disadvantaged students attain results at or above national averages. The approach is characterized by high challenge and high expectations (Accelerated Schools Project, 2002). A second movement, Authentic Pedagogy, was developed in the United States to promote high-quality learning and high achievement through a focus on four aspects of classroom instruction: higher order thinking (which research indicates is less evident in disadvantaged and ESL classrooms); *substantive conversation,* or sustained interaction, between students and with the teacher; deep knowledge, or the development of complex understandings in topics or discipline areas; and the making of connections to the world beyond the classroom. The model also requires that the tasks students engage in involve higher-level organization of information, consideration of alternatives, elaborated written communication, and development of understanding of disciplinary content and processes. Authentic pedagogy has been the basis for similar Australian projects such as Productive Pedagogies and Quality Teaching. Although all of these approaches were developed in culturally and linguistically diverse educational contexts, none paid specific attention to issues of language.

Recent research has built on the American work in second language teaching and learning. The work has been based on three research projects:

- *Putting Scaffolding to Work for Language and Literacy Education: New Perspectives for ESL Education* (Hammond, 2008)
- the *ESL Pedagogy Action Inquiry Project* (2002–2007), a one-year action learning program involving ESL and class teachers (Kindergarten to Grade 11) with groups of ESL students in their classes
- *Challenging Pedagogies: Engaging ESL Students in Intellectual Quality* (2006–2008)

The studies and projects explored the implications of quality teaching for second language learners. A key finding has been in importance of scaffolding, both "designed-in" in the program planning and "contingent" at point of need (Hammond, 2001). For scaffolding to be effective for second language learners, teachers should use a range of diverse semiotic systems in building linguistic and conceptual understanding. They also need to focus on metalanguage and metacognitive awareness in developing learners' abilities to talk about and reflect on the nature of their own learning. Teachers developed a range of oral and written mediating texts to facilitate the scaffolding process. Finally, they need to implement sequences of tasks involving pair and group work drawing on ESL pedagogies. The key theoretical concepts in this work have been:

- *Rich tasks* that are problem-based, requiring deep understanding and featuring a real world–like setting; their "end product" is for an audience beyond the classroom; they require collection, organization, synthesis, and transformation of substantial amounts of information; rich tasks are also built into the learning process; a rich task is the "big idea" from a unit of work, relating to the essential questions that the teacher poses

(Gibbons, 2002, 2006). The notion of rich tasks has enabled discipline outcomes and content to be negotiated and clarified. Rich tasks have also enabled the identification of genres and language features integral to the achievement of the rich tasks.

- *Backward mapping,* the practice of working back from the rich tasks to devise a unit of work, the sequence of teaching/learning activities, and the genres and language skills needed.

- *Substantive conversation,* the interaction between teacher and students around conceptual understandings. This interaction builds and reflects communities of practice.

The projects implementing this approach involve groups of classroom teachers undertaking action inquiry with a particular focus on how students' oracy and literacy development can be integrated with content area learning. The majority of projects focused on science, history, geography, and business studies in Grades 4 to 9, and the research foci have been varied. Many have worked on issues relating to subject-specific genres such as exploring assumed cultural understandings, developing more formal spoken language and vocabulary, and working on sentence level grammar.

Case Study

Connell Park is a Sydney inner city working-class secondary school of some 800 students, 90 percent of whom are from language backgrounds other than English. Maha, a science teacher, and Stella, an ESL teacher, were working with a Grade 7 science class on a unit of work focused on gravity and friction. They chose their rich task from the Grade 7 science syllabus: Students needed to design, carry out, and report orally and in writing on their own science experiment relating to forces, gravity, and friction. This task involved their understanding scientific method, dependent and independent variables, and being able to apply these understandings to real life problems. Backward mapping forced the teachers to pare down much of the textbook content in order to focus on developing deep understanding of forces and also the skills relating to scientific method. Backward mapping gave teachers the tools to negotiate, select, and sequence subject skills, understanding, and knowledge along with the language and genres important in communicating these understandings. The unit drew on students' understanding of forces in everyday life through cars and football. The teachers worked through a range of TESOL activities such as dictogloss, sequencing tasks, group brainstorms, and other collaborative tasks to develop students' use of technical language and scientific understanding. There was constant recycling of key concepts such as dependent and independent variables. The teachers tracked the development of student language and literacy and conceptual understandings over the term. The team teaching, the nature of the action research, and the teacher inservice component have been keys to the program's success.

Whole School Change: Institutional Provision for TESOL

A third development has been the focus on whole school change and organizational issues in secondary TESOL. The specific institutional context is a key factor in any attempt to improve the educational outcomes and experiences of the students. External curriculum, teaching, and professional development initiatives and policies are re-contextualized differently in each institution. Goldenberg (2004) gives one of the few accounts of how the settings for change in culturally diverse schools can be established. His account of the failure of initial attempts to improve outcomes at Freeman elementary school with a large Hispanic population indicated the problem in adopting generic models of change. The key concept for Goldenberg was that of agency or setting, defined as "any instance in which two or more people come together in new relationships over a sustained period of time in order to achieve certain goals" (Goldenberg, 2004; Sarason, 1996). The elements that helped create a school context that was supportive of working to improve student academic outcomes were:

• goals that were set and shared
• indicators that would measure success of these goals
• assistance by capable other
• leadership that supported and pressured

These elements were used to influence teacher attitudes (such as their expectations for student learning) and classroom teaching (how and what they teach). Goldenberg and the school principal formed an academic expectations committee that developed common goals and indicators and linked with a set of other structures and initiatives in the school: teacher workgroups, grade meetings, and whole staff meetings. Over a five-year period, students' educational experiences improved and academic outcomes rose to be at or above state averages. The failure of the initiative to effect any sustained change because of change of personnel, funding cuts, and new district priorities led Goldenberg to conclude:

> the model did not work in the abstract nor disconnected from specific contexts . . . the model worked in settings—situations where people came together over a period of time to accomplish specific goals. (2004, p. 171)

Case Study: Organizational Change Working from Second Language Learner Needs

In 2001 Kotara High School was a school in Sydney, Australia, of 300 students of whom 95 percent were of Arabic-speaking backgrounds. The school had a retention rate of 40 percent to Grade 12 and on all tests the students were in the lowest 20 percentile in the state. Staff morale was low, partly because declining enrolments meant that positions were being lost. In 2005 the school population had grown to 800 and was culturally and linguistically very diverse. Student outcomes in standardized tests were at or above state average. The curriculum had expanded with a greater range of school subjects and additional offerings such as debating, drama, chess, and excursions. There was strong parental involvement and staff were participating in a range of committees. There was much more support for students in terms of developing English and their first language. How had this happened?

The new principal came from an inner city boys' school that had implemented radical changes in school management and teaching. Teachers and parents were engaged in developing policies, deciding on the type of school they wanted, and determining how they would achieve this. Policies addressed issues such as resources, classroom teaching, staff, and student attitudes and behaviors. Several initiatives emerged from this process:

- A leadership team with direction and involvement developed. The principal also worked with head teachers to promote various school improvements.
- Teachers and students initiated debating, drama, chess, dance, and performance groups.
- The curriculum was maintained and expanded even with small student classes: senior chemistry, physics, and advanced mathematics were kept going.

- There were workshops on planning and teaching, with a focus on implementing a more challenging, more scaffolded, and more language-inclusive curriculum. Each month teachers and principal would try out and report on different classroom strategies such as jigsaw learning, alternate questioning techniques, or the use of contracts. Successful strategies were continued.

Maria and Sen are two of the four ESL teachers at Kotara. Each year they undertake a whole school assessment to identify second language learning needs. They also consult with local elementary schools to target students in need of ESL. These students are then placed in a limited number of mainstream classes with native speakers and experienced subject teachers. Maria and Sen can then organize team teaching since their ESL students make up some 30 percent of targeted classes. Each of the ESL teachers specializes in different subject areas: Maria focuses on mathematics and science and Sen concentrates on history and geography. Their role in team teaching is usually as equals, taking joint responsibility with the subject teachers for planning, discipline, teaching, and grading. The teaching role depends on the class; sometimes they take an initial ten minutes on language work, sometimes they plan and run groupwork activities. They find that they tend to be involved in the teaching of genres and writing. The students are pre- and post-tested with each unit and Maria and Sen find this gives them a good idea of students' progress.

Maria and Sen also have parallel classes (or sheltered English instruction) in Grades 8, 9, and 10 for ESL students who need more help. They act as the English teachers, teaching the mainstream English curriculum but with greater support. Students requiring more intensive help are often directed toward additional elective language support classes: ESL teachers have offered courses in "Word Power," writing, grammar, and other areas. Finally, the school has initiated English classes for parents who have officially enrolled part-time at the school. Maria and Sen find this an exciting innovation for parents, many of whom had only one or two years schooling in their countries of origin. This case study exemplifies the importance of organizational strategies in secondary EAP. The effectiveness of specific programs relies on working from the needs, constraints, and resources in the institutional contexts in which programs are developed.

Current Issues and Future Directions

The example of Kotara High School is not common. TESOL programs in the United States, United Kingdom, Canada, Australia, and New Zealand have developed along different lines in response to system constraints more than in response to the needs of their international and immigrant learner groups, which in fact are similar across national boundaries. There is a need for a dialogue in each country to be initiated between secondary and post-secondary EAP so that the needs of learners can be addressed more effectively at both levels of education. Secondary EAP would learn from the flexibility and responsiveness of post-secondary EAP in meeting specific learner needs. Post-secondary EAP could benefit from the work done in exploring the language-content nexus in terms of classroom teaching and program organization.

Such a dialogue has become increasingly important in light of the changing migration and study patterns. The international student population is becoming increasingly diverse. Students are making their careers and lives between their countries of origin and their adopted countries. International students are also entering at secondary school levels more than ever before. In the past five years there have been dramatic increases in migration from West Africa, Sudan, Iraq, and Afghanistan, especially of refugee students with disrupted educational backgrounds. It has been difficult to shift resources to new areas of settlement. Established programs have had to be flexible in adapting to different needs. Program goals have also needed to be re-examined in light of changing global migration patterns. Increasingly, people are living and working across national boundaries; families are no longer defined geographically. Many ESL students will now spend their careers living and working between their parents' countries of origin, their adopted country, and elsewhere: the "tangled cultural experiences" and complex sets of affiliations that typify migrant families in modern society (Clifford, 1997; Inda & Rosaldo, 2002). The implications of this for EAP programs are that they need to provide access to educational opportunities and beyond; the goal is not just fluency in English for a specific course but fluent bilingualism and biliteracy for life and career. Secondary EAP teachers in both ESL and EFL contexts are facing a student population with vastly divergent English language learning needs and experiences.

The dialogue between secondary and post-secondary EAP also needs to occur in teacher education. Large numbers of second language learners have been in the schools since the migration programs of the 1950s, and yet it is still the case across the English-speaking world that the vast majority of teachers have no training in second language teaching and learning or second language development. With demographic changes and the shift in focus to second-generation migrants, it is increasingly the case that language needs must be addressed through mainstream classes. Second, ESL teachers are increasingly moving across sectors, between school, college, and other positions. Teacher education can no longer afford to focus on preparing graduates for one sector alone. The final issue is the globalization of teacher education itself. Teacher shortages in the United Kingdom, United States, and Canada have meant that TESOL/EAP teachers seek teacher education and teaching positions overseas. The push for English teaching in Asia and elsewhere has meant that many teachers also seek pre-service teacher education in the United States and United Kingdom. The increase in internationally educated EAP teachers has meant that the divide between native and non–native speaking teachers of English may finally be breaking down.

The final issue is the need for research drawing on the different research traditions in a principled way. Mixed method approaches, drawing on quantitative, qualitative, and linguistic tools provide interesting ways to frame research. Examples of these are EAP studies addressing the issues of text and context and studies in the United States and Europe exploring the language and learning needs and teaching programs of ESL students in specific locations. These research approaches provide ways to move beyond program-specific evaluations.

*   *   *

KEN CRUICKSHANK lectures in applied linguistics and teacher education in the Faculty of Education, University of Wollongong, Australia. He has taught ESOL for many years to teenagers and adults. His main research interest is literacy practices and second language learning and his most recent book is *Teenagers, Literacy and School: Reading and Writing in Multilingual Contexts*.

REFERENCES

Accelerated Schools Project. (2002). Retrieved November 2007 from www.acceleratedschools.net

Anstrom, K., & Kindler, A. (1996). *Federal policy, legislation and education reform: The promise and the challenge for language minority students* (NCBE Resource Collection Series No. 5). Washington, DC: National Clearinghouse for Bilingual Education. Retrieved November 2007 from www.ncbe.gwu.edu

Bachman, L. (1990). *Fundamental considerations in language testing.* Oxford, UK: Oxford University Press.

Barnes, D. (1976). *From language to communication.* Harmondsworth: Penguin.

Britton, J. (1979). *Language and learning.* Harmondsworth: Penguin.

Bruner, J. (1986). *Actual minds, possible worlds.* Cambridge, MA: Harvard University Press.

Cahill, D. (1996). *Immigration and schooling in the 1990s.* Canberra: Australian Government Publishing Service.

Callaghan, M., Knapp, P., & Noble, G. (1993). Genre in practice. In B. Cope & M. Kalantzis (Eds.), *The powers of literacy: A genre approach to teaching writing* (pp. 179–202). London: Falmer Press.

Callaghan, M., & Rothery, J. (1988). *Teaching factual writing: Report of the Disadvantaged Schools Program Literacy Project.* Sydney, Australia: Metropolitan Disadvantaged Schools Program.

Canale, M., & Swain, M. (1980). Theoretical bases of communicative approaches to second language teaching and testing. *Applied Linguistics, 1*(1), 1–47.

Chamot, A., & O'Malley, M. (1992). The cognitive academic language learning approach: A bridge to the mainstream. In P. Richard-Amato & M. A. Snow (Eds.) *The multicultural classroom: Readings for content-area teachers.* New York: Longman.

———. (1994). *The CALLA Handbook.* Reading, MA: Addison-Wesley.

Christie, F. (2002). The development of abstraction in adolescence in subject English. In M. Schleppegrell & C. Colombi (Eds.) *Developing advanced literacy in first and second languages: Meaning with power* (pp. 45–66). Mahwah, NJ: Lawrence Erlbaum.

———. (2005, September). *Advanced literacy development for the years of adolescence.* A plenary paper given at the Symposium on 'Imagining Childhood', Research Centre for Social and Policy Research, Charles Darwin University.

Christie, F., & Martin, J. R. (Eds.) (1997). *Genres in institutions: Social processes in the workplace and schools.* Henden, VA: Academic Press.

Clifford, J. (1997). *Routes: Travel and translation in the late twentieth century.* Cambridge, MA: Harvard University Press.

Coffin, C. (2003). Reconstruals of the past—settlement or invasion? The role of Judgment Analysis. In J. R. Martin & R. Wodak (Eds.), *Re/reading the past: Critical and functional perspectives on time and value* (pp. 219–246). Amsterdam: John Benjamins.

Cummins, J. (2000). *Language, power, and pedagogy: Bilingual children in the crossfire.* Clevedon, UK: Multilingual Matters.

Davison, C., & Williams, A. (2001). Integrating language and content: Unresolved issues. In B. Mohan, C. Leung, & C. Davison (Eds.), *English as a second language in the mainstream: Teaching, learning and identity.* Harlow, UK: Pearson.

Department of Education and Science. (1975). *A language for life* (Bullock Report). London: HMSO.

———. (1985). *Education for all* (Swann Report). London: HMSO.

Derewianka, B. (2003). Grammatical metaphor in the transition to adolescence. In A. Simon-Vandenbergen, M. Taverniers, & L. Ravelli (Eds.), *Grammatical metaphor: Views from systemic functional linguistics. Amsterdam studies in the theory and history of linguistic science. Series IV—Current issues in linguistic theory* (Vol. 236, pp. 185–219). Amsterdam: John Benjamins.

Gibbons, P. (2002). *Scaffolding language, scaffolding learning: Teaching second language learners in the mainstream classroom.* Portsmouth, NH: Heinemann.

———. (2006). *Bridging discourses in the ESL classroom: Students, teachers and Researchers.* London: Continuum.

Goldenberg, C. (2004). *Successful school change: Creating settings to improve teaching and learning.* New York: Teachers College Press.

Goodman, K. (1986). *What's whole in whole language?* Portsmouth, NH: Heinemann.

Halliday, M. A. K. (1975). *Learning how to mean: Exploring in the development of language.* London: Edward Arnold.

———. (1976). *System and function in language.* London: Oxford University Press.

Hammond, J. (Ed.) (2001). *Scaffolding: Teaching and learning in language and literacy education.* Sydney: Primary English Teaching Association.

———. (2008). Challenging pedagogies: Engaging ESL students in intellectual quality. *Australian Journal of Language and Literacy, 31*(2), 128–154.

Haque, Z., & Bell, J. (2001). Evaluating the performance of minority ethnic pupils in secondary schools. *Oxford Review of Education, 27*(3), 357–368.

Harklau, L., Losey, K., & Siegal, M. (Eds.) (1999) *Generation 1.5 meets college composition: Issues in the teaching of writing to U.S.-educated learners of ESL.* Mahwah, NJ: Lawrence Erlbaum.

Hymes, D. (1972). On communicative competence. In J. B. Pride & J. Holmes (Eds.), *Sociolinguistics* (pp. 269–293). London: Penguin.

Inda, J. & Rosaldo, R. (Eds.) (2002) *The anthropology of globalization: A reader.* London: Blackwell.

James, C., & Schecter, S. (2000). Mainstreaming and marginalisation: Two national strategies in the circumscription of difference. *Pedagogy, Culture and Society, 8*(1), 23–40.

Johns, A. M. (Ed.) (2002). *Genre in the classroom: Multiple perspectives*. Mahwah, NJ: Lawrence Erlbaum.

Kindler, A. (2002). *Survey of the states' limited English proficiency students and available educational programs and services 2000–2001 summary report*. Washington, DC: National Clearinghouse for Bilingual Education. Retrieved March 2008 from www. ncbe.gwu.edu/ncbepubs/sea reports/97-98

Khoo, S., McDonald, P., Giorgas, D., & Birrell, B. (2002). *Second generation Australians*. Report of the Department of Immigration, Multicultural and Indigenous Affairs. Canberra, Australia: DIMIA.

Krashen, S. (1988). *Second language acquisition and second language learning*. New York: Prentice Hall.

Lave, J., & Wenger, E. (1991). *Situated learning: Legitimate peripheral participation*. Cambridge, UK: Cambridge University Press.

Leung, C. (2003). *Integrating school-aged ESL learners into the mainstream curriculum*. (Paper 21, Working Papers in Urban Language and Literacies). London: Kings College.

Levin, H. (1987). New schools for the disadvantaged. *Teacher Education Quarterly 14*, 60–83.

———. (1998). Accelerated schools: A decade of evolution. In A. Hargeaves, A. Lieberman, M. N. Fullan, & D. Hopkins (Eds.), *International handbook of educational change* (pp. 807–830). New York: Teachers College Press.

Lo Bianco, J. (1998). ESL . . . Is it migrant literacy? . . . Is it history? *Australian Language Matters, 6*(2), 1 and 6–7.

Macken-Horarik, M. (2002). "Something to shoot for": A systemic functional approach to teaching genre in secondary school. In A. M. Johns (Ed.), *Genre in the classroom: Multiple perspectives* (pp. 17–42). Mahwah, NJ: Lawrence Erlbaum.

Martin, J. R. (1984). Language, register and genre. In F. Christie (Ed.), *Language studies: Children writing: Reader*. Geelong, Australia: Deakin University Press.

———. (2003). Making history: Grammar for interpretation. In J. R. Martin & R. Wodak (Eds.), *Re/reading the past: Critical and functional perspectives on time and value* (pp. 19–60). Amsterdam: John Benjamins.

Meltzer J., & Hamann, E. (2005). *Meeting the literacy development needs of adolescent English language learners through content-area learning: Part 2. Focus on classroom teaching and learning strategies*. Providence, RI: The Educational Alliance, Brown University.

Mohan, B. (1986). *Language and content*. Reading, MA: Addison Wesley.

Mohan, B., Leung, C., & Davison, C. (Eds.). (2001). *English as a second language in the mainstream: Teaching, learning and identity*. Harlow, UK: Pearson.

Moore, H. (1995). Telling the history of the 1991 Australian Language and Literacy Policy. *TESOL in Context* 5(1), 6–20. Queensland: Australian Council of TESOL Organizations.

NSW Board of Studies. (2000). *Stage 6 ESL syllabus.* Sydney, Australia: Board of Studies.

NSW DET (Department of Education and Training). (2004). *ESL guidelines for schools.* Sydney, Australia: Author.

Ogbu, J., & Simons, H. (1998). Voluntary and involuntary minorities: A cultural ecological theory of school performance with some implications for education. *Anthropology and Education Quarterly, 29*(2), 155–188.

Portes, A. & Zhou, M. (1993). The new second generation: Segmented assimilation and its variants among post-1995 immigrant youth. *Annals of the American Academy of Political and Social Science, 530,* 74–98.

Sarason, S. (1996). *Revisiting the culture of the school and the problem of change.* New York: Teachers College Press.

Schmid, C. (2001). Educational achievement, language-minority students, and the new second generation. *Sociology of Education* (Extra Issue), 71–87.

School Curriculum and Assessment Authority (1996). *Teaching English as an additional language: A framework for policy.* London: Author.

TESOL. (1997). *ESL standards for pre-K–12 students.* Alexandria, VA: Author.

Thomas, W., & Collier, V. (1997). *School effectiveness for language minority students.* Washington, DC: National Clearinghouse for Bilingual Education.

Van Ek, J., & Alexander, L. G. (1980). *Threshold level English.* Oxford, UK: Pergamon Press.

VCE Victorian Curriculum and Assessment Authority. (2006). *English/English as a second language: VCE study design.* Melbourne, Australia: Author.

Vygotsky, L. (1986). *Thought and language* (A. Kozulin, Trans). Cambridge: MIT Press.

Wilkins, D. (1976). *Notional syllabuses.* Oxford, UK: Oxford University Press.

2

Tertiary Undergraduate EAP: Problems and Possibilities

ANN M. JOHNS
San Diego State University

Abstract

Arguing that the principal purposes of undergraduate EAP literacy courses should be to promote rhetorical flexibility, enabling students to develop an awareness of, and sensitivity to, a variety of texts and tasks, the author explores three genre "schools" (Hyon, 1996) for their potential, finding that each has both strengths and limitations. Finally, she notes that work by Carter (2007) may provide important pedagogical insights, and she builds upon his "macro-genre" categories to suggest classroom approaches.

Definitions and Delivery Systems

EAP at the undergraduate level is difficult to define, for it is considerably more complex and elusive than most other ESP categories, particularly for the first two years of university, which will be the focus of this chapter.[1]

---

[1] I have decided to write about the first years of college and university education because these EAP issues are the most varied and controversial. As students take up their majors (in the United States) or become more initiated into their majors (in many other countries), the ESP required begins to resemble EAP for graduate students, especially master's degrees.

This complexity stems, for the most part, from the diversity of the target situations in which students will be employing academic English. As Bartholomae (1985) noted:

> Every time a student sits down to write for us, he [sic] has to invent the university for the occasion—invent the university, that is, or a branch of it, like History, Economics or Anthropology or English. He has to learn to speak our language . . . to try on the particular ways of knowing, selecting, evaluating, arguing, reporting, or concluding that define the discourses of our communities. (p. 134)

For these and other reasons, many who teach or develop curricula for these tertiary contexts do not think of themselves as ESP practitioners, though for the purposes of this volume and my argumentation, I will use the term.

In most parts of North America and in countries in which North American textbooks are used, EAP is delivered initially through freshman or sophomore composition courses, though reading is integral to these curricula as well. The teaching of composition at this level in North America has a long history (Silva, 1990; Johns, 1990). Nonetheless, considerable controversy continues about the focus and the value of these courses, the educational backgrounds of the instructors, instructors' abilities to prepare students for other university classes, and the relationship, or lack thereof, between the tasks assigned and literacies taught in composition classes and those found in disciplinary classrooms (see Leki & Carson, 1997). Practitioners continue to ask: Should composition courses prepare students for university tasks, if this is even possible, or should they provide stand-alone enrichment (Spack, 1988)? Should students be encouraged to "assimilate" into the university, acquiring the cultures of the academy, or should they be "empowered" by critical pedagogies to resist disciplinary and administrative hegemonies (Benesch, 2001)? In her useful volume *Controversies in Second Language Writing* (2004), Casanave discusses at some length these and other questions about the teaching of composition, so they will not be discussed further here.[2]

Though the history of academic literacy instruction in North American tertiary education is a long one, the necessity for additional EAP preparation during tertiary education is new to some universities in other parts of the

---

[2]There is much more involved in student academic success than reading and writing, of course. Listening to lectures, taking appropriate notes, and several types of oral activities are essential as well.

world. This is particularly true in Europe, where increasing numbers of students are speakers of second/foreign languages and/or are not well prepared in secondary schools (Johns, 2003). In many parts of Europe and in other parts of the EFL world, university administrators balk at the prospect of devoting full classes to academic English, as is the case in North America, so EAP is often delivered through writing centers, with services offered concurrently with the students' major courses.[3] There are problems with writing centers as well. For example, the backgrounds of writing center tutors may not be sufficiently in L2 training or consistent with the students' needs and their major disciplines. In addition, the centers often become dumping grounds for students who, according to their instructors in the disciplines, "can't write."

What, then, is EAP for the undergraduate student, particularly during the initial years of post-secondary education? What should be its purposes? I will attempt to answer these questions here, based on my more than 30 years of research, teaching, and teacher training in a number of contexts. I will argue that the principal purposes of EAP instruction in the first years of tertiary education should be to prepare students to be rhetorically flexible, to empower them to develop an awareness of, and sensitivity to, whatever contexts, texts, and tasks their courses and instructors present (Johns, 2008). By taking this stance, I may be admitting that EAP for undergraduates is *not* ESP in the traditional sense, since identifying *specific* needs and focusing on *analyzable target situations,* and then *completing discourse analyses,* are all difficult, if not impossible, to carry out.

Relevant Theory and Research (Genre)

Two areas of theory and research seem to be most prevalent among the practitioners who discuss the first tertiary years: critical theory (see Benesch, 2001; Canagarajah, 2002) and genre theory. Because genre theory is more characteristic of ESP in that it implies learner adaptation to, or negotiation of, context, rather than resistance, genre will be the focus of the discussion here.

---

[3]Students may also be given a combination of the two types of programs. As I write this, I am completing a Fulbright appointment in South Africa, at the University of Limpopo (formerly the University of the North), where students who are deemed "unprepared" are given a foundation course in study skills. All students take a "general" EAP course, and two more EAP courses, for more advanced students, are being designed. In time, students will also be given opportunities to visit a Writing Center, which is in the planning stage.

Hyon (1996) separated the genre theoreticians into three "schools," a taxonomy that continues to be useful. In this short chapter, I am making a particular argument, and in the process, I cannot do justice to the work of any of the schools; so I advise those interested to examine the works by experts from each in order to develop their own opinions about the schools' potential (see Johns, 2002).

One of the schools, the New Rhetoric (NR) can be found principally in North America among composition teachers of native speakers of English who have been trained in literature, composition, or rhetoric. New Rhetoricians argue that "genre" is not the text itself, but is a socio-cognitive concept stored in the schemas of expert writers who apply and vary these schemas as they read or write for specific contexts (Bazerman, 1997; Coe, 2006). Russell (1997) has explained the roles of genres in this way: "genres predict—but do not determine—the nature of a text that will be produced in a situation" (p. 522). Research areas in the New Rhetoric relate to the context of texts and the influences upon writers within these contexts, exploring how writers use "generic resources to act effectively on a situation through a text" (Freeman & Medway, 1994, p. 11). Researchers are also concerned with how genres evolve, who owns them, and what ideologies are embedded in their production (Berkenkotter & Huckin, 1995). Influenced by Bakhtin (see Eagleton, 2007), they speak of the hybridity of genres, of the intertextual influences upon the writer and the text, and the resultant heteroglossia within every text.

Theoreticians from another genre school, founded by the Systemic Functional Linguists (Halliday & Hasan, 1985), argue that genres, and the language of meaning-making, *are* found in the texts themselves, and that certain genres, such as "exposition," and "historical account" can, and should, be taught systemically to diverse students entering the culture (Martin 1993). Their extensive theory and research is devoted to the exploration of the language and structures of texts, particularly to how these elements reflect and imply social processes (Christie, 1998). Research directly related to EAP pedagogy in this school tends to center on student acquisition of genres and classroom ethnographies as the pedagogies unfold (Macken-Horarik, 2002; Unsworth, 2000; Williams 1999) or upon how language and texts function within disciplinary texts (Schleppergrell, 2004; Halliday & Martin, 1993).

Proponents of the English for Specific Purposes (ESP), the third "school," are more ambivalent about where genres are located, though theorists and researchers tend to move from a text to its context, thus giving texts predominance in research and theory. As is the case for Systemic Functional Linguistics, much of the ESP research can be applied to EAP pedagogies, but at the graduate level. Swales' moves analyses in texts (1990) and corpus-based studies of the language that indicate writer/reader interactions (Hyland, 1998, 2005) are especially applicable (see Feak, this volume; Jordan, 1997; Paltridge, 2001, for a more thorough discussion of ESP research and pedagogies.).

Another theoretical issue for all of the schools is genre naming. The New Rhetoricians contend that genres can only be named by those in power within a given community of readers and writers; and even then, naming is transitory (Prior, 1998). In academic contexts, the powerful are faculty and the reviewers and editors for whom the faculty produce their valued texts; so these are the people who name the valued genres of a community. Experts from the ESP school generally agree with the New Rhetoricians on the naming issue, supporting the view that "genre names are inherited and produced by discourse communities" (Swales, 1990, p. 58).

Particularly for pedagogical purposes, naming is considered differently by the Systemic Functionalists, who identify, analyze, and teach as "key genres" a list of text types (Rose, 2006) such as "exposition" and "description." Bhatia (2004), an ESP theorist, sorts out the differences between the staged pedagogical texts of Systemic Functionalism and the named texts of the ESP and New Rhetoric camps, claiming that the former are "independent" and "decontextualized" rhetorical *devices*, useful in composing genres but *not* the genres themselves. Instead, he notes, authentic genres, such as the research article, the business plan, or the book review, are possessed, and named, by those in power in the communities in which they function.

A third topic raised in theoretical discussions is the *social* nature of genres. Although theorists in all three schools speak of genres as social, the ways in which they conceptualize what this term means are varied; and this variance influences the pedagogies that result. For the New Rhetoricians, the buffeting effects of context are paramount to understanding what "social" means. Theorists are most interested in the situational factors that influence the texts produced: the reader and writer roles and ideologies, genre hegemonies, and intertextual influences, as well as other factors. They argue, then, that genre "conventions . . . (are) discursively generated constructs that are multiple and in flux" (Shi & Kubota, 2007). Thus Prior, after an extensive study of writing in a graduate class, concluded that "writing and disciplinarity are locally situated, extensively mediated, deeply laminated, and highly heterogeneous" (1998, p. 275).

What does "social" mean for Systemic Functionalists? These linguists are most concerned with language, specifically language as meaning making within a social framework. Williams (2007) describes this group's position-ing of the social in this way, following Halliday:

> Halliday's interest is specifically in language as a meaning-making resource. His general term for the theoretical orientation is "language as social semiotic." Because the theory is oriented to exploring meaning-making in social contexts, it is now being used for research in educational linguistics . . . (and other fields).

It is the language, then, that creates meaning in a social context, and the "key genres" embody this language at the discourse level for the literacy classroom.

Somewhat like the SFL theorists, ESP theorists seem to discover the social first in the texts themselves. This is particularly true in the work of Hyland (1998, 2005), and Myers (1989, 1992), who hypothesize about writer/audi-ence relationships from data taken from different academic genres. Swales, in *Other Floors, Other Voices* (1998), completed research in which text, context, writer, and discipline were viewed as interacting; however, the lan-guage and structure of texts still predominates in much of his work.

As I conclude this section, I must again remind the reader that this is a brief overview, constructed by this author to make the arguments that fol-low. I urge the reader to go beyond this discussion to the work of research-ers and theoreticians in the three schools. It is, of course, much richer and more nuanced than it can be portrayed in this single chapter.

Exemplar Practices

What is an exemplar practice in EAP for the tertiary student? As I have noted, this is a controversial question for practitioners. Since I have limited my discussion here to genre theories and pedagogies and since this is an ESP volume, I will talk about practices that assist students to "assimilate" into university cultures (see Benesch, 2001, for an opposing view) and their genres, through target situation analysis in particular (see Dudley-Evans & St. John, 1998).

Studies of Target Tasks

Target situation analyses in EAP for novice tertiary students, though difficult, have been important to understanding the gaps or convergences between what is taught in composition classes and/or tutorials and the expectations of the university at large. The most useful of these attempts classify the tasks that students perform across the curriculum and advocate for a variety of textual experiences, beyond the traditional essay, within an academic literacy program. What continues to be one of the best task taxonomies is by Horowitz (1986), who classified writing assignments into categories that "have enough specificity to capture essential differences among tasks and enough generality to place into the same category essentially similar tasks which might appear to be quite different" (p. 449). Some of Horowitz's seven tasks contain academic or pedagogical genres, since they have names and some identifiable conventions (summary/reaction to a reading or a case study); however, others are more generally categorized (research project) or more specific to the principal purposes of the task (connection of theory and data; synthesis of multiple sources). Nonetheless, this was an excellent beginning, one that has been built upon over the years.

Horowitz's study was limited in that it took place at one university. With the popularization of computer technologies, much more extensive studies of tasks have been completed. Melzer (2003), for example, studied 787 writing assignments across the disciplines from 48 different tertiary institutions in the United States, focusing upon the rhetorical elements of these tasks: their aims, their audiences, and the genres. Figure 2.1 presents a composite of his findings.

Considering the centrality of in-class examination responses in undergraduate tasks, it is important to mention Melzer's somewhat disturbing discussion of the demands of many of these prompts:

> One pattern I noticed in both the short answer and essay exams is the extraordinarily broad scope of questions that are supposed to be answered in a few sentences or in an hour or less. Three examples follow from history classes. Write on one of the following two questions:
> 1) It is argued by some that the Soviet-American Cold War from 1947 through 1991 was inevitable, given the results of World War II and the ideological conflict between the two countries. Evaluate that argument.
> 2) Discuss the impact of American liberal democratic values on American national security policy during the Cold War.
> 3) Discuss the evolution of the American Republic from 1782–89.

Of course, there were other, more realistic and focused prompts mentioned in Melzer's study, but this predominance of vague, global questions

FIGURE 2.1

Rhetorical Elements of Undergraduate Tasks

TASK ELEMENTS	MAJOR FINDINGS
Aims	Informative aims were much more common than others (574), with exploratory (117) and persuasive (90) coming second and third.
Audiences	Examiner/instructor audiences topped the list (654) with all other audiences (peer, self, wider audiences) occurring in fewer than 50 tasks.
Genres	Short-answer, in-class examinations (184) and journal/learning log entries (106) led the list, with all other genres (abstract/summary, lab report, review) occurring in less than 30 examples. *300 of the assignments included no recognizable genre.*

Source: Adapted from Melzer, 2003.

should be of concern to literacy instructors—and to instructors in the disciplines.

Melzer is not alone, of course, so my colleagues and I have reviewed other EAP task literature and conducted studies on our own campus, a large, comprehensive North American university. We have concluded that the features in Figure 2.2 are common to undergraduate tertiary writing tasks in the first two years (McClish & Johns, 2006).

Pedagogical Strategies and Curricula

Given the nature of EAP literacy tasks for this population, what are the appropriate pedagogical strategies for genre-based classes? What should the central goal for genre-based literacy pedagogy be? Russell and Fisher (2008) juxtapose two possible goals. The first and most common is the **acquisition of expository text types,** often called "genres" in textbooks or curricula. North American practitioners will be most familiar with this goal, realized in many composition textbooks: the teaching and re-teaching of the pervasive single genre, the five paragraph essay. Five paragraph essays are commonly taught in text templates: "illustration, exemplification, comparison, contrast, classification, and so on" (Silva, 1990, pp. 14–15). Unfortunately, this common pedagogical genre, carried over from 1950s structuralism

FIGURE 2.2

Common Features of Undergraduate Writing Tasks

- They are *short*: 2–3 pages for out-of-class, shorter for in-class.
- They are *often completed in class,* in timed essay examinations.
- They *vary unpredictably,* in text structure and content. [Note: Faculty tend to call all types of undergraduate texts *essays,* so identifying the required text structure, the argumentation, and other features of a task can be difficult for students.]
- Tasks require the *integration of sources.* Even if this requirement is not mentioned in the prompt, students are expected to integrate class readings, lectures, and discussions into their writing. This integration requires students to demonstrate their understanding of the sources as well as their ability to integrate sources into their own texts.
- Most require *concise, impersonal, academic writing.* Belletrism (showy, overly elaborate prose) is not valued by most instructors. Instead, writing should be straightforward, precise, and efficient . . . and backed by appropriate evidence.
- Many tasks call for the students' *deep understanding* of class objectives and concepts, as related to the disciplines, the readings, and the lectures.
- Tasks require *selective and purpose-driven reading, as well as critical thinking* at a number of levels: summary, analysis, synthesis, and critique.
- Tasks often can ask students to *identify arguments in texts, compare arguments or concepts, respond to an author's argument, or summarize.*

(Johns, 1990), does not appear as is in classes across the curriculum, though of course much of what students acquire when practicing this genre could be transferred. A much more varied and research-driven approach to this goal is exemplified by the Systemic Functionalists, whose pedagogies focus on the **acquisition of "key" genres,** through a study of the purposes, language, and the "stages" that characterize the text exemplars. As noted earlier, practitioners of this school assume that if students can control these text types ("genres") such as "exposition," "discussion," and "historical recount," they can, in fact, work within any genres from the culture.

A second, quite different, goal for a tertiary undergraduate EAP program is **genre awareness,** best exemplified by the New Rhetoric tradition (see Russell & Fisher, 2008), one which views genres as constantly variable and thus reformulated for immediate social contexts. Though, as Tardy (2006) has shown, understanding the "scenes" of writing and developing expert genre awareness strategies is difficult for the novice student, I will insist that despite the challenges, genre awareness should be the principal goal of novice undergraduate EAP courses. The acquisition of specific decontextualized texts, such as those suggested by Systemic Functional Linguists or the compositionists who advocate for the five paragraph essay, cannot give students either the rhetorical flexibility or the analytical skills that would enable them to adapt to the large variety of textual possibilities, both named and unnamed, that they are confronted with in academic contexts. One example of the limitations of teaching genre acquisition may illustrate this point. When my students new to university first take "essay examinations" in their academic classes, they tend to perform poorly. Assuming that all "essays" have five paragraphs and a particular move structure, they often ignore the prompts given and produce the traditional five paragraphs. Their instructors in the disciplines are exasperated, awarding these students poor grades (see Johns, 2002).

Given the findings about the complex tasks and variable target situations in which students will be using language and texts, what should be included in literacy curricula? First of all, EAP students need to be actively researching and negotiating each of their new literacy sites, each classroom in which they enroll, since the influences upon the classroom are so varied that they cannot generalize from one classroom to another (see Johns, 1997, pp. 92–105). One of the goals of our reading/writing classes should be to assist students to be researchers.

What does being an active researcher and negotiator in a classroom mean? For about fifteen years, my colleagues and I taught in a learning communities program for first-year tertiary students at my university (see Johns, 2001). Our research goal in these classes was to determine what influenced the students' academic success. In one learning community, Guleff (2002) asked her literacy students to become observers/ethnographers in the sociology class in which they were enrolled. In reporting her study, Guleff discusses the students' writing processes as they took, and assembled, their research notes. First, they examined a professional ethnography that the sociology instructor had assigned, noting that one of the important elements was the classification of activities; then they took notes in the sociology class, focusing, in particular, on the interactions between the instructor and students. Here are one student's notes on a typical class day:

> The professor continued his lecture on the seven step development of a hypothesis that is incorporated into a research paper. . . . The reaction of the class was not all that big due to the fact that some were sleeping, reading, reading the newspaper, or doing other homework. You could see that the professor was not too happy with the class by his facial expressions.

In addition to producing a paper in their literacy class that paralleled the ethnography they had studied, the students also researched themselves—and how they might succeed in the sociology class. They noted that even though the professor wasn't always fascinating (!), if they had listened and taken better notes, they would then be able to understand the assignment. It would do no good, they reckoned, to ask the professor about the assignment during his office hours, since he had already discussed it in class while they (presumably) slept or read the paper. They also reflected on their growing understanding of their roles as writers in producing ethnographic texts. Like the writer of the professional ethnography they had studied, they were able to create their own categories for analysis of student and professor classroom activities for the EAP class. Later, when they completed an ethnography for the instructor about their work at a child care center, they again created their own categories. Their writing processes were complex, appropriate to the production of what was for them a new genre, the ethnography.

As faculty researchers, we were most interested in what factors assisted some of the diverse students in these classes to succeed. In a 1992 publication, I report on a case study of an immigrant student, new from Laos, the only student in my learning communities class who achieved an A grade in the anthropology class in which they all were enrolled. Why did she succeed? She carefully listened to lectures and interviewed the instructor to determine the focus of the course. In the process, she discovered that anthropological concepts such as "assimilation" and "adaptation" were most important to the instructor—and to the instructor's assessments—and she organized her notes around these concepts, clustering information from both lectures and readings on the "conceptual pages" of her notebook. When she was confronted with an in-class essay prompt such as "Tell how the Yanamamo adapted to their environment," she had already organized her ideas for a response.

The students from the learning communities discussed here began with observing the academic scene and its instructor and then investigated that scene in depth. Other students have begun with the texts they are assigned to read and the papers they write—again in an effort to understand the classroom scene. They are encouraged to take drafts of their papers to their instructors who assigned them and to ask if they are on the right track. They are told to read some of the assignments for their "content" classes, such as anthropology or sociology, summarize them, and then go to the disciplinary instructor to ask if they have understood the readings. As literacy instructors, we cannot predict what will be valued in students' disciplinary classrooms;

however, we can predict how instructors will react to student questions *if* they know that students are making an effort to complete and understand classroom tasks. Therefore, an essential practice in tertiary EAP classrooms is to assist students to research new academic "scenes" and to role-play or take notes in order to better understand or negotiate these scenes.

But perhaps I am getting ahead of myself. The first question about a tertiary academic class or tutorial should probably be, "What should the curriculum look like?" As should be clear, we should not be confining our teaching to the "academic essay" or other text artifacts, but instead, we should be destabilizing students' genre theories (Johns, 2002) and preparing them to study the values, tasks, and texts in their undergraduate classes. In addition to teaching the research skills already discussed, we suggest (Figure 2.3) other elements of literacy classes in which genre awareness is central (McClish & Johns, 2006).

FIGURE 2.3

Essential Elements in an EAP Literacy Class for Tertiary Undergraduates

> Students need to
> - Read *a variety of texts for a variety of purposes,* for summary, identification of an argument, analysis, and synthesis—and to search for appropriate citations for their own writing.
> - *Analyze a variety of prompts,* some of which, as Melzer (2003) notes, are not very revealing. If these prompts are incomplete or vague, they need to know what questions to ask instructors about them.
> - *Write short, well-crafted papers, responding to prompts under* both timed and untimed conditions. The long research paper for first- and second-year tertiary students seems to be a thing of the past.
> - *Integrate sources into their papers and discussions.* The practice of formal and informal citations is central to students' success.
> - *Accurately paraphrase, summarize, and interpret the readings* for their own texts and class discussions.
> - *Build precise academic vocabulary,* both the "mortar" words that cross disciplines and the "brick" words that represent the central concepts of the discipline (Dutro & Moran, 2003).
> - *Research literacies* in their disciplinary classes.
> - *Reflect frequently* upon their literacy experiences.

Source: Adapted from McClish & Johns, 2006.

These may be the essential elements, but what is the framework for such a class? How should it be assessed? Ideally, since a variety of readings and writings are assigned and reflection is central, students should prepare an academic portfolio (Johns, 1997, pp. 131–136) in which textual variety is the central focus. One way to achieve this textual variety while considering disciplinary contexts is to adopt the taxonomy by Carter (2007), a writing-across-the-curriculum specialist who has developed a four-part classification of writing processes and responses in "macro-genres" across the disciplines. In my view, this is the most useful of the EAP target situation analyses completed in recent years. Carter has found that there are clusters of response types, "macro-genres," that parallel disciplines and their genres, responses that will enable both instructors and students to understand the values and texts of disciplines. Figure 2.4 outlines these types, the disciplines in which they are found, and the genres that result.

This is a very useful analysis in that Carter shows the relationships between disciplines, their responses, and their genres, providing for EAP instructors methods for entering disciplinary practices without becoming too precise or focused upon a single discipline.

Given the Carter framework, we might establish the following goals for students:

1. Write under a variety of conditions following a variety of prompts related to the response types.
2. Using the response types and, ideally, interviews with disciplinary faculty, practice questions to ask of their readings and writing tasks in disciplinary contexts.
3. Enter their texts that mirror response types into a portfolio, their final assessment.
4. Reflect frequently upon their literacy experiences.

Certainly there is much more that could be said of curricula and assessment in EAP within the confines of genre theory and practice. But why go on? After 30 years in the literacy teaching business, I am very pleased to have discovered the Carter framework, which seems to embody both authenticity and accessibility for students, a framework that may actually open the way to genre awareness.

FIGURE 2.4

Response Types ("Macro-Genres") in the Disciplines

---

1. A <u>problem-solving/system-generating</u> response
   Disciplines: Business, social work, engineering, nursing

   a) Identify, define, and analyze the problem
   b) Determine what information and disciplinary concepts are appropriate for
      solving the problem
   c) Collect data
   d) Offer viable solutions
   e) Evaluate the solutions using specific discipline-driven criteria
   Genres: *case studies, project reports and proposals, business plans*

2. A response calling for <u>empirical inquiry (an IMRD paper)</u>
   Disciplines in the sciences, nursing, and the social sciences

   a) Ask questions/formulate hypotheses
   b) Test hypotheses (or answer questions) using empirical methods
   c) Organize and analyze data for verbal and visual summaries
   d) Conclude by explaining the results
   Genres: *lab reports, posters, a research report or article*

3. A response calling for <u>research from sources</u>
   Disciplines in the humanities: English and other literatures, classics, history

   a) Pose an interesting research question
   b) Locate relevant (often primary) sources for investigating the question
   c) Critically evaluate the sources "in terms of credibility, authenticity,
      interpretive stance, audience, potential biases, and value for answering
      research questions"
   d) Marshall evidence to support an argument that answers the research
      question
   Genre: *"The quintessential academic genre: the research paper"* (MLA style)

4. A response calling for <u>performance</u>
   Disciplines: Art, music, composition (writing)

   a) Learn about the principles, concepts, media, or formats appropriate for
      the discipline
   b) Attempt to master the techniques and approaches
   c) Develop a working knowledge and process
   d) Perform and/or critique a performance

<u>Source</u>: Adapted from Carter, 2007.

Current Issues/Future Directions

It may appear to readers in other parts of the world that the comments made in this chapter are too North American to be very useful in EFL contexts or in tertiary institutions where writing classes are not offered. However, I have found that what is said here may have value in the rest of the world as well. I have been working in a variety of international contexts (most recently: Mexico, Turkey, and South Africa; see also www.rohan.sdsu.edu/~annjohns where there are different types of academic and linguistic challenges. It is remarkable to find most of the same characteristics in target EAP literacy situations as reported above and the same questions about what it means to be literate as an undergraduate. I have also found that many literacy instructors across the world, like those in North America, would much prefer to teach genres as templates, thus emphasizing genre acquisition rather than genre awareness. They find the Systemic Functional materials and the American materials that teach the five paragraph essay both accessible and reassuring because they seem to provide specific answers to complex literacy questions. Others find that a cognitive approach, rather than the socio-literate one presented here, is more useful to their classrooms (e.g., Bruce, 2005). However, if we are to be true to the ESP goals of preparing students for their future language-related experiences, then the somewhat ambiguous and socially oriented curricula suggested here appear to be much more appropriate.

But whatever happens, research by both students and instructors must continue. Questions such as the following need to be answered: Will a curriculum based upon the Carter scheme be accessible to students and teachers across the world? What strategies should we use to assist students to research and negotiate their literacy situations? Do the proposals made here result in increased student motivation and transfer of learning? How can we more intelligently imbed the study of language into the responses and genres of the disciplines (see Schleppegrell, 2004, and Zwiers, 2006)?

I have been asking questions like these for more than thirty years, as have others involved in teaching academic literacies to novice tertiary students, and I expect the questions and arguments to grow in number as academic literacy in English and other languages becomes increasingly important across the world. With the more sophisticated target situation analyses, we seem to be getting closer to the answers. If, by some intellectual miracle, an agreement is reached about what EAP literacy is at this novice tertiary level, then more work continues to be necessary to produce theoretically sound but student- and teacher-accessible curricula.

* * *

ANN M. JOHNS is Professor Emerita of Linguistics & Writing Studies, San Diego State University (CA/USA). She has published four books and more than 50 articles on literacies, genre, and ESP, and has taught or consulted in 20 countries. Since her retirement, she has been consulting with, and writing literacy curricula for, diverse, college-bound secondary students.

REFERENCES

Bartholomae, D. (1985). Inventing the university. In Rose, M. (Ed.), *When a writer can't write: Studies in writer's block and other composing process problems* (pp. 134–165). New York: Guilford Press.

Bazerman, C. (1997). The life of genre, the life in the classroom. In W. Bishop & H. Ostrom (Eds.), *Genre and writing issues, arguments and alternatives* (pp. 19–26). Portsmouth, NH: Boynton/Cook.

Benesch, S. (2001). *Critical English for academic purposes: Theory, politics, and practice.* Mahwah, NJ: Lawrence Erlbaum.

Berkenkotter, C., & Huckin, T. N. (1996). *Genre knowledge and disciplinary communities.* Hillsdale, NJ: Lawrence Erlbaum.

Bhatia, V. K. (2004). *Worlds of written discourse: A genre-based view.* London: Continuum.

Bruce, I. (2005). Syllabus design for general EAP writing courses: A cognitive approach. *Journal of English for Academic Purposes, 4,* 239–256.

Canagarajah, A. S. (2002). *Critical academic writing and multilingual students.* Ann Arbor: University of Michigan Press.

Carter, M. (2007). Ways of knowing, doing, and writing. *College Composition and Communication, 58,* 385–418.

Casanave, C. P. (2004). *Controversies in second language writing: Dilemmas and decisions in research and instruction.* Ann Arbor: University of Michigan Press.

Christie, F. (Ed). (1998). *Pedagogy and the shaping of consciousness: Linguistic and social processes.* London: Cassell.

Coe, R. M. (2006). Crossing the borders of genre studies: Commentaries by experts. (With co-presenters A. Johns, A. Bawarshi, K. Hyland, B. Paltridge, M. J. Reiff, and C. M. Tardy.) *Journal of Second Language Writing, 15,* 234–249.

Dudley-Evans, T., & St. John, M. J. (1998). *Developments in English for specific purposes: A multi-disciplinary approach.* Cambridge, UK: Cambridge University Press.

Dutro, S., & Moran, C. (2003). Rethinking English language instruction: An architectural approach. In G. Garcia (Ed.), *English learners: Reaching the highest level of English literacy* (pp. 227–258). Newark, NJ: International Reading Association.

Eagleton, T. (June, 2007). I contain multitudes. *London Review of Books, 12,* 13–15.

Guleff, V. (2002). Approaching genre: Prewriting as apprenticeship to communities of practice. In A. M. Johns (Ed.), *Genre in the classroom: Multiple perspectives* (pp. 211–224). Mahwah, NJ: Lawrence Erlbaum.

Halliday, M. A. K., & Hasan, R. (Eds.) (1985). *Language, context, and text: Aspects of language in a social semiotic perspective.* Geelong, Australia: Deakin University Press.

Halliday, M. A. K., & Martin, J. R. (1993). *Writing science: Literacy and discursive power.* London: Falmer Press.

Horowitz, D. (1986). What professors actually require: Academic tasks for the ESL classroom. *TESOL Quarterly, 20,* 445–462.

Hyland, K. (1998). *Hedging in scientific research papers.* Amsterdam: John Benjamins.

———. (2005). Stance and engagement: A model of interaction in academic discourse. *Discourse Studies, 7,* 173–192.

Hyon, S. (1996). Genres in three traditions: Implications for ESL. *TESOL Quarterly, 30,* 693–722.

Johns, A.M. (1990). L1 composition theories: Implications for developing theories of L2 composition. In B. Kroll (Ed.), *Second language writing: Research insights for the classroom* (pp. 24–36). New York: Cambridge University Press.

———. (1997). *Text, role, and context: Developing academic literacies.* New York: Cambridge University Press.

———. (2001). An interdisciplinary, interinstitutional, learning communities program: Student involvement and student success. In I. Leki (Ed.), *Academic writing programs* (pp. 61–72). Alexandria, VA: TESOL.

———. (2002). Destabilizing and enriching novice students' genre theories. In A. M. Johns (Ed.), *Genre in the classroom: Multiple perspectives* (pp. 237–248). Mahwah, NJ: Lawrence Erlbaum.

———. (2003). Academic writing: A European perspective. *Journal of Second Language Writing, 12,* 313–319.

———. (2008). Genre awareness and the novice student: An on-going quest. *Language Teaching, 41,* 239–254.

Jordan, R. R. (1997). *English for academic purposes: A guide and resource book for teachers.* Cambridge, UK: Cambridge University Press.

Leki, I., & Carson, J. (1997). Completely different worlds: EAP and the writing experiences of ESL students in university courses. *TESOL Quarterly, 31,* 231–255.

Macken-Horarik, M. (2002). "Something to shoot for": A systemic functional approach to teaching genre in secondary science. In A. M. Johns (Ed.), *Genre in the classroom: Multiple perspectives* (pp. 17–42). Mahwah, NJ: Lawrence Erlbaum.

Martin, J. R. (1993). Genre and literacy—modeling context in educational linguistics. *Annual Review of Applied Linguistics, 13,* 141–172.

McClish, G., & Johns, A. M. (2006, March 10). *College writing tasks across the curriculum.* Paper presented at the College for All Conference, San Diego, CA.

Melzer, D. (2003). Assignments across the curriculum: A survey of college writing. *Language and Learning across the Disciplines, 6,* 86–110.

Myers, G. (1989). The pragmatics of politeness in scientific articles. *Applied Linguistics, 10,* 1035.

———. (1992). Textbooks and the sociology of scientific knowledge. *English for Specific Purposes, 11,* 3–17.

Paltridge, B. (2001). *Genre and the language learning classroom.* Ann Arbor: University of Michigan Press.

Prior, P. A. (1998). *Writing/disciplinarity: A sociohistorical account of literate activity in the academy.* Mahwah, NJ: Lawrence Erlbaum.

Rose, D. (2006, March). *Reading to learn; learning to read.* Presentation at the University of Kwazulu-Natal, Pietermaritzburg, South Africa.

Russell, D. (1997). Rethinking genre in school and society: An activity theory analysis. *Written Communication, 14,* 504–554.

Russell, D., & Fisher, D. (2008). On-line multimedia case studies for professional education: Revisioning concepts of genre recognition. *Proceedings of SIGET, 4th Simpósio International de Estudos de Genĕros Textuais.* Universidade do Sul de Santa Catarina, Brazil. Retrieved from www3.unisul.br/paginas/ensino/pos/linguagem/cd/index.htm

Schleppegrell, M. (2004). *The language of schooling: A functional linguistics perspective.* Mahwah, NJ: Lawrence Erlbaum.

Shi, L., & Kubota, R. (2007). Patterns of rhetorical organization in Canadian and American language arts textbooks: An exploratory study. *English for Specific Purposes, 26,* 180–202.

Silva, T. (1990). Second language composition instruction: Developments, issues, and directions in ESL. In B. Kroll (Ed.) *Second language writing: Research insights for the classroom* (pp. 11–23). New York: Cambridge University Press.

Spack, R. (1988). Initiating ESL students into the academic discourse community: How far should we go? *TESOL Quarterly, 22,* 29–52.

Swales, J. M. (1990). *Genre analysis: English in academic and research settings.* Cambridge, UK: Cambridge University Press.

————. (1998). *Other floors, other voices: A textography of a small university building.* Mahwah, NJ: Lawrence Erlbaum.

Tardy, C. (2006). Crossing the boundaries of genre studies: Commentaries by experts. (With co-presenters R. M. Coe, A. Johns, A. Bawarshi, K. Hyland, B. Paltridge, & M. J. Reiff.) *Journal of Second Language Writing, 15,* 234–249.

Unsworth, L. (Ed). (2000). *Researching language in schools and communities: Functional linguistic perspectives.* London: Cassell.

Williams, G. (2007). *Researching language use in education: Systemic Functional Linguistics* (LLED 601A Syllabus). University of British Columbia, Dept. of Language and Literacy Education.

————. (1999). The pedagogic device and the production of pedagogic discourse: A case example in early literacy education. In F. Christie (Ed.), *Pedagogy and the shaping of consciousness: Linguistic and social processes* (pp. 88–111). London: Cassell.

Zwiers, J. (2006). Integrating academic language, thinking and content: Learning scaffolds for non-native speakers in the middle grades. *Journal of English for Academic Purposes, 5,* 317–332.

3

Setting the Stage for Scholarly Evaluation: Research Commentaries in the EAP Graduate Writing Curriculum

CHRISTINE FEAK
University of Michigan

Abstract

A cursory look at syllabi of graduate-level courses across all disciplines will reveal that a frequent goal of instruction is for students to become aware of and sufficiently engaged with significant issues in their chosen fields so as to be able to a adopt a critical stance toward their disciplines. Often students are expected to demonstrate their ability to adopt a critical perspective through writing assignments that require them to evaluate one or several published papers in their field. How to best help students develop strategies for responding to texts in a critical manner has been the focus of ongoing discussion in the English for Academic Purposes literature. This paper contributes to this discussion by first exploring current perspectives regarding the difficulties students face when evaluating the scholarship of their field and providing examples of student approaches to writing critically. The paper then considers some potential drawbacks of using book reviews as exemplars of evaluative writing, suggesting the need for providing graduate students yet another evaluative genre, namely the research commentary. Certain kinds of research commentaries, particularly those that initially begin as spoken, public commentaries, may indeed provide a good starting point for helping graduate students work toward understanding the underlying goals of evaluation and take a critical stance in their writing.

As observed by Hyland (2005), academic writing, particularly the research article (RA), was once thought to be "objective, faceless, and impersonal." This view has largely been abandoned as discourse studies have revealed that persuasion, evaluation, and argumentation are indeed central features of research writing that are subject to disciplinary norms. Evaluation and argumentation are not only important in the writing of RAs for publication, but also for success in a student's course of study at English-medium colleges and universities. Although most often examined in terms of undergraduate success (e.g., Dobson & Feak, 2001), critical thinking, in particular the ability to evaluate scholarship in one's chosen discipline, is typically a stated goal of the graduate curriculum as well and, as Cheng (2006) indicates, integral to academic survival. A quick review of course syllabi available through a search of most English-medium university websites clearly reveals that evaluation plays a central role in most graduate courses, whether through classroom discussion, writing assignments, or both. Thus, it is not unusual for a graduate level syllabus to include statements such as the following from the syllabus for Families and Health, a graduate-level course offered at the University of Michigan.

> This course provides a context within which participants can critically and actively explore a broad range of information concerning the nature of families in the U.S. As part of your professional socialization and development, the course will provide you with directed opportunities to develop your skills in the areas of critical thinking and writing. In order to accomplish this, we attempt to establish an environment in which individuals actively and thoughtfully participate in discussions and class presentations. Further, it is expected that written assignments reflect the standards of critical analysis and will be evaluated and graded accordingly.

While we might expect courses in the social sciences to emphasize evaluation, this emphasis seems to run across all graduate programs. Courses in engineering and the hard sciences also design their syllabi to include an emphasis on critique and evaluation, as indicated in the syllabus for a graduate course in Electrical Engineering and Computer Sciences, entitled Advanced Artificial Intelligence.

> This course has two main purposes. One is to provide students who want to become AI researchers and practitioners with a deeper and broader appreciation of the field. The other is to give students experience in reading and understanding cutting-edge research results as presented in recent papers rather than in textbook form. Students will demonstrate mastery of both of these goals by working through exercises, critiquing papers, discussing ideas and approaches in class, and completing a course project.

Courses in dentistry, nursing, and medicine also place a similar emphasis on critical evaluation, as stated in the syllabus of a medical ethics course.

> My goals in this course are for you to:
> 1. become informed about and engage critically with substantive issues in medical ethics;
> 2. sharpen your practical reasoning skills by:
>   – analyzing arguments,
>   – reasoning analogically,
>   – and applying theory and general principles to specific cases;
> 3. demonstrate your learning through discussion and writing.

Despite the important goal of helping graduate students learn to critically engage with the scholarship in their fields, achieving this goal poses a challenge for instructors and students alike. The professor of the Family Behavior course cited above observes that there is a portion of her class "that can be described as critical thinkers when they begin, a portion of emerging critical thinkers," and, she laments, "a group that is not there yet that remains virtually untouched by what goes on in the course" (Linda Chatters, e-mail, January 13, 2007). On the student side, a recent survey of fourteen first- and second-year graduate students (both Ph.D. and master's) in one of my advanced EAP writing courses revealed that they did not know ($n = 10$) or were unsure of ($n = 4$) how to critically analyze scholarship in their fields. Yet, at the same time, eleven of the fourteen students indicated that they would be writing papers in which some evaluation of scholarship would be required.

Students face numerous challenges when expected to evaluate scholarship (Cheng, 2006; Hyland, 2002; Swales & Feak, 2004). For example, students may have difficulty taking on the unfamiliar persona of a supposed expert (Dobson & Feak, 2001; Swales & Feak, 2004). Students also report anxiety arising from their lack of sufficient content knowledge (Belcher, 1995; Caffarella & Barnett, 2000). Further, unlike senior academics, students often lack a conceptual framework from which to view work in a particular field or may have a framework that differs from that of the discipline, which can also lead to uncertainty as to what critical analysis should entail (Lea & Street, 1998). In some cases, students may harbor misconceptions about the role of critique in their disciplines. While students in the social sciences acknowledge that they will need to be able to evaluate scholarship in their chosen field, students in the other fields, particularly mathematics, engineering, and the natural sciences, often believe that the norm in their field is to build upon, rather than critique, the work of others (Belcher, 1995) (but note the excerpt from Advanced Artificial Intelligence syllabus earlier). Finally, for L2 learners in particular, culture may also influence their ability and/ or willingness to evaluate (Ahmad, 1997; Atkinson & Ramanathan, 1995; Cadman, 1997; Canagarajah, 2002; Cheng, 2006; Kaplan, 1988). In this case, students may feel that it is inappropriate to criticize the work of others.

Whether or not culture is a primary factor contributing to the difficulties of L2 students remains open to discussion; what is clear, however, is that when asked *whether* they find evaluation difficult, they often respond that they do because they think they know what they are supposed to do, but do not know how to do it. This confusion has also been described by Lea and Street (1998), whose research revealed that students often did not understand what they should be doing when writing academic papers, despite an awareness that different writing tasks required different approaches. Not only do the students themselves not always understand how to write a successful paper, but instructors as well are not always able to clearly articulate their expectations. In this regard, Lea and Street (1998) describe a writing tutor who expected students "to be critical, to evaluate, to try and reach some sort of synthesis," but was unable to move beyond the descriptive terms *criticism*, *evaluation*, and *synthesis* to explain how students should engage in these cognitively demanding activities. No doubt, these are difficult concepts to unpack (Woodward-Kron, 2002).

This then raises the question, if students do not know what to do, what are they doing when they are expected to write a critical evaluation of scholarship? Insights into this question can be found in one recent study of novice and experienced journal manuscript reviewers. Godoy (2006) conducted a controlled experiment in which seventeen new engineering faculty members were given instruction on peer review and then asked to review a paper that had already been reviewed by three experienced reviewers. After reading the paper, the novices were asked to write a review, indicating whether the manuscript should be accepted as is, accepted with revision, or rejected. Although one can reasonably assume that the experienced reviewers would do a better job than inexperienced reviewers, the study identified significant differences in the reviews of the novices and experienced reviewers. The experienced reviewers focused primarily on the weaknesses (e.g., models chosen and comprehensiveness). The experts also commented on the interpretations of the data as well as on how limitations of the study under review were addressed. Finally, although all of the experts rejected the paper, they suggested ways the manuscript might be improved; only one of the novices recommended that the paper be rejected and offered suggestions for improvement. In their reviews, the novices tended to focus on superficial aspects of the paper, looking at the paper largely in terms of the quality of writing style, as opposed to commenting on the strengths and weaknesses of the study design, methods, and interpretations. Interestingly, one area where the novice writers did outperform the experts was in their efforts to write their reviews in a manner that was respectful to the manuscript author.

While the new faculty members' attention to superficial matters in the manuscript review does seem somewhat surprising, this finding would hold true for many first- and second-year graduate students. For instance, when asked to evaluate scholarship in their field, students at this level may primarily engage in information transfer (Bereiter & Scardamalia, 1987)—that is, summarizing the work, limiting their evaluation to a concluding comment in which they simply express their like or dislike of the article. Some L2 students may offer overly positive, sometimes enthusiastic evaluation, assuming that this is what an instructor wants, as in the following example.

> I think the logic of the design and discussion is very clear and convincing. It is definitely a wonderful investigation which provide invaluable evidence to help us understand the association between taste and odor. (WZ)

Other L2 students may tend toward reacting rather than evaluating.

> According to Saxonhouse, who was a great professor in University of Michigan and died last Wednesday, some surveys suggest that American high-technology companies have disadvantages, compared with Japanese. It is particularly discussed the optoelectronics industry, products of which are assembled from light and electronics devices, such as LASER, CD players and Video cameras, because Japanese government supports it by aid, loan, and so on. Krugman implies that such supports promote retaliation from Japan's trading partners. *However, these arguments are ridiculous.* (EK)
>
> (<u>Note</u>: No further explanation was given.)

Students who are familiar with book reviews may know that these texts frequently highlight the relevant sections of the volume under review so as to give readers an overall sense of topics covered. However, if this same strategy is applied to a review of a research article following the common Introduction, Methods, Results, and Discussion (IMRD) structure, L2 students may merely identify the sections along with their purpose, rather than explore the content of each section.

> The research is divided into five sections, which are Abstract, Introduction, Experimental, Results and Conclusive discussion. In the abstract section, it summarizes all descriptions within the journal such as the objective of this paper, the equipment used to investigate the result and also present the summary of the paper. The purpose of this section is to make the reader understand roughly about the journal and easily to follow up. In the introduction section, the authors provided a background about Pd which is used as a catalyst in the past and also much research which have already done. (PP)

While having an understanding of generic features of an RA is important, an evaluation that does not move beyond superficial description will not likely succeed.

L2 students may also be influenced by book review commentary on writing style. Lacking experience in regard to the stylistic features worthy of mention, one L2 student wrote the following:

> This paper is appealing because buzz words such as NGOs, network, accountability, and other terminologies appear everywhere in this article and not so much difficult technical terms.
> (PC)

Although the above observation is focused on terminology, this student also seems to be indicating that the paper is good because she can understand it, a strategy not uncommon among L2 students, as further revealed by the next example.

Many L2 students also offer their commentary with an imagined reader in mind. This is not in itself necessarily an unwise strategy. In fact, references to an abstract reader are employed in book reviews and other evaluative genres to distance the reviewer from the criticism being made or to establish solidarity with a particular community or its standards (Hyland, 2000). However, in the case of newer students this strategy is often adopted to simply reveal their own understanding.

> In addition, they explained the method to do the experiment step by step which is quite easy for the reader to understand.
> (PP)

One might argue that this last example does offer some evaluation (i.e., the text is easy to understand); however, this kind of evaluation may be relevant only if the target audience of the text under review includes outsiders or newcomers to a field—for example, perhaps a neuroscientist writing an article about brain function for linguists or psychologists. In discussing use of "the reader" in her text, my student revealed that she simply wanted to say that because she had understood the article, it must be good (PP, personal communication).

These excerpts were taken from a small corpus of 45 critiques submitted in two of my credit-bearing graduate student writing courses, Academic Writing II and Academic Writing and Grammar. Students in these two courses are fully matriculated, typically in their first or second year of a master's or Ph.D. program, and taking a full academic course load. They are enrolled in one of these writing courses because either a re-evaluation of their academic language skills led to a requirement to take an academic writing course or they themselves have identified a need to work on their writing. Most students in these two courses can be considered emerging critical thinkers or "not quite there yet." Students in Academic Writing II are inexperienced writers, but have fairly good control of grammar and vocabulary. Their writing difficulties tend to center more on choosing language for the best effect, the flow and development of ideas, as well as appropriately using source materials. Students in Writing and Grammar have these same difficulties, but are additionally challenged by problems with vocabulary and grammar, which tend to interfere with their ability to communicate their ideas in writing.

Although the writing ability of the students in the two courses differs, the writing tasks that they are expected to complete in their degree programs *do not differ*. In other words, regardless of their ability, linguistic or otherwise, all students enrolled in, say, the Family and Health course previously mentioned will need to be able to write critical evaluations. Surveys of my L2 students' writing requirements in their degree programs show that common writing assignments include research papers for seminars, critical evaluations of current scholarship, analyses of single papers, project reports, lab reports, and position papers. Given that so many of these assignments require students to evaluate scholarship in their fields, critique writing is a central feature in Academic Writing II and Writing and Grammar. For one assignment, students are given the option of turning in a paper from one of their content courses that involves evaluation (with the permission of the content instructor) or evaluating a journal article of their choice from their own field.

To help L2 students understand the purpose of and approaches to evaluating scholarship, the courses have traditionally spent time on academic book reviews, which are available for every discipline and can easily be found online (Belcher, 1995). Book reviews are a highly evaluative genre that examines the extent to which the book contributes to the knowledge of a field, relates to established theory, and offers something that other books do not. The structure of book reviews proposed in Motta-Roth (1998) is particularly useful in helping L2 students realize the importance of first summarizing content before evaluating. A modified version of Motta-Roth's move analysis appears in Figure 3.1.

By analyzing book reviews, L2 students can also begin to understand some of the scholarly values of their fields (preferred models, particular methodologies, certain approaches to argumentation, or even whether

FIGURE 3.1

Aims and Elements of a Book Review

GENERAL AIM		SPECIFICALLY ACCOMPLISHING THAT AIM
Introducing the book	by	establishing the topic *and/or* describing potential readership *and/or* providing information about the authors *and/or* making generalizations about the topic *and/or* establishing the place of the book in the field
Outlining the book	by	highlighting the general organization of the book *and/or* describing the content of each chapter or section *and/or* referring specifically to non-text material such as graphs, tables, and appendices
Highlighting parts of the book	by	providing focused evaluation by making general, positive commentary *and/or* offering specific, negative commentary
Providing final commentary and recommendations	by	commenting on price or production standards (good binding, paper quality, size) *and/or* specifying the scope of the usefulness of the book *and/or* recommending (or not recommending) the book, despite limitations, if any

Source: Swales & Feak, 2004.

books themselves are valued by the discipline), the scope of the praise and criticism, metadiscourse (Chapter One examines . . .), as well as vocabulary (how positive is *useful* within the context of a book review?) and grammar choices. In addition, book reviews can serve as a springboard for discussions of audience, purpose, and strategy. (For a more detailed discussion of book reviews see Belcher [1995] and Hyland [2000].)

Despite the richness of book reviews as potential models for the evaluation of scholarship, some of their characteristics can pose difficulties for new graduate student writers with little experience writing evaluations. Book reviews may tend more toward praise than criticism, devote undue attention to writing style, or be seen as an opportunity for reviewers to espouse their own views on a topic. In addition, since book reviews are evaluating a product, they may include comments on production quality and a recommendation as to whether others in the field should read or purchase a volume (Hyland, 2000), topics that a student would generally not be expected to address in a for-class evaluation of an RA. Finally, some reviews include evaluation that could be considered overly positive/negative for a paper written for a course, as in these excerpts from two published reviews.

> Reading each section is *fascinating*. They are [*sic*] full of facts, new ideas and reasoned argument as to where the future might lead us (Steen, 1999).

> Other sections, particularly in Chapters 4 and 5 on nonlinear theory and the mathematical appendices are, for the most part, far too brief to be comprehensible even if correct. The reputation of neither the author nor the publisher will be enhanced by this book and I cannot recommend it to anyone (Craik, 2000).

Given some of these unique characteristics of book reviews, using only book reviews as models of evaluative scholarship can sometimes lead L2 students (and perhaps all new graduate students) astray. Despite instruction to the contrary, they may incorporate features of book reviews that might best be avoided, as demonstrated by the following excerpts from student papers.

> I highly recommend this article to extremely busy politicians all over the world because the volume of this article is only two pages. Furthermore, the very catchy title may attract other people, too. (YH)

> I would have no hesitation in recommending this paper as a must reading for all those concerned with the fatigue behavior of concrete. (YW)

> Moreover, this article is well produced with high quality figures, from which the clue of model developing can be easily grabbed by reader. (BH)

Book reviews may be a useful starting point for helping first- and second-year L2 students learn to write evaluations of scholarship in their disciplines, but other evaluative genres can serve as useful models as well. Actual reviews of manuscripts submitted to journals are valuable, but these may be difficult to obtain and issues of ownership and use may arise (but see Belcher,

2007). Journal editorials are another potential source of teaching material, but these are not likely to offer much negative criticism of a particular piece of scholarship. RAs may contain some evaluation, but generally not enough sustained evaluation of a single study or paper to be of significant value as models for evaluation. Published annual reviews of a specific discipline (e.g., *Annual Review of Applied Linguistics* or *Annual Review of Information Science and Technology*), which one might expect to offer a fair amount of evaluation, are also of limited value. Such publications generally require a fair amount of background knowledge to follow, they deal with very recent (perhaps cutting edge) research, and they highlight studies perceived as having made a positive contribution to the field. Finally, annual reviews may in fact be more descriptive than evaluative.

One under-explored evaluative genre that we can look to is the published research commentary, which may be referred to as Commentary, Correspondence, Discussion, or Letters. The descriptive label assigned to research commentaries varies from journal to journal and in some cases the label used in one journal may be used in another journal, but for a very different kind of text; in other words, in one journal a discussion may be a research commentary, while in another a Discussion may in fact be more like an editorial. For the purposes of this discussion, a research commentary (RC) is a short, solicited or unsolicited, published evaluation of or critical response to a conference presentation or journal article, as opposed to an evaluative review of an area of inquiry. In some journals RCs are a regular feature, especially journals in medicine and some in psychology, and appear immediately after the article being reviewed; in others they appear only when an article generates some controversy and thus the commentaries may appear in subsequent issues. In some journals, again particularly those in medicine, the commentaries can consist of the oral exchanges following the presentation of the research at a conference. In this latter kind of published commentary, the speakers' comments are transcribed for eventual publication in the same issue in which the research paper will appear. The speakers review their comments and at this point become authors who tweak their comments to improve the language, focus, or intent of the comments (John Benfield, MD, personal communication, December 2004). RCs may be considered part of a single genre chain (Räisänen, 2002; Swales, 2004) that includes the conference proposal (in some cases), the conference paper (in some cases), the original article, the commentary, and then a response by the author of the original article. In some cases an article may spark such controversy (consider the responses to Firth and Wagner's 1997 critical assessment of second language acquisition research) that the ensuing responses create a genre *cluster* of many responses, not unlike the many separate conference abstracts that are generated in response to a call for proposals or reviews of a manuscript submitted to a journal for publication.

To demonstrate how RCs may be incorporated into an academic writing course, here I provide two sample RCs. The first is an RC that perhaps more closely resembles the kind of written evaluation that students think they may be expected to create for a course paper. This RC appeared in the *Journal of Autism and Developmental Disorders*, immediately following the article that prompted the response. Given that the original article and the RC appear in the same issue, the response may have been invited, perhaps in recognition of the controversy surrounding the interventions for autism and funding sources to support them. The RC title, "Benefit-Cost Analysis and Autism Services: A Response to Jacobson and Mulick," is quite typical in that it is a general to specific colon-type title that includes the post-colon phrase *a response to*. An awareness of this title structure can enable students to find their own RCs through online resources such as Google Scholar using the search "a response to * and *," allowing them to build a corpus of evaluative writing in their own field.

Below are excerpts from the RC that focus on the evaluation of the model proposed in the original article. The first paragraph is the opening paragraph, while the second and third paragraphs presented here are in fact the fifth and sixth paragraphs of the commentary.

> In their article on system and costs issues in programs for children with autism, Jacobson and Mulick (2000) deal with the importance of examining the economic environment surrounding provision of effective services. However, their arguments are based on faulty assumptions, inadequate research findings, and misuse of benefit-cost analysis methods. Rather than providing an objective, systematic review of what is known and accepted about existing early intervention programs, the article comes across as a promotion for one approach, early intensive behavior intervention (EIBI). By invoking the technical jargon of economics, the authors attempt to leave the impression that both the autism scientific community and funding agencies should embrace this treatment methodology. By framing complex issues in this way, the authors do a disservice to the children, families, and professionals struggling to find answers to difficult questions. In this commentary, we raise questions about the assumptions and several points in Jacobson and Mulick's article.

. . . the authors attempt to demonstrate that the provision of EIBI services will sufficiently increase the long-term income of recipients to cover costs. Using income as a measure of long-term benefit of EIBI is questionable. As Mikesell (1991) stated, "There are questions both about what earning pattern to use and whether that narrow production view truly gauges the social worth of an individual; this approach is seldom used in current benefit-cost analysis" (p. 193).

In addition to the questionable use of income as a measure of benefit, Jacobson *et al.* (1998) made a number of assumptions having no substantial empirical or theoretical foundation. . . . They also assumed that "Without EIBI the majority of children with autism . . . will manifest enduring dependency on special education and adult developmental disability services." This critical assumption is made without reference to any substantiating research. The authors further assumed in their model that children with autism . . . who achieve normal functioning will no longer need any special services after 3 years of EIBI and will earn average wages during their lifetime. A cost-benefit model that is based almost entirely on conjecture and speculation offers little insight into reality and is of little use. In fact, poorly constructed models may be more damaging because of improper and misleading conclusions. Basically, Jacobson and Mulick (2000) attempt to demonstrate that EIBI is cost-benefit effective because they *assume* EIBI is the most effective treatment. Basing resource decisions on this type of model is clearly the type of deception about which Mikesell was warning. . . . (Marcus, Rubin, & Rubin, 2000)

RCs of this type can be particularly useful when we work on evaluation in an EAP writing course. This RC, like many RCs, begins with direct citation to the published paper and a brief general summary. The transition to evaluation is marked by *however* and the perceived main weaknesses are generally stated along with the effect of these weaknesses. The authors conclude their introduction by stating that they will call into question the assumptions underlying the work by Jacobson and Mulick. In the end, the RC authors' stance is quite clear.

Bloch (2003) also argues that published letters to journals editors (i.e., those written in response to a published paper) can be a valuable source of materials for teaching evaluative writing, particularly in terms of organization and content. In his analysis of letters to journal editors he identified several categories of evaluative commentary that could prove useful to graduate student writers and revealed that the content of most letters are of these types.[1]

- Negative criticism of some research claims
- Positive evaluation of some research claims
- Giving limited support or criticism to some research claims

Bloch also points out that in his letter corpus, methodologies and discussions of the results are commonly criticized as is the failure to cite relevant research in the field. This awareness of the RA sections that are most likely the target of criticism can be quite helpful to students, who may mistakenly believe that their evaluation should address all parts of an RA.

As with book reviews, however, RCs such as the one excerpted on autism could also potentially lead students astray. It is quite negative, offering little positive evaluation. The authors state that the research in question

> [is] based on faulty assumptions, inadequate research findings, and misuse of benefit-cost analysis methods
>
> do[es] a disservice to the children, families, and professionals struggling to find answers to difficult questions
>
> [engages in the] questionable use of income as a measure of benefit
>
> [introduces] a cost-benefit model that is based almost entirely on conjecture and speculation, offers little insight into reality, and is of little use

These are indeed harsh criticisms of research on a highly controversial issue among autism experts. Unlike more established members of a field, even if new graduate students possessed the disciplinary knowledge to engage in such scathing criticism, many would likely hesitate to do so, thus perhaps somewhat limiting the value of such a text. Alternatively, after working with such a text, some students may incorrectly assume that their job in evaluating scholarship is to be as harsh as possible, joining the ranks of what John Swales has described as "the Young and the Cruel" (John Swales, personal communication). Thus, if RA commentaries are used in the teaching of eval-

---

[1]RCs of this type may also include general statements as to why the research is important and citations to the letter writer's own research, but such commentary is less frequent.

uation, it is also important to discuss the students' purpose in evaluating a piece of scholarship. Is the goal to find as many weaknesses as possible in a given paper? Should both negative and positive comments be included? To what extent should students strive to offer a fair assessment, recognizing both strengths and weaknesses. In recognizing weaknesses, students should also be encouraged to develop some understanding as to why or how those weaknesses may have evolved.

Perhaps a better starting point for new students would be an RC similar to this second example. This RC began as an oral response to a conference paper on sleep deprivation. The paper was presented at the Fortieth Annual Meeting of the Society of Thoracic Surgeons in January 2004 and was subsequently published in the *Annals of Thoracic Surgery* in September that same year. The research examined whether surgeon sleep deprivation affected cardiac surgery outcomes and concluded that sleep deprivation had no impact on morbidity or mortality. The presentation, supported by slides, was only ten minutes long and followed by brief comments by an invited respondent. After the invited response the floor was opened for a short Q and A session. The first of several audience members who had questions for the presenter and first author (Dr. Ellman) was Dr. Ungerleider, who spoke spontaneously.[2] Below is the published exchange between the two, which has been slightly edited to reduce its length.

> DR ROSS UNGERLEIDER (Portland, OR): This is an important study, and it is important because of the work hours issue that we all now confront and wrestle with.
>
> I would like to point out that there has been considerable work on this topic. Bud Baldwin, . . . who is an authority on this topic, has actually been on the surgeon's side, and he points out the distinction between work hours and sleep hours, and I think it is important for us, because the big difference is that future studies probably should focus on this distinction. . . .
>
> True sleep deprivation will affect outcomes in surgery, and we need to be careful, I believe, not to suggest that we don't need sleep. There are, however, some individuals who do need less sleep than others, but we all need sleep. We all need REM sleep to reorder our brains.
>
> And so I have these questions for you and perhaps a suggestion. First of all, what really constitutes sleep deprivation and how do we measure it? Were your surgeons really sleep-deprived? The database, as far as I can

---

[2] I was at the conference and in the audience when the paper was given.

understand it, doesn't say anything about sleep. It only says things about work hours. And so I wonder if you can review your data in terms of work hours as opposed to sleep hours, since we really don't know much about the sleep of your surgeons, and the issue that we confront is one about work hours.

It is important for us to evaluate our ability to work and perhaps not dispute the well-known data that we need sleep. This would be a much more helpful "spin" on your data. If we acknowledge that sleep is important and look at data regarding work hours, we may be better able to construct what our futures as CT surgeons would look like. I wonder if you could rephrase your comments and your paper's conclusions with respect to work hours?

Thanks for having the courage to stand up there and present this paper.

DR ELLMAN: . . . Dr Ungerleider, thanks for your comments . . .

We are not trying to assert that surgeons don't need sleep. In fact, what we are trying to assert is the idea that surgeons should not have mandatory restrictions on their work hours. A part of the process of becoming a trained surgeon is realizing your limits and knowing when you have to sleep. Now, some people would obviously argue that self-restriction like that wouldn't necessarily work. Our attempt in this study was to at least demonstrate that sleep deprivation didn't lead to medical errors.

In terms of the sleep hours, it is literally impossible in a retrospective study to actually tell how much sleep these surgeons had over this time period. With our guidelines, we felt that we limited it in such a way that the only possible amount of sleep that they could have had was no greater than four hours. Many authors suggest that less than 5 hours of sleep constitutes sleep deprivation, and this was the definition we used. Moreover, we designed our study based on the Accreditation Council for Graduate Medical Education work-hour guidelines that essentially forbid operating the day after a night's call.

With regards to looking back over these data as a means to assess work hours rather than sleep, I think that would bring in even more problems and confounding factors than we already have. Objectively, we only really knew when the surgeon was in the operating room, and thus used these data as the main determinants for sleep deprivation in our study. Future studies regarding work hours would be very helpful, but would most likely require a prospective study design. Again, I appreciate your comments. (Ellman et al., 2004)

An exhaustive analysis of this type of commentary is not possible within the scope of this chapter, but generally a conference commentary at the Society of Thoracic Surgeons meeting will begin with some thanks and a compliment to the author, after which some background information is given in preparation for the questions. Commentators generally indicate how many questions they will ask, presumably to help the paper presenter formulate his or her response. After asking the question(s), the commentator then generally concludes by again thanking the presenter for his or her contribution. Thus, in addition to being exemplars of critical evaluations of research, such commentaries can also serve to demonstrate typical conference etiquette in a question and answer session. In this latter regard, as a public response, these commentaries are very polite, unlike some other occluded evaluative genres such as peer reviews of manuscripts where reviewers may be less concerned about possible face threatening acts (FTAs) (see Belcher (2007) and Kourilova (1996) for more on manuscript reviews). Dr. Ungerleider simply asks a question about the definition of sleep deprivation, rather than directly stating that the definition employed in the study could have skewed the results. Thus, an added benefit of introducing RCs of this type is that they may somewhat dispel the notion that North Americans, particularly those in the United States, are always direct in their communications with others. The goal of softening possible FTAs can be further explored by examining the organization of Dr. Ungerleider's commentary and Dr. Ellman's response. As is often the case in other kinds of evaluative texts such as published reviews (Belcher, 1995), Dr. Ungerleider adopted a "good news–bad news" approach to organizing his comments so as to soften the criticism. Dr. Ellman's response is equally careful so as to not directly dismiss the concern regarding the definition of sleep deprivation.

In the RC Dr. Ungerleider is concerned about two aspects of the study: the definition of sleep deprivation and the greater importance of work hours as opposed to the amount of sleep a surgeon has had. These concerns reveal the importance of how key study concepts are defined, as these definitions could have affected the robustness of the findings and hence conclusions.

The exchange between the two surgeons can be used to draw students' attention to how such factors as definitions can influence the outcomes of a study and are therefore worthy of consideration when evaluating research.

In addition to examining the kind of criticism being made, students can also usefully look at how positive or negative Dr. Ungerleider's commentary is overall and how Dr. Ellman explains that changing the focus to work hours cannot be done. (This aspect of the exchange can in fact be particularly important for students who may eventually need to respond to reviewer comments on a paper for publication.) Dr. Ellman's use of both *I* and *we* in his response can also be highlighted, as this is important to distinguish his own opinion, particularly at the end of his response, from the thinking of his group. Another feature worth noting is how Dr. Ellman speculates about future studies incorporating work hours, specifically his use of *would*.

To encourage students to both understand and engage in some critical inquiry, a task such as the one below may be useful.

Task One

At many professional meetings or conferences it is common to provide audience members an opportunity to ask questions or comment on the research that was presented. Read the commentary, which followed a conference paper on sleep deprivation and surgical outcomes. With a partner discuss the questions that follow.

1. Dr. Ungerleider does not begin his commentary with his questions. Why? How would you characterize his comments before the questions?

2. How important are the compliments at the beginning and end of Dr. Ungerleider's commentary?

3. How critical or negative are Dr. Ungerleider's comments? What expressions does he use to soften his comments?

4. There are a number of aspects of a study that can be scrutinized. Which of the following seem to be of most concern to Dr. Ungerleider? The data? The interpretations of the data? Assumptions underlying the study? How important are such concerns in your field?

5. In his final comment Dr. Ungerleider states that, "It is important for us to evaluate our ability to work and perhaps not dispute the well-known data that we need sleep. This would be a much more helpful 'spin' on your data." What does he mean by *spin*?

6. Suppose you were preparing a written evaluation of a published RA. Do you think you would use the word *spin* to talk about the perspective used to characterize some data? Why or why not? Can you think of any alternatives to *spin*?

7. How well does Dr. Ellman address the concerns raised by Dr. Ungerleider?

8. How important is it for Dr. Ellman to thank Dr. Ungerleider for his comments?

9. Dr. Ellman begins his response by saying, "We are not trying to assert. . . . In fact, what we are trying to assert is. . . ." Do you think this sequence with the repetition of *trying to assert* and the use of the progressive would be useful for both spoken and written academic English? Why or why not?

10. How would you characterize the exchange between the two? How important do you think it is to maintain a similar level of respect in a written review for a course assignment? What about a manuscript review for a journal?

11. What could Dr. Ungerleider ask as a follow-up question?

12. Take Dr. Ungerleider's concerns about whether the surgeons were actually sleep deprived and write them up as if you were reviewing the study for homework in one of your courses.

Recognizing the kind of reasonable criticism that could be levied against a study is an important initial step toward becoming engaged with the scholarship of one's field (Cheng, 2006). Recognition alone, however, may not lead to the actual production of criticism. To establish the foundation for critical inquiry, students can consider the following set of questions provided in *Academic Writing for Graduate Students* (Swales & Feak, 2004).

1. Who is the audience?

2. What is the purpose of the article?

3. What research question(s) is (are) being addressed in the article? (Stating the research question as a *yes* or *no* question will help you identify the focus of a paper. In our experience a question such as *Does herbal tea cause tooth decay?* can be more useful in guiding your thinking than can a simple statement establishing the topic, as with *This paper is about herbal tea and tooth decay.*)

4. What conclusions are drawn from the research?

5. What kind of evidence is offered in support of the conclusions? Is there any evidence that could or should have been included, but was not?

6. Are the conclusions valid or plausible based on the evidence? Why or why not?

7. Are there any important assumptions underlying the article? How do these influence the conclusions?

8. Does the paper make an original contribution to the field? Why or why not?

If we consider Dr. Ungerleider's comments again, we can see how the eight questions (particularly Questions 3–7) relate to the concerns that he raises, further demonstrating that interacting with some given information, whether spoken or written, can help them determine the extent to which the associated claims and conclusions are credible. Moreover, these questions can help students begin to formulate their own deeper understanding or interpretation of a text that may be distinct from that of the text author (Gillen, 2006).

Apart from their value in examining the authors' stance, including the use of hedges, boosters, attitude markers, and self-mention (see Hyland, 2005) as well as reporting verbs, placement of *by* V-*ing* clauses, and tense, the two RCs can help L2 students understand that assumptions will influence a study and that these assumptions in turn can affect whether the claims or conclusions emerging from that study are persuasive. Although highly relevant for understanding the reasoning and conclusions of an article, assumptions can be particularly difficult to identify because they may be unstated or presumed.

Cheng's (2006) case study supports this approach to developing materials to help L2 students become better equipped to evaluate scholarship. His case study of Fengchen revealed that, contrary to the view that native culture interferes with students' ability to successfully engage in critical evaluation, L2 students are not necessarily so constrained by culture as may be envisioned and suggested by earlier research. This is not to say that culture has no influence, but perhaps we should focus somewhat less on cultural differences and rather more on lack of experience so that we might provide students in EAP writing courses opportunities to develop strategies for academic criticism. We need to look at many types of scholarly evaluation—look beyond RAs, which may offer minimal evaluation of a specific study or a broader area of research (Cheng, 2006), and book reviews, which may evaluate aspects of a book that are not highly relevant for the scholarly evaluation of an RA, and include such texts as the RC (both those written in response to an RA and those generated initially in response to a conference presentation) since their primary purpose is to evaluate a piece of scholarship.

Like book reviews, RCs are a site where there is an open, explicit encounter with the author(s) of a particular piece of scholarship. However, unlike book reviews, which examine the treatment of many facets of a topic, the intent of the RC engagement is typically to call some very specific aspect of the work into question, to alert readers to alternative perspectives, or to even warn readers to treat the results cautiously. Thus, if book reviews are considered to be a "source of friction" within a field and potentially threatening to the author(s) (Hyland, 2000), RCs are even more so. RCs have considerable potential as examples of how experts execute the type of analysis expected of graduate students in a U.S. university, but there is a need for research on this neglected genre so that we can create suitable teaching materials. By starting with an RC that takes a more moderate and less confrontational approach to criticism (such as the conference paper RC), we can help even the most reluctant of new graduate student writers begin to see the importance of evaluating the work of others in creating disciplinary knowledge and to see that the goal of evaluation is not to wage an attack. By exposing students to many different kinds of academic evaluation, we will be better able to help our L2 students develop rhetorical and linguistic strategies to critically engage with the scholarship in their fields and help them realize that evaluation can lead them to communicate not only what they know, but also what they themselves think.

*   *   *

CHRISTINE FEAK has been a lecturer at the English Language Institute, University of Michigan, since 1988, where she is the lead lecturer for writing courses. She is co-author of *Academic Writing for Graduate Students* and *English in Today's Research World*.

REFERENCES

Ahmad, U. K. (1997). *Scientific research articles in Malay: A situated discourse analysis*. Unpublished doctoral dissertation, University of Michigan—Ann Arbor.

Atkinson, D., & Ramanathan, V. (1995). Cultures of writing: An ethnographic comparison of L1 and L2 university writing/language programs. *TESOL Quarterly, 29,* 539–568.

Belcher, D. (1995). Writing critically across the curriculum. In D. Belcher & G. Braine (Eds.), *Academic writing in a second language: Essays on research and language pedagogy* (pp. 135–154). Norwood, NJ: Ablex.

―――. (2007). Seeking acceptance in an English-only research world. *Journal of Second Language Writing, 16*(1), 1–22.

Bereiter, C., & Scardamalia, M. (1987). *The psychology of written composition.* Hillsdale, NJ: Lawrence Erlbaum.

Bloch, J. (2003). Creating materials for teaching evaluation in academic writing: Using letters to the editor in L2 composition courses. *English for Specific Purposes, 22*(4), 347–364.

Cadman, K. (1997) Thesis writing for international students: A question of identity? *English for Specific Purposes, 16*(1), 3–14.

Caffarella, R. S., & Barnett, B. G. (2000). Teaching doctoral students to become scholarly writers: The importance of giving and receiving critiques. *Studies in Higher Education, 25*(1), 39–52.

Canagarajah, A. S. (2002). *Critical academic writing and multilingual students.* Ann Arbor: University of Michigan Press.

Cheng, A. (2006). Analyzing and enacting academic criticism: The case of an L2 graduate learner of academic writing. *Journal of Second Language Writing, 15*(4), 279–306.

Craik, A. D. D. (2000). [Review of the book *Flow Instability*]. *Journal of Fluid Mechanics, 424,* 378.

Dobson, B., & Feak, C. B. (2001). A cognitive modeling approach to teaching critique writing to nonnative speakers. In D. Belcher & A. Hirvela (Eds.), *Linking literacies: Perspectives on L2 reading-writing connections* (pp. 186–199). Ann Arbor: University of Michigan Press.

Ellman, P., Law, M., Tache-Leon, C., Reece, T. B., Maxey, T., Peeler, B., et al. (2004). Sleep deprivation does not affect operative results in cardiac surgery. *Annals of Thoracic Surgery, 78*(3), 906–911.

Firth, A., & Wagner, J. (1997). On discourse, communication, and (some) fundamental concepts in SLA research. *Modern Language Journal, 81*(3), 285–300.

Gillen, C. M. (2006). Criticism and interpretation: Teaching the persuasive aspects of research articles. *Life Sciences Education, 5*(1), 34–38.

Godoy, L. A. (2006). Differences between experts and novices in the review of Engineering journal papers. *Journal of Professional Issues in Engineering Education and Practice, 132*(1), 24–28.

Hyland, K. (2000). *Disciplinary discourses: Social interactions in academic writing.* London: Longman.

———. (2002). Activity and evaluation: Reporting practices in academic writing. In J. Flowerdew (Ed.), *Academic Discourse* (pp. 115–130). New York: Longman.

———. (2005). Stance and engagement: A model of interaction in academic discourse. *Discourse Studies, 7*(2), 173–192.

Kaplan, R. B. (1988). Contrastive rhetoric and second language learning: Notes toward a theory of contrastive rhetoric. In A. Purves (Ed.), *Writing across language and cultures: Issues in contrastive rhetoric* (pp. 275–304). Newbury Park, CA: Sage.

Kourilova, M. (1996). Interactive function of language in peer reviews of medical papers written by non-native users of English. *UNESCO ALSED-LSP Newsletter, 19*(1), 4–21.

Lea, M., & Street, B. (1998). Student writing in higher education: An academic literacies approach. *Studies in Higher Education, 23*(2), 157–172.

Marcus, L. M., Rubin, J. S., & Rubin, M. A. (2000). Benefit–cost analysis and autism services: A response to Jacobson and Mulick. *Journal of Autism and Developmental Disorders, 30*(6), 595–598.

Motta-Roth, D. (1998). Discourse analysis and academic book reviews: A study of text and disciplinary cultures. In I. Fortanet, S. Posteguillo, J. C. Palmer, & J. F. Coll (Eds.), *Genre studies in English for academic purposes* (pp. 29–59). Castellon, Spain: Publicaciones de la Universitat Jaume I.

Räisänen, C. (2002). The conference forum as a system of genres. In E. Ventola, C. Shalom, & S. Thompson (Eds.). *The language of conferencing* (pp. 69–93). Frankfurt: Peter Lang.

Steen, W. M. (1999). [Review of the book *Laser Welding*]. *Optics and Laser Technology, 31*(7), 529.

Swales, J. M. (2004). *Research genres.* Cambridge, UK: Cambridge University Press.

Swales, J. M., & Feak, C. B. (2004). *Academic writing for graduate students: Essential tasks and skills, 2nd ed.* Ann Arbor: University of Michigan Press.

Woodward-Kron, R. (2002). Critical analysis versus description? Examining the relationship in successful student writing. *Journal of English for Academic Purposes, 1*(2), 121–143.

4

English for Professional Academic Purposes: Writing for Scholarly Publication

KEN HYLAND
University of Hong Kong

Abstract

With English now established as the international language of research and scholarship, EAP practitioners are increasingly asked to assist junior academic staff with the academic literacy skills demanded by publication and conference presentation in a foreign language. In this chapter I address this growing area of academic literacy support by focusing on English for Professional Academic Purposes (EPAP): research and instruction with the goal of facilitating academic publication and presentation in English. The chapter first maps out the domain of EPAP and discusses why it is needed and then goes on to provide a theoretical underpinning for work in the area and some instructional practices.

English is now unquestionably the language of international scholarship and an important medium of research communication for non–native English speaking academics around the world. While accurate figures are hard to come by, perhaps one in five of the world's population now speaks English with reasonable competence (Crystal, 2003), and the language is rapidly coming to dominate the dissemination of knowledge. Universities in many countries now require staff to present at international conferences and, more crucially, publish in major, high-impact, peer-reviewed Anglophone journals as a prerequisite for tenure, promotion, and career advancement. As a consequence, EAP practitioners increasingly find themselves called upon to venture into this unfamiliar terrain to improve the writing for publication skills of colleagues from other departments. In this chapter I address this growing area of academic literacy support, focusing on English for Professional Academic Purposes (EPAP): research and instruction with the goal of facilitating academic publication and presentation in English.

Scholarly Publication and EAP: Mapping the Territory

Research shows that academics all over the world are increasingly less likely to publish in their own languages and to find their English language publications cited more often. References to English language publications, for example, have reached 85 percent in French science journals, and English makes up over 95 percent of all publications in the *Science Citation Index*. Swales (2004) observes that many leading European and Japanese journals have switched to publishing in English, and this Anglicization of published research can also be seen in the dramatic increase in papers written by non–native English speakers in leading English language journals (e.g., Wood, 2001). Many prestigious Chinese universities, for example, stipulate that their Ph.D. students must have at least one paper accepted by an international journal before they can graduate, while the Chinese Academy of Sciences supplements the salaries of researchers who have published internationally (Cargill & O'Connor, 2006). With libraries increasingly subscribing to online versions of journals, the impact of English becomes self-perpetuating, since it is in these journals where authors will be most visible on the world stage and receive the most credit.

While the driving forces behind this global spread of English in academic life are complex and often tied to political and commercial interests, one can view these developments in two contrasting ways. It is possible to see the growth of English as establishing a neutral lingua franca, efficiently facilitating the free exchange of knowledge across the globe, or as tool of linguistic hegemony and cultural imperialism (e.g., Pennycook, 1994). It takes on additional importance for scholars, however, who want their work to be widely read and frequently cited. Participation in this global web of scholarship is now an obligation for many academics as publication has become inseparable from the process by which prestige and credibility are assessed. Publication equals "productivity" and is used as a crude measure of worth, with institutions conferring promotion and tenure on the length of personal bibliographies. Additional pressure to publish comes from institutional sources as publication is often a key element in department reviews and Research Assessment Exercises in many countries link government funding directly to individual publication.

The challenges of writing for publication are, however, considerable in today's competitive climate where it is not unusual for journals in some fields to receive ten times more submissions than they can use. Moreover, for writers it not only involves developing the research craft skills and "ways of knowing" of a discipline, but also control of its specialized discourse conventions. A paper will only find its way to publication if it frames ideas and employs forms of argument that readers are likely to find familiar (Hyland, 2000/2004).

These requirements are daunting to all academics as native English speakers also struggle to produce polished prose (Casanave & Vandrick, 2003) and editors frequently point out that many of the difficulties experienced by NNSs are also shared by NSs (e.g., Gosden, 1992). Swales (2004, p. 56), in fact, argues that the most important distinction in publishing is not between native (NES) and non–native English speakers (NNES), but

> between experienced or "senior" researcher/scholars and less experienced or "junior" ones—between those who know the academic ropes in their chosen specialisms and those who are learning them.

There is certainly something to this view, as the growing proportion of papers by L2 authors in refereed English language journals testifies. Native English speakers rarely receive help with academic writing during their university careers and are often less "academically bilingual" than many NNESs, and we should not exclude them from EPAP classes. Our writing for publication classes for doctoral students in London, for example, usually contained as many domestic as international students.

This, then, is the territory that EPAP occupies: conducting research and developing materials and activities designed to facilitate the participation of novice scholars in the global research network of English.

Evidence for Need

Despite the fact that all newcomers feel challenged and intimidated by writing for publication, attention has largely focused on the obstacles faced by non–native English speaking researchers in getting into print. This is certainly the view of journal publishers and editors who have viewed the surge of NNES activity in the publishing arena with some alarm. This extract from an editorial in *Oral Oncology* is typical of this concern:

> An emerging problem facing all journals is the increasing number of submissions from non-English-speaking parts of the world, where the standard of written English may fall below the expectations of a scientific publication. (Scully & Jenkins, 2006)

Research shows that while editors concur that "acceptance or rejection of a manuscript is primarily based on scientific merit" (Gosden, 1992, p. 129), editors in many disciplines insist on having submissions vetted by native English speakers, often requiring writers to pay copyeditors to correct their prose before it is accepted. Referees and editors, in fact, offer a great deal of unsolicited language assistance, and suggestions for would-be authors regularly occur in the pages of science journals (e.g., Jaffe, 2003; Tychinin & Kamnev, 2005).

A central cause of difficulty for novice writers, particularly those working outside the metropolitan centers of research, is their isolation from current literature and the demand that they situate their work in a rhetorical tradition. Gosden (1992, p. 115) summarizes the views of his sample of science journal editors in this way:

> The broad term 'isolation' covers many causes, for example: not carefully reading 'Instructions to Authors'; unfamiliarity with the journal and its academic level; not previewing previous literature well and relating to others' work, possibly due to a lack of literature/library facilities; a lack of awareness of what constitutes publishable research; and unfamiliarity with the broad (and unwritten) 'rules of the game'.

Many of these disadvantages apply equally to NES outsiders.

Research has also revealed similar concerns among non–native English scholars themselves. Over two-thirds of the 585 Cantonese L1 academics in Hong Kong who responded to Flowerdew's (1999) questionnaire, for example, felt they were at a disadvantage compared with NESs, with about half citing language issues as the main problem. Follow-up interviews with 26 respondents showed that many felt hampered by "less facility of expression" and a "less rich vocabulary." While it is difficult to say whether these self-perceptions represent actual disadvantage, they may have an impact on writers' confidence and how they set about drafting and revising academic papers to the rhetorical standards demanded by editors, referees, and other gate-keepers.

Research into the writing processes adopted by novice NNES academics also suggest that writing for publication can be a laborious task. St. John (1987), for instance, found that her sample of Spanish researchers rarely undertook structural revision and focused instead on precise expression in English through changes in word order and lexis, sometimes via translation from Spanish. Similarly, Li's (2006) account of a Chinese doctoral student of physics shows how advice from supervisors, a journal editor, and reviewers helped guide the student through six drafts and several painstaking resubmissions before her paper was finally accepted for publication. Gosden (1995) also found considerable text revisions by seven Japanese post-graduate students. In response to journal reviewers and colleagues, they made over 320 changes between the first draft and published paper, changes that Gosden sees as a movement toward more mature writing characterized by a greater range of cohesive devices, explicitness, hedging, and subordination.

Essentially then, revisions represent a reworking of the rhetorical goals of a paper to more clearly meet the perceived needs of readers. This is shown even more clearly in a later study in which Gosden (2003) points out that the majority of critical feedback from reviewers to NNESs writing for a scientific publication addressed interpersonal features of the presentation rather than technical or ideational material. In a context where editors are overwhelmed with submissions and are often looking for reasons to reject manuscripts, non-standard language may serve as good a reason as any to justify this.

Theoretical Understandings: Situated Learning and Social Constructionism

The issues faced by newcomers to academic publishing have largely been seen in the theoretical context of the social practices of disciplinary communities, drawing on both a situated learning and social constructionist theories. These perspectives help show how the re-drafting process can be seen not just as the transformation of a text, but also the apprenticing of an individual writer into the knowledge constructing practices of a discipline. Gatekeeping genres such as research articles are of particular interest in this context because they can be viewed as sites of disciplinary engagement (Hyland, 2000/2004), where insiders are able to make use of their cultural knowledge to gain advantages over novices. The final product is seen as a social act that can only occur within a particular community and audience. More specifically, by focusing on scholarly writing as a situated practice and by examining the local interactions that occur in negotiating the passage of a paper to publication, it becomes possible to see how participation functions as a mode of learning.

This process of writing and publishing research papers reveals both the regulating mechanisms of a particular discourse community and the dynamism of its practices, at least partly because the norms of the discipline are constantly defined and changed through the participation of newcomers to the discipline. Most centrally for EPAP, however, is the fact that learning to write for a professional peer audience is the process by which novices are socialized into an academic community: it is the recognized route to insider status.

This perspective draws on Lave and Wenger's (1991) well-known work on situated learning and the idea that we acquire the skills and practices of our professions mainly by participating in these practices and not just by being taught about them. The metaphor of "apprenticeship" has been used to describe this process, although Lave and Wenger talk of "legitimate peripheral participation" to conceptualize learning as engagement in the sociocultural activities of "communities of practice." In other words we learn by doing, gradually developing an academic identity as we come to write and think in ways compatible with those of our discipline under the guidance of more senior members, more experienced peers, and the comments of editors and reviewers (Casanave & Vandrick, 2003). When considering writing for publication, this apprenticeship involves a careful negotiation with two principal audiences: the community of scholars who will read the finished paper and hopefully cite it and use it in their own research and the journal gatekeepers who will judge the paper as ready for publication.

In terms of the larger community audience, we need to see texts as the outcome of interactions among academics engaged in a web of professional and social associations. The ways writers present their topics, signal their allegiances, and stake their claims represent careful negotiations with, and considerations of, their colleagues so their writing displays a professional competence in discipline-approved practices. In other words, writers must be aware of the distinctive ways of identifying issues, asking questions, addressing a literature, criticizing colleagues, and presenting arguments that readers anticipate in their field (Hyland, 2000/2004, 2005; Myers, 1990). An important consideration here is the need to balance a personal stance against the demands and expectations of the professional discourse community. Novice writers often believe that they have to strive for an original voice in order to be noticed, but this fails to grasp the essentially social nature of writing for publication. Originality is not the expression of an autonomous self but of writing that is embedded in and built on the existing theories, discourses, and topics already legitimated in the community.

Disciplinary socialization, however, is most immediately and locally revealed in the process of negotiating revisions to a paper and incorporating the feedback of editors and reviewers. The process of revising a paper and responding to editorial changes can be a fraught one for novice writers. Not only must they rewrite and polish what may have taken months to craft in order to situate their work more centrally in the concerns of the discipline, but they must also incorporate others' views, relinquishing some of their textual ownership (Lee & Norton, 2003). Equally difficult on this learning path is understanding and responding to the comments of editors and reviewers (Gosden, 1992, 1995). Rejection or requests for major rewriting are never welcome and comments may seem overly critical, condescending, or dismissive. On the other hand, hedged criticism and obliqueness can be misunderstood by NNESs and may lead novice authors to underplay criticisms and fail to make necessary changes (Gosden, 2003).

I have only sketched some of the issues raised by research and theory into NNES publishing, but the discussion reveals some of the complexities involved and helps to establish a framework for EPAP pedagogy. I turn to some of the teaching implications in the next section.

Instructional Practices

Clearly the advanced literacy competencies and insider knowledge involved in crafting a paper for publication and negotiating editorial correspondence present considerable challenges for many early-career scholars, whatever their first language. There is, however, a large and growing literature concerning the characteristics of published articles in different disciplines and it would be remiss of us as EAP practitioners not to make this knowledge explicit to those seeking to publish in English. Notwithstanding that the practices of publication and associated expectations differ markedly from one field to another, teaching should, I would argue, focus principally on isolating key features of texts and making these explicit to writers. This involves both raising awareness of the ways language is used to most persuasive effect and encouraging reflection on writers' own preferred argument practices. In addition, however, I think it is productive to assist novice writers with the strategies they might employ in the publication process itself, giving particular attention to the analysis of their target publications and the navigation of the revision process.

Targeting a Journal

One of the most important findings of research into successful writing is that writers consider their readers, even before they begin to write. For publishing authors a key aspect of this involves writing with a specific journal in mind (revising for another journal if it is subsequently rejected). This means researching target journals to ensure that their paper both addresses the relevant audience and is presented in the appropriate way. While this might be a somewhat tedious part of publishing, there is really no way around this, and a few hours of intensive surfing of publishers' websites getting to know the requirements and kinds of submissions they are looking for can help avoid an editorial rejection before reviewers have even seen the paper. There are a number of useful activities that can help raise an awareness of these strategies among inexperienced writers.

Esteem

Among the issues that novices can usefully be encouraged to consider is the hierarchy of esteem that attaches to journals. All publications have a subjective ranking in a discipline from the blue chip through the solidly respectable to the third tier commendable, the locally creditable, and beyond. Such discriminations are part of the intellectual stock-in-trade of the successful academic, and an understanding of them is important both in terms of a successful publishing outcome and the degree of credit that is likely to accrue to the writer from acceptance.

Students in EPAP courses can draw up a list of the journals in their area and rank them according to their relative prestige into, say, four or five categories, such as those suggested in the last paragraph. They can then discuss their decisions with peers from the same discipline or with more experienced disciplinary insiders who are likely to be familiar with the fine gradations that distinguish journals. They might then check these impressions against the journal impact factors in the Science Citation Index (SCI), available online through the *Web of Science* www.isinet.com/journals, and perhaps draw up a list of the different criteria they would use to judge the quality of a journal (impact, rejection rates, publishing times, etc.). In this way students can gain a better understanding of the relative risks and rewards of seeking to publish in particular journals and make more accurate assessments of their possible chances of success.

Journal Readership and Specialism

Successful papers also reveal the writer's knowledge of the market for the paper in the sense that it is relevant to the audience and timely in its appearance. These two factors may be more important than originality in getting a paper published, and while such decisions clearly involve knowledge of the field and its current literature, they also relate to the question of finding the right niche for the topic. In other words, the author of a successful paper *knows the journal* to which the paper is submitted. This involves knowing the academic level at which the journal is pitched, knowing the sort of papers it publishes, and knowing its intended readership. The author can then respond accordingly and choose a journal that most closely fits the level, subject matter, and proposed audience of his or her paper.

EPAP instructors can encourage writers to be clear as to the focus of their target journal in order to improve the chances of successful publication. In turn, of course, this also means that they need to clearly understand the direction of their own work so they are able to position themselves in relation to the literature and to see how it fits the orientation and interests of the readers of the target journal. To accomplish this fit, students can summarize core aspects of their (planned) paper with a series of one-sentence responses to questions such as:

- What is the topic of the paper?
- What theoretical/methodological approach does it use?
- What issues does it address in the prior literature?
- What is novel in the paper?
- Who will it most interest?

This reflection on, and explicit understanding of, one's own paper makes it easier to then target a range of potential journals for their likely interest in the paper. This can be done as a mini-research activity through library and web searches by looking at back issues to establish the relevance and suitability of the paper for a journal. Students can gain familiarity with the type of papers a journal publishes, the stance or approach it favors, the background knowledge and orientation of its readers, and the composition of its editorial board. As editors often send papers to be refereed by members of the board who may be in the reference list of the submitted paper, additional attention can be given to researching the views and possible responses of this group to the paper.

Journal Format

Publishing requirements, which address formatting, word length, referencing style, submission information, and so on are often publication-specific and usually posted on the publisher's website. It is worthwhile for writers to peruse the Instructions to Authors (ITA) and Aims and Scope statements of the journals they wish to target. These documents, particularly the ITA, should guide a writer's construction of a paper as it is frustrating to have a script returned because it fails to follow the submission guide. To ensure that a script meets these requirements, writers can carry out an Internet search of journal home pages on their target list and check their papers against the submission guidelines.

Writing a Paper

Current theory and research contains a wealth of information on professional academic discourse that can be translated into means of supporting scholars writing in English, either through workshops, personal tutoring, or creation of self-help materials. Unlike earlier intuition-driven practices, this support is based on careful analysis of actual language behaviour, typically employing the techniques of genre and corpus analysis, to make clear how patterns of language work to shape meanings.

I don't want to imply that our teaching should simply help writers to accommodate themselves blindly to the publication machine. We have a responsibility both to students and to the ethical principles of the discipline to ensure that our students are aware of the consequences of their different language choices. Our goal, it seems to me, should always be to enhance writer empowerment and agency without disadvantaging their acceptance within their communities. This means providing support for individual understanding and expression within institutional expectations and conventions, following the sort of advice that Kubota gives to novice writers:

> In my experience, the more the publishing community recognises the credibility of my work, the more I feel empowered to explore alternative ways of expressing ideas. Thus it is advisable for a writer to follow closely the conventions at least in the initial stages of writing for publication in order to gain the cultural capital that will facilitate her or his initiation into the academic community. (Kubota, 2003, p. 65)

This kind of support is provided by an encouraging environment in which writers can reflect on, become aware of, and try out the persuasive options their disciplines make available. I will mention here a few key areas where novice research writers might be brought closer to the patterns of their disciplinary discourses.

Reflecting on Strategies

First, assisting participants of an EPAP writing course must involve, as a necessary starting point, some element of rhetorical consciousness raising and linguistic meta-awareness. I have found it useful to begin EPAP courses with a series of preliminary tasks designed to heighten awareness of writing as a situated disciplinary practice, introducing some basic techniques of genre analysis and encouraging reflection on some of the ways that language is used to communicate research. One way of raising different possibilities to novices is to invite them to share their concerns and introduce them to the practices of established academics found in the ethnographic research literature (e.g., Myers, 1990) or in published first-hand accounts (e.g., Casanave & Vandrick, 2003). They can be asked to respond to ideas such as supervisor mentoring (Lee & Norton, 2003), adapting Ph.D. chapters for publication, the pros and cons of co-authorship, and using good papers as models (Swales & Luebs, 2002).

Another useful task of this kind is suggested by Swales and Feak (2000, p. 16), who bring some key aspects of academic writing in English to students' attention and then encourage reflection on these:

American academic English, in comparison to other research languages, has been said to:

___ 1. be more explicit about its structure and purposes

___ 2. be less tolerant of asides or digressions

___ 3. use fairly short sentences with less complicated grammar

___ 4. have stricter conventions for sub-sections and their titles

___ 5. be more loaded with citations

___ 6. rely more on recent citations

___ 7. have longer paragraphs in terms of number of words

___ 8. point more explicitly to "gaps" or "weaknesses" in the previous research

___ 9. use more sentence connectors (words like *however*)

___10. place the responsibility for clarity and understanding on the writer rather than the reader

 • Reflect on your own first academic language. Place a checkmark (√) before those points where academic writing in your L1 and American academic English differ. If you do not think the difference holds for your language, leave it blank.

 • Are there other differences that you think ought to be mentioned?

 • If you are writing for an American audience how much do you think you need to adapt to an American style? Do you think you need to fully "Americanize" your writing, or can you preserve something of your own academic culture in your academic writing?

Contrastive tasks such as this can focus writers' attention on some recurring organizational patterns and conventions in English that may be familiar to them in their own language, raising issues of effective argument structure, reader awareness, appropriate disciplinary interactions, and cultural identity. Each of these features has attracted considerable attention in recent research, and an explicit awareness of them can be essential to successful academic writing.

Finally, it is also important for writers to consider issues of purpose and audience in their writing before moving on to look in detail at what these might mean for their rhetorical choices. Novices can have difficulties in recontextualizing themselves as writers in the research community rather than as graduate students. Essentially, writing for publication differs from student genres in that it is what Swales (1990) refers to as a *norm developing* practice, concerned with persuasive reporting through the review process and engagement with the professional world, rather than *norm developed*, which simply displays what the student knows. This is often a difficult transition to make, and students are often puzzled why a thesis that meets the requirements of a reputable university fails the criteria of professional journals. Clearly, studies addressed to an expert audience can never just report what was done or what was found, but must textualize work in a way that colleagues recognize as "doing biology" or "doing sociology."

Students might be asked to brainstorm how these requirements for length, generalizable relevance, contextualization in current debates, and so on can be achieved. Additionally, comparative consciousness-raising tasks can again be helpful in revealing how the purpose and audience of a text can differ, and these suggestions can be implemented by students working in groups:

- Compare titles, abstracts, sub-headings, etc., from papers in the fields of group members.
- Compare a relevant research article with an equivalent popularization of the same topic, focusing in particular on how arguments are framed in relation to audience knowledge and possible response to claims.
- Compare a chapter from a thesis with a final published paper, looking at audience, cohesion, argument development, level of detail, and so on.
- Outline a methods or introduction section for an article based on the corresponding section from a thesis (preferably the students' own if possible), discussing what changes have been made to address a different audience and purpose.

Focusing on Structure

The schematic structures of research articles in a range of (largely scientific) disciplines have been described, together with their rhetorical moves and steps, and these can be made explicit to students as a framework for creating their own texts. Swales' (1990) three-part CARS (Creating a Research Space) model of article introductions has been joined by other descriptions for methods (Swales, 2004), results (Brett, 1994), discussion sections (Lewin, Fine, & Young, 2001), and abstracts (Hyland, 2000/2004). Although descriptions offer conflicting analytic schemes for what are essentially similar texts, some have proved remarkably robust and can be extremely useful in helping novice writers both identify rhetorical units and recognize how these perform communicative functions.

These descriptions suggest a number of pedagogic tasks. Students can, for instance, be presented with a diagrammatic representation of the move structure of a typical article that, as far as possible, corresponds to one in the student's discipline. Weissberg and Buker's (1990) *Writing up Research,* for example, offers some useful diagrams of the experimental research paper format that can be discussed and compared with actual articles in students' fields, looking for similarities and differences. These diagrammatic representations can then be fleshed out by looking at individual sections, arranged according to what is assumed to be the order of increasing writing difficulty: methods, abstracts, results, introductions, and discussions (e.g., Swales & Luebs, 2002). This helps writers to see the rhetorical unfolding of a paper and how language is related to particular functions. Within particular article sections, discussions can then revolve around text reconstruction activities, where students put jumbled sentences into their likely original sequence, and matching exercises, where they identify moves and steps and see how these are realized.

Academics intending to write less prosaically patterned social science papers can explore the possible range of options found in presenting key recurring functions. Lewin et al. (2001) define these functions as follows (with the corresponding science sections in parentheses):

1. Motivating the research (introduction)

2. Describing the collection (methods)

3. Reporting results (results)

4. Evaluating results (discussion)

These communicative purposes can be identified in research papers and then explored for possible sub-functions such as *limitations, unexpected results, summarizing results,* and *recommendations,* all of which may be found in Discussion sections. Both Introductions and Discussion sections tend to be especially problematic for novice writers and warrant particular attention by EAP instructors. By first modeling the different moves suggested in the literature and then asking students to identify the individual steps of moves in sample papers, teachers can raise awareness of conventional patterns of realization. Students can then brainstorm the points they want to include in their paper, consider how these might be expressed, and decide where they would be best included in the paper. Swales and Feak (2004, chap. 8) is a particularly valuable resource in this regard, suggesting a number of tasks for pedagogically exploiting the CARS introduction model.

The insights produced by these kinds of activities, into the links between forms and functions and the possible variations in expressing these functions, are frequently a revelation to writers. They can be particularly useful if the EAP instructor's expertise is used in tandem with that of experienced disciplinary colleagues. Cargill and O'Connor (2006), for instance, report the success of a "collaborating-colleague" approach designed for groups of novice Chinese researchers working in this way. Questionnaire returns showed that this collaboration was the most valued aspect of the writing-for-publication course and that students felt they had benefited most from learning about the structure of the article genre and its sections.

Analyzing Sentence and Discourse Features

In addition to an understanding of the rhetorical structure of the research paper, writers need to develop sentence- and discourse-level strategies for expressing meanings. Again, the research literature directs us to the most productive forms. The fact that most novice writers are already skilled analysts in their fields can be put to good effect here by encouraging them to analyze the features of the genres they wish to write.

Concordance software can be very useful in this regard, revealing frequently used ways of expressing meanings. One such productive pattern, for example, is "evaluative *that*" (Hyland & Tse, 2005) (as in *We believe that* or *It seems that*), which allows writers to mark their main argument, summarize the direction of the research, and highlight their stance as the theme of the sentence. Entering the expression *it * that* into a concordancer will search for the word *it* followed by *that* in the near vicinity, producing examples such as these in a corpus of research papers:

it is likely that	*it shows that*	*it is worth noting that*
it seems that	*it is claimed that*	*it is shown that*
it is clear that	*it is true that*	*it suggests that*

When these examples are studied more carefully, they reveal that academic writers use this phrasing extremely frequently to express their evaluation of whether the following statement is likely to be true or not. Advanced students are likely to benefit from exploring the kinds of predicates used in the construction, the degree of certainty conveyed, and different ways to present the source of the evaluations (Hyland, 2006).

An important feature of much recent research is an attempt to reveal how persuasion is accomplished not only through representing ideas, but also by the construction of an appropriate authorial self (Hyland, 2005). These features include, for example, imperatives, personal pronouns, hedging and boosting, and citation practices. The importance of all these items can be highlighted using corpus searches for common items and then concordancing these. For instance, the frequency of **self-mention** (I, we, our, etc.) (Hyland, 2001) can be identified in a relevant corpus and then individual instances analyzed in concordance lines to see the particular function they are associated with. Students may decide, for example, whether the form is used to express one of the following functions:

- explaining what was done (*We interviewed ten teachers from schools in . . .*)

- structuring the discourse (*First, I will discuss the methodology used . . .*)

- showing a result (*Our findings show that the . . .*)

- making a claim (*I think two factors are significant . . .*)

In turn, this could lead to a discussion concerning the degree of acceptable personal intrusion and commitment in a given discipline.

Hedges represent one of the most frequent rhetorical features of academic writing in all disciplines. These are devices such as *possibly, might,* and *likely,* which withhold complete commitment to a proposition, allowing information to be presented as an opinion rather than fact. They imply that a claim is based on plausible reasoning rather than certain knowledge and so indicate the degree of confidence it might be wise to attribute to a claim while allowing writers to open a discursive space for readers to dispute interpretations. The most frequent hedges and their functions can be identified using a concordance program, and then students can be asked to speculate on why writers chose to hedge at certain points and whether they chose to express the hedge personally or objectively.

An awareness of hedges can also be approached through the use of text extracts (Hyland, 1996). To discover the effect of hedges on statements students can:

- examine a text and distinguish statements that report facts from those that are unproven
- identify all hedges in a text, circling the forms used, and account for their use at that point
- locate and remove all hedges and discuss the effect on the meaning of the text
- identify hedging forms and compile a scale ranking the amount of certainty they express
- consider a series of reformulations that vary the levels of certainty of a text and evaluate whether they accurately report the original statements
- determine whether the forms vary cross-culturally by translating them into the L1

In addition to raising consciousness of forms, students also need to see the importance of hedges as discourse-based strategies and how they relate to the writer's overall text plan. One way of illustrating the effect of hedges on a text is to examine the same content in different evidential contexts. Thus students can be asked to compare an article with a popularization of the same topic, as a text with all hedges removed clearly becomes a different type of text, altogether more certain.

Another key feature of research papers well covered in the literature is that of **citation** (Hyland, 2000/2004). The inclusion of references to the work of others is obviously central to academic persuasion as it both grounds a text in previous work in a discipline and displays the writer's status as an insider. It helps align him or her with a particular community or orientation, confirming that this is someone who is knowledgeable about the topics, approaches, and issues that currently interest and inform the field. But because discourse communities see the world in different ways, they also write about it in different ways, with disciplines employing different frequencies and forms. Essentially, we not only find a heavier use of citations in the humanities and social sciences, but also a preference for reporting verbs such as *discuss, suggest, argue*, etc., which refer to *discourse activities* and often carry an evaluative element in reporting others' work. Engineers and scientists, in contrast, tend to use fewer citations and prefer verbs that point to the research itself like *observe, discover, show, analyze,* which remove interpretation and emphasize real-world actions.

In terms of pedagogy, students can examine a research paper in their field to study where reference is made to previous work, *why* the author has decided to cite at that point, what material has been cited, and what can be safely left uncited. Participants can also look at the forms used, listing the reporting verbs used and the evaluative weight they carry—that is, what they suggest about the writer's attitude to the cited material. Attention can also be drawn to whether citations are mainly integral (cited author is in the citing sentence) or non-integral (cited author is in parenthesis) (Swales, 1990, p. 148) and why these choices have been made. Several studies have also sought to explain tense choices in citing the work of others, and students might wish to examine Swales and Feak's (2004, pp. 254–255) analysis of this issue:

- Pattern I: reference to single study—researcher as agent—past tense
- Pattern II: reference to areas of inquiry—researcher not as agent—present perfect tense
- Pattern III: reference to state of general knowledge—reference to current knowledge—present tense

Citation patterns should be followed up by more intensive work on how to organize an effective literature review that builds an argument toward the issues the writer intends to address.

Finally, a major area of academic writing often mentioned by reviewers and analysts as an area of difficulty for novice writers is that of **interactive metadiscourse** (Hyland, 2005; Hyland & Tse, 2004). Sometimes called *textual metadiscourse* or *metatext,* these linguistic devices allow writers to shape their arguments to the needs and expectations of their target readers, managing the information flow of their text by judicious use of these features:

- *frame markers,* which refer to text boundaries or structure, including items used to sequence, label stages, state goals, and indicate topic shifts *(this is in four parts, in sum, we will now)*
- *transitions,* mainly conjunctions, used to assist comprehension by marking additive, contrastive, and consequential steps in the discourse *(in addition, in contrast, therefore)*

- *endophoric markers*, which make additional material salient to the reader by referring to other parts of the text *(see table two, in the previous section)*
- *evidentials*, which indicate the source of information originating outside the current text (citations)
- *code glosses*, which signal the restatement of information *(for example, that is, in other words)*

Tasks that can sensitize students to the rhetorical effects of metadiscourse include:

- comparing two texts on a similar topic written for different audiences (e.g., a textbook and a research paper) and discussing how each audience is addressed by textual choices
- locating all transitions in a text, classifying them as either addition *(and, furthermore)*, comparison *(similarly, on the other hand)*, or consequence *(therefore, because)*, and seeing which types and forms are most common; comparing these with another text to draw conclusions about the type of argument or audience expectations
- completing a gapped text from which metadiscourse items have been removed and considering the effect of including them
- locating and removing all cases of a particular feature and discussing the effect this has on the comprehensibility, impact, and reader-orientation of the text
- using a concordancer to locate and identify all code glosses or all frame markers in a corpus of research abstracts or introductions and discussing their use

Revising and Negotiating

A final area of reported difficulty for apprentice scholars is navigating the quality-assurance mechanisms of peer-review and editorial commentary (Gosden, 1992, 1995). While the majority of reviewers take considerable care to frame negative reviews in a helpful, collegial way, many novice writers are so disheartened by criticism that they give up at this point. Learning to accept criticism, understand comments, and negotiate the demands of reviewers requires both open-mindedness and determination; these are key strategies of publishing success.

It is helpful if writers can see their submission not as a single text but as part of a *genre set*, the productive and receptive genres that together contribute to a paper's eventual acceptance. Some of these, such as the ITA, editorial board list, and the paper itself, I have mentioned earlier, but other genres that ensure that a journal paper is not just shaped by the author but is influenced by the professional community through the suggestions of reviewers and editors include:

- referees' reports
- editor's summary and directions
- cover letter from the writer listing the changes made, noting where these appear in the revised script, and pointing out which suggestions have not been followed and why

While these genres are occluded, or hidden from wider view, it is important that students have opportunities to see and understand them.

Frequently NNES writers complain that they can't understand the point behind reviewers' comments or the action the editor is recommending. Criticisms are often hedged, phrased as questions, or put in the form of gentle suggestions rather than as required changes (Hyland & Hyland, 2001), and while motivated by politeness, this doesn't help the writers to see what changes they need to make. Tasks that focus on the expression of commentary and suggestion, such as those mentioned above for hedges, for example, can sensitize students to the understatement and mitigation often found in reviews. Other activities might include students working in pairs to respond to the "reviewers" (or, other students') comments on a passage of their work; interpreting editors' letters, deciding whether the overall tone is an encouraging "revise and resubmit" or contains the implicit advice to submit elsewhere; and deciding which comments on a draft should lead to revision and which not, making the case for not making the changes in a cover letter.

Endnote

In this chapter I have outlined aspects of what may be a new and challenging area for EAP practitioners: that of engaging in EPAP and helping professional academics achieve their publication goals. With the growth of English as the language of scholarship and research and the scramble to publish now a career imperative, English for Professional Academic Purposes is fast becoming a central part of EAP's research and teaching activity. Having sketched out the research evidence for taking this area seriously and the relevant theoretical perspectives that inform our approach to it, I have presented some ways that current genre, corpus, and ethnographic research into disciplinary discourses can be translated into classroom support for novice scholars.

I should point out here that this is an area where linguistic research has probably outstripped pedagogic practice. While we have a large and growing understanding of disciplinary discourses and writing practices, we are still far from understanding the specific needs of this group and, indeed, whether the linguistically, socially, and disciplinarily heterogeneous individuals we lump together in this category actually form a single group at all. We are, in other words, flying by the seat of our pants here, and both more research into our students' needs and more understanding of what actually works with different students is required to perfect our practices. What is certain, however, is that this growing and important area is both professionally rewarding and urgently needed, and I look forward to seeing the innovative ways that practitioners will respond to the challenge.

* * *

KEN HYLAND is Professor of Applied Linguistics and Director of the Centre for Applied English Studies at the University of Hong Kong, having recently moved from the University of London. He has taught Applied Linguistics and EAP for more than 30 years in Asia, Australasia, and the UK and has published more than 130 articles and 14 books on language education and academic writing. He was founding co-editor of the *Journal of English for Academic Purposes* and is now co-editor of *Applied Linguistics.*

REFERENCES

Brett, P. (1994). A genre analysis of the results section of sociology articles. *English for Specific Purposes, 13*, 47–69.

Cargill, M., & O'Connor, P. (2006). Developing Chinese scientists' skills for publishing in English: Evaluating collaborating colleague workshops based on genre analysis. *Journal of English for Academic Purposes, 5*, 207–221.

Casanave, C., & Vandrick, S. (Eds.). (2003). *Writing for scholarly publication*. Mahwah, NJ: Lawrence Erlbaum.

Crystal, D. (2003). *English as a global language*. Cambridge, UK: Cambridge University Press.

Flowerdew, J. (1999). Problems of writing for scholarly publication in English: The case of Hong Kong. *Journal of Second Language Writing, 8*(3), 243–264.

Gosden, H. (1992). Research writing and NNSs: From the editors. *Journal of Second Language Writing, 1*(2), 123–139.

———. (1995). Success in research article writing and revision: A social-constructionist perspective. *English for Specific Purposes, 13,* 37–57.

———. (2003) Why not give us the full story? Functions of referees' comments in peer reviews of scientific research papers. *Journal of English for Academic Purposes, 2,* 87–101.

Hyland, F., & Hyland, K. (2001). Sugaring the pill: Praise and criticism in written feedback. *Journal of Second Language Writing, 10*(3), 185–212.

Hyland, K. (1996). Nurturing hedges in the ESP curriculum. *System, 24*(4), 477–490.

———. (2001). Humble servants of the discipline? Self-mention in research articles. *English for Specific Purposes, 20*(3), 207–226.

———. (2004). *Disciplinary discourses: Social interactions in academic writing.* Ann Arbor: University of Michigan Press. (Originally published 2000, London: Longman)

———. (2005). *Metadiscourse.* London: Continuum.

———. (2006). *English for academic purposes: An advanced resource book.* London: Routledge.

Hyland, K., & Tse, P. (2004). Metadiscourse in academic writing: A reappraisal. *Applied Linguistics, 25*(2), 156–177.

———. (2005). Evaluative *that* constructions: Signalling stance in research abstracts. *Functions of Language, 12*(1), 39–64.

Jaffe, S. (2003). No pardon for poor English in science: Written and spoken language skills are critical to careers. *Scientist, 17,* 44.

Kubota, R. (2003). Striving for original voice in publication? A critical reflection. In C. Casanave & S. Vandrick (Eds.), *Writing for scholarly publication* (pp. 61–69). Mahwah, NJ: Lawrence Erlbaum.

Lave, J., & Wenger, E. (1991). *Situated learning: Legitimate peripheral participation.* Cambridge, UK: Cambridge University Press.

Lee, E., & Norton, B. (2003). Demystifying publishing: A collaborative exchange between graduate student and supervisor. In C. Casanave & S. Vandrick (Eds.), *Writing for scholarly publication* (pp. 17–38). Mahwah, NJ: Lawrence Erlbaum.

Lewin, B., Fine, J., & Young, L. (2001). *Expository discourse: A genre-based approach to social science research texts.* London: Continuum.

Li, Y. (2006). A doctoral student of physics writing for publication: A sociopolitically-oriented case study. *English for Specific Purposes*, *25*, 456–478.

Myers, G. (1990). *Writing biology: Texts in the social construction of scientific knowledge.* Madison: University of Wisconsin Press.

Pennycook, A. (1994). *The cultural politics of English as an international language.* London: Longman.

Scully, C., & Jenkins, S. (2006) Editorial: Publishing in English for non-native speakers. *Oral Oncology*, *42*(7), 753.

St. John, M. J. (1987). Writing processes of Spanish scientists publishing in English. *English for Specific Purposes*, *6*, 113–120.

Swales, J. (1990). *Genre analysis: English in academic and research settings.* Cambridge, UK: Cambridge University Press.

———. (2004). *Research genres.* New York: Cambridge University Press.

Swales, J., & Feak, C. (2000). *English in today's research world: A writing guide.* Ann Arbor: University of Michigan Press.

———. (2004). *Academic writing for graduate students: Essential tasks and skills, 2nd ed.* Ann Arbor: University of Michigan Press.

Swales, J., & Luebs, M. (2002). Genre analysis and the advanced second language writer. In E. Barton & G. Stygal (Eds.), *Discourse studies in composition* (pp. 135–154). Cresskill, NJ: Hampton Press.

Tychinin, D., & Kamnev, A. (2005). Beyond style guides: Suggestions for better scientific English. *Acta Histochemica*, *107*(3), 157–160.

Weissberg, R., & Buker, S. (1990). *Writing up research: Experimental research report writing for students of English.* Upper Saddle River, NJ: Prentice Hall.

Wood, A. (2001). International scientific English: The language of research scientists around the world. In J. Flowerdew & M. Peacock (Eds.), *Research perspectives on English for academic purposes* (pp. 71–73). Cambridge, UK: Cambridge University Press.

Part 2

ENGLISH FOR
OCCUPATIONAL PURPOSES

5

English for Specific Business Purposes: Intercultural Issues and the Use of Business English as a Lingua Franca

BRIGITTE PLANKEN
Radboud University, the Netherlands

CATHERINE NICKERSON
Indian Institute of Management Bangalore

Abstract

An important characteristic of business discourse research is that many researchers in the field are also active in teaching. As a result, many of the methodologies associated initially with LSP/ESP research, such as needs analysis surveys, genre analysis, and close text analysis, have also been used in investigating business discourse. Unlike LSP/ESP research, however, business discourse research on the whole has been motivated less by pedagogical concerns and more by the desire to gain an understanding of how people communicate effectively and strategically in an organizational context. This has led to an increasing interest in the use of

Business English as a Lingua Franca (BELF) and in the impact of the intercultural on international business communication. This chapter will discuss the findings of a number of studies that represent these two areas of interest, with particular reference to spoken business discourse. It argues that such findings can be used as a starting point for the development of materials for the teaching of English for Specific Business Purposes (ESBP) that reflect "business talk" in the real world.

This chapter discusses recent studies in the field of business discourse, in particular involving Business English as a Lingua Franca (BELF), whose findings could inform Business English (BE) teaching and the development of BE materials. Research on business discourse is particularly relevant as a source of inspiration for English for Special Business Purposes (ESBP) teaching, as business discourse "is all about how people communicate using talk or writing in commercial organizations in order to get their work done" and can be regarded as "language as social action in business contexts" (Bargiela-Chiappini, Nickerson & Planken, 2007, p. 3). Central to the discussion will be two lines of research: investigations that have thrown light on the characteristics and use of BELF, and contextualized investigations of the pragmatic, intercultural, and language policy issues that play a role in international business communication where BELF is used. Throughout, our emphasis will be on research into spoken BE (for a discussion of research that has influenced the teaching of written BE, see Nickerson & Planken, this volume). First, however, we will briefly consider ESP and business discourse research, the incongruence between BE teaching materials and real-life BE, and the nature of BELF itself.

ESP and Business Discourse Research

An important characteristic of business discourse research is that many researchers in the field are also active in teaching. This means that applied linguistics, LSP (Language for Specific Purposes), and ESP in particular have been influential, especially outside the North American context where many researchers interested in business discourse research also teach English or other languages for specific business purposes (for an overview, see Swales, 2000, and also Gollin & Hall, 2006). As a result, many of the methodologies associated initially with ESP research, such as needs analysis surveys, genre analysis, and close text analysis (cf. Belcher, 2004), have also been used in investigating business discourse, and researchers interested in business discourse have referred to a number of fields and disciplines in their investigation of language at work, such as genre theory, discourse analysis, organizational communication, and applied linguistics, in addition to ESP (see also Bhatia, this volume, for an example of the application of genre theory to legal discourse). This has led to different ways of thinking about business language and the different contextual variables that can influence how business people talk (and write) at work.

Unlike ESP research, however, business discourse research on the whole has been motivated less by pedagogical concerns and more by the desire to gain an understanding of how people communicate effectively and strategically in an organizational context, with an increasing interest in recent years in the use of BELF and the impact of the intercultural on international business communication. The potential of this type of business discourse research for ESBP, BE, or BELF teaching would thus seem obvious. It aims at understanding why, when, and how business professionals communicate in different (intercultural) settings, more often than not in BELF, and how the (BELF) discourse they use is shaped or impacted by, for instance, national and corporate cultures, corporate policy, and language competencies. In addition, as the findings from such studies reflect and describe new developments in business communication practice, they can be used as a starting point for teachers to give direction to, or determine potential areas of interest for, BE teaching curricula, and also as a way of ensuring that BE teaching materials stay abreast of the impact that globalization and communication technologies, for example, have had—and are having—on business communication, particularly in international contexts.

Business English in Books versus Business English in Practice

Diane Belcher has pointed out that the very fact that ESP teaching tends traditionally toward setting narrow objectives is regarded by its critics as "the essence of the shortcomings of the ESP approach to English language teaching" (Belcher, 2004). In the critics' view, by narrowing the focus of ESP to cater to the specific needs of a specific target group, ESP training teaches learners "enough English to survive" in certain pre-defined contexts, but "not enough to survive in the world at large," while ESP materials remain "too far removed from the real-life contexts that learners aim for" (Belcher, 2004, p. 165). Indeed, some research would seem to back up at least the latter assumption, about the incongruence between ESP materials and "real" ESP, at least with regard to BE. As early as 1988, for example, Williams noted the (mis)match between the English used by native speakers in real-life business meetings she analyzed and the "language for meetings" presented in BE teaching materials (30 textbooks) that were widely available at the time of the study. There was almost no correspondence between the language in the meetings and in the books, and the speakers' use of English in real life was far more complex, varied, and dynamic than the way in which it was represented for the student (Williams, 1988).

More recently, Mike Nelson conducted an extensive corpus-based study of real-life BE and BE teaching materials (2000b) that was concerned with two main questions: whether the lexis of BE differs from everyday general English, and whether the lexis found in BE in published materials is different from that occurring in business contexts in real life. Nelson's data consisted of a Published Materials Corpus (PMC) drawn from 33 published BE course and resource books and a BE Corpus (BEC) representing British and U.S. native speaker discourse, divided between spoken and written genres used to discuss and speak about business, like business newspapers and radio reports, and spoken and written genres that are used to actually do business, like emails and meetings. With the British National Corpus (BNC) as a reference corpus, he examined how BE differed from general English, and similarly, how the BE in published materials differed from authentic BE used in real-life business. He found that the BEC lexis represented a limited number of semantic categories (and collocates) compared with the BNC lexis and related largely to business people, companies, institutions, money, business events, places of business, time, modes of communication, and technology. Also, the key lexis of authentic BE (BEC) was more positive in nature than the key lexis in the BNC. For example, the BEC contained only positive interpersonal adjectives, such as *new, best,* and *successful,* as keywords, whereas the BNC contained both positive and negative keywords, such as *nice* and *lovely* (as positive interpersonal adjectives) and *dead* and *dark* (as negative interpersonal adjectives). In addition, most adjectives in the BEC referred to things such as products and companies, and emphasized "action" and "dynamism," rather than "emotion." Overall, Nelson's analyses suggest that there are indeed specific areas of lexis that can be considered as central to authentic BE and as semantically distinct from general English, although still attached to it. (For a more detailed discussion of the study and its implications for ESBP, see Bargiela-Chiappini, Nickerson, & Planken, 2007).

Nelson's comparison of authentic BE (BEC) with the BE presented in teaching materials (PMC) showed that the PMC reflected mainly "problem-solving" situations, and in doing so emphasized a set of lexis that was different from that found in the real-life BE in the BEC. The PMC, for instance, focused on meetings, presentations, travel, and food, and presented positive and negative lexis in equal proportions. In addition, unlike the BEC lexis, lexis in the PMC emphasized the personal and interpersonal dimension, and reflected politeness. The project website[1] provides several examples of how Nelson (2006a) has referred to the findings of his analysis of the BEC to develop relevant teaching materials that represent real-life business language for learners of BE. As Nelson notes:

> It is not enough for [BE] materials writers to sit down and write what they think happens in business. They need to look at the actual language being used. Publishers will say that they now include many authentic texts in their books, but these authentic documents tend to be related to "talking about" business (interviews with a CEO are a common example). They do not include the language used at the "hard end"—the kind of language actually used to "do business" in real meetings, real emails and real negotiations. The main reason for this is the difficulty of access to them, but without it we are just scrambling about in the dark. (Nelson, 2003)

The analysis of published BE materials in particular confirms the findings of other studies of published EFL materials (e.g., Nickerson, 2005; St. John, 1996), suggesting that not much seems to have changed since Williams concluded in 1988 that there was a disconnect between the language actually used in business and the language taught for business (see also discussion in Nickerson & Planken, this volume, specifically related to written communication). At the same time, Nelson's analyses seem to confirm that authentic BE indeed covers a limited scope, which would go some way to justifying the narrower focus in ES(B)P teaching pedagogy, while at the same time countering some of the criticisms of ESP more generally that were highlighted by Belcher (2004). Still, the mismatch between authentic BE and coursebook BE remains worrying, in that it suggests not only that little has changed with respect to the authenticity—and thus the relevance—of BE materials but also that potential sources of information that could be used

---

[1]http://users.utu.fi/micnel/BEC/downloadable_materials.htm

as a basis to give direction to ESBP pedagogy, to identify areas of interest for ESBP curricula, and to make BE teaching materials more authentic, relevant, and up to date, would seem to have been left largely untapped, even despite suggestions on how to bridge the gap between theory and practice in a number of the edited volumes that have appeared in the course of the past decade (e.g., Connor & Upton, 2004; Hewings & Nickerson, 1999). We refer here in particular to research in the field of business discourse (for a recent overview, see Bargiela-Chiappini et al., 2007) that has been conducted on various business genres (e.g., in meetings, negotiations, presentations) over the past few decades, and in particular to those investigations that have considered (spoken) business discourse in international settings, where BE is used as the lingua franca, more often than not by non-native speakers (see also Lockwood, Forey & Elias, this volume, for a discussion on the use of English in call center communication in a non–English speaking context).

What Is Business English?

As previously noted, one of the primary aims of Nelson's study was to compare BE, as represented in the BEC, with general English, as represented in the BNC. This raises the interesting issue of what BE actually is. The BEC, for instance, consisted of texts collected from native speaker sources—Britain and the United States (see Nelson, 2006, for details). As many have observed, however, English is used as an international business language by native, second and foreign language speakers in a wide variety of interactions and, of course, not only by British and American native speakers. Recently, Barbara Seidlhofer (e.g., Seidlhofer, 2002, 2004) has emphasized the need to work toward an empirically based description of *lingua franca* English (in general) in order to provide appropriate BE teaching approaches and materials and to distinguish between BE characteristics that are likely to cause (communication) problems and those that are not. Her 2003 overview of a number of *lingua franca* characteristics (co-authored with Jennifer Jenkins), provides preliminary suggestions as to what aspects of BE/BELF might warrant attention in teaching and, more important, what aspects might not. The authors describe a successful ELF interaction in which virtually none of the language produced was "correct" or idiomatic by native speaker standards. They observe that "for the purpose at hand, the kind of English that is employed works and it serves the participants quite adequately for doing the job they have to do" and further, that their analyses of other lingua franca interactions confirm "that a great deal of ELF communication is conducted at comparable levels of proficiency, and that quite often it is features which are regarded as 'the most typically English', such as third-person –s, tags, phrasal verbs and idioms, as well as the sounds /θ/ and /ð/ and weak forms, that turn out to be non-essential for mutual intelligibility" (Seidlhofer & Jenkins, 2003, p. 151).

For business contexts specifically, a large-scale corpus-based investigation of the language used in BELF interactions would be a useful complement to work like Nelson's based on native speaker sources, in that it would help to determine areas where native and non-native varieties of BE are different and thus potentially problematic. Also, comparative micro-level investigations of BELF speakers from different cultures would also be useful, in that, like Seidlhofer and Jenkins' work for general ELF interactions, they help not only in pinpointing problematic areas, but also in identifying characteristics that do not necessarily need to be a teaching or training focus since they are "non-essential for mutual intelligibility" (Seidlhofer & Jenkins, 2003, p. 151). Such information on features of BE/BELF could be usefully incorporated into BE/BELF teaching materials by, for example, collating cross-cultural *lingua franca* data and comparing and contrasting it with native speaker data.

In recent years, a growing group of researchers has investigated the BE that is used as a common language in business interactions involving people who are speakers of languages other than English. Such BELF can be seen "as a 'neutral' and shared communication code": neutral because "none of the speakers can claim it as his/her mother tongue" and shared as "it is used for conducting business within the global discourse community, whose members are BELF users and communicators in their own right—not 'non-native speakers' or 'learners'" (Louhiala-Salminen, Charles, & Kankaan-ranta, 2005, pp. 403–404). Examples of studies with a focus on BELF (discourse) include Louhiala-Salminen et al. (2005) on the effects of introducing BELF as a corporate language in two Nordic mergers, Planken (2005) on BELF as it is used in intercultural sales negotiations, Briguglio (2005) on BELF at multinational companies in Malaysia and Hong Kong, and Poncini (2004) and Rogerson-Revell (2007) on BELF in multicultural (European) meetings. A number of these studies will be discussed in more detail, and in particular, how their findings inform BE(LF) teaching. For starters, the studies by Louhiala-Salminen et al. and Planken (both 2005) provide examples of investigations that reveal the influence of national culture (Louhiala-Salminen et al.) on the one hand, and business experience (Planken) on the other, as determining factors in the inclusion of certain discourse (strategies) in business interactions in BE/BELF. The studies also offer insights into the cultural and situational factors that play a role in shaping business relationships across different cultures. As such, they form a useful source of information regarding both the nature—and consequences—of BELF as it is used in intercultural business settings, and they suggest aspects of BELF (use), or other issues that are relevant to BELF (use), that could be incorporated into BELF teaching.

The Consequences of Choosing BELF as a Corporate Language

The 2005 publication by Louhiala-Salminen et al. reports on an investigation of the consequences of introducing English as a corporate language for Finnish and Swedish employees working together in two cross-border corporate mergers in Scandinavia (forming Paper Giant and PankkiBanken/Scandi Bank), each between a Swedish and a Finnish company. The investigation focused on the perceptions the two cultures held of each other's communication cultures, offset against the BELF discourse they produced in their new corporations when working together on a day-to-day basis. In their introduction, the authors note the dramatic rise in cross-border mergers in recent years, especially in the Nordic countries, that has caused many newly formed corporations to increasingly opt for English as their official corporate language instead of the traditional lingua franca in this region, *scandinaviska*. In practice, this means that "corporate documentation and all reporting is done in English" and that English is also used in most "communication between different units" (2005, p. 402). This observation in itself provides further evidence that English continues to advance as the preferred lingua franca in the international business arena.

First, a written survey and interviews were conducted to investigate communicative practices in both corporations, and to tap the perceptions the Finnish and Swedish employees held of each other. The issues covered included, for example, daily routines of communication, language choice in specific situations, and the characteristics of what the respondents considered to be "typically" Swedish or Finnish styles of communication. Second, the team investigated whether the characteristics that the respondents had identified as typical were reflected in the discourse used by the members of each national culture. To do this, the sources they analyzed included the discourse characteristics of videoed meetings, involving both nationalities, in both corporations. Here, the researchers were particularly interested in manifestations of BELF, about which they hypothesized that although it may be regarded as a "neutral" code in the sense that everyone who uses it is a non-native speaker, and thus starts out on an equal footing with every other BELF user, this by no means means that BELF is "culture-neutral." In other words, despite sharing a "neutralizing" language, BELF speakers will continue to bring to business interactions "their own culture-bound views of how encounters should be conducted," as well as "discourse practices" inspired by their respective first languages (2005, p. 404).

The daily communication routines and the use of languages in both corporations, and in both countries, were found to be largely similar; around 80 percent of employees' time was spent in internal (mostly spoken) communication, and more than half the employees across the board reported that they were involved in cross-border—intercultural—communication on a weekly or daily basis. The use of English had increased for both nationalities (Finnish and Swedish), and in both companies, from the pre-merger situation to the present (2004), and accounted for around 20 percent of all communication. In addition, there were employees at all levels (not just in higher-level designations), and in all business units of the two multinationals, who used English for practically all internal communication, including in all telephone calls and meetings. Their language choice seemed above all pragmatic, depending on the target group and the group members' language skills (e.g., in the presence of non-native speakers of Finnish or Swedish, English was used), the status of English as the new corporate language (e.g., some Finnish employees of ScandiBank, where Swedish had been the official language of the merger before the switch to English, continued to speak Swedish with Swedish colleagues), and medium and genre of communication (i.e., written versus spoken, meetings versus dinner table conversations, etc.). Respondents reported difficulties with foreign languages (which included BELF for both groups, and Swedish for the Finnish) in situations such as using the telephone, in finding nuances, in "ordinary small talk," and in giving an opinion in meetings (see also the discussion of findings from Planken's and Rogerson-Revell's studies below). Overall, the use of foreign languages included BELF in spoken rather than written communication seems to have been the most problematic across the two multinationals and for both nationalities.

With regard to what was "typically" Swedish or Finnish communication, "Swedes were seen to be 'discussive' and 'wordy'," while "Finns were 'direct' and 'economical with words'" (2005, p. 408). Interestingly, their perspectives on their own and each other's communication were found to largely refer to the same features, although each group used different evaluations to characterize them, and by extension, to characterize effective communication. Whereas the Finns considered themselves as "factual" and "direct," implying that these characteristics make them effective communicators, the Swedes referred to essentially the same traits in the Finns as "blunt," "pushy," and "few-worded." The Swedes described themselves as "discussive" and "democratic" communicators, implying that these traits made them effective, but the Finns perceived them as "wordy" people who "talked endlessly" (2005, p. 409). This confirmed the authors' assumption that BELF in intercultural contacts may ensure "neutrality" in the sense that all participants start off on an equal basis as non-native speakers, but that participants still bring to any interaction their own cultural background, reflected in the fact that they continue to regard the other speakers from the perspective of their own national framework. Furthermore, their assumption that BELF users transfer mother tongue language patterns to BELF was backed up by the observation that, in meetings between the two nationalities, the Swedish exhibited an interpersonal orientation, characterized by the use of queries, questions, hedging, and other forms of meta-discourse intended to orient the hearer to the discourse, whereas the Finns tended toward issue orientation, and a relatively low level of interpersonal orientation. Furthermore, the Swedish speakers relied much less than the Finnish on shared context or values, such that they used "more explicit rhetoric and conversational gambits than do Finnish speakers" (2005, p. 413).

This publication is useful because it provides a multi-layered picture of the real-life BELF communication that takes place in a multinational corporation, and because it contributes to a richer understanding of the challenges posed by opting for BELF as an official corporate language, even in countries where the standard of English proficiency can be assumed to be high. The study also pinpoints at least one important characteristic of BELF: The differences in BELF communication styles found between the Finnish and Swedish at the two corporations cause the researchers to conclude that BELF is not "cultureless" but that "[r]ather, it can be seen to be a conduit of its speaker's communication culture" (2005, p. 417). This observation not only points the way forward to a fruitful line of inquiry in many other corporations around the world where BELF is used between speakers that represent different national cultures, but it also has a number of potential implications for ESBP pedagogy, particularly where BELF is concerned. First, the notion of BELF as a shared, highly functional code needs to be balanced against the fact that BELF users will still incorporate their own, not necessarily shared, mother tongue patterns, culture(s), and culturally determined conventions and practices within the BELF discourse. What this might imply for BELF teaching, for example, is that native-speaker or near–native speaker norms for English (i.e., levels of competence in various domains, including grammar, pronunciation, etc.) are not the most directly relevant basis for setting course objectives or for other issues such as determining domains, which language aspects require attention, what type of grading is necessary, or which materials should be created. Ideally, such criteria and objectives relate specifically to BELF and its users and should follow from a consideration of BELF characteristics (see also Seidlhofer's comments on pages 112–113 on determining "essential" and "non-essential" aspects of BE), the interactional settings in which BELF is used, and the specific difficulties, needs, and motivations associated with BELF use (see pages 122–124 for difficulties BELF users were found to experience in Rogerson-Revel's case study). Louhiala-Salminen et al. note as much, and more, when they suggest that in teaching learners to use BE around the world, the BELF perspective should always be foregrounded. Learners should be trained first and foremost "to see themselves as communicators who have real jobs to do and needs to fulfil"; as a result, it is "these jobs and needs that should be emphasized [in courses], not the language they use to carry them out" (2005, pp. 418–419).

Second, given the potential variation in cultural frameworks that BELF users bring to an intercultural interaction, learners should be made aware of "how to use contextual clues" and to recognize the "situational presuppositions of their counterparts in an interaction" (Louhiala-Salminen et al., 2005, p. 419). This assigns added importance to training listening skills in BELF courses, because it is only through listening to what other BELF users "say and imply" that these objectives can be achieved. A related aim of BELF courses, according to Louhiala-Salminen et al., should be to create awareness among BELF learners of their own and others' cultural patterns of communication, and of the relevant discourse practices and conventions, so that they "learn to appreciate the need to be flexible," an essential prerequisite to survive in today's rapidly changing, unpredictable, global business community.

Rapport across Cultures: Comparing Professional and Aspiring Negotiators' BELF

The 2005 publication by Planken details an investigation of BELF in intercultural sales negotiations, which focused in particular on how participants managed their business relationship through BELF discourse. Her investigation compared two BELF corpora of simulated negotiation discourse, one produced by professional negotiators with between five and thirty years of experience in conducting intercultural negotiations in BELF and the other by ten students of international business communication with relatively little negotiating experience, that is, aspiring or pre-experience negotiators. As its starting point, the study uses Helen Spencer-Oatey's model of rapport management (Spencer-Oatey, 2000a, 2000b), which provides a comprehensive treatment of intercultural, relational communication, with a specific focus on language use in business settings. As an approach to interaction, it is sensitive to issues of face and interpersonal perceptions and assumptions, and how these may impact (intercultural) communication; essentially, the model seeks to provide a contextual framework that can explain how (business) language is used to manage (business) relationships. As in Gina Poncini's work on multilingual business meetings, discussed below, the emphasis in Spencer-Oatey's approach is on how participants work together to find a solution despite different cultural backgrounds, rather than on defining cross-cultural misunderstanding or communication breakdown (see also Spencer-Oatey & Xing, 2003, 2005, on Chinese-British business encounters).

According to Spencer-Oatey, rapport—or "harmony-disharmony"— needs to be managed across five interrelated, but discrete, domains of interaction: the illocutionary domain (the performance of speech acts), the discourse content domain (e.g., choice of topic, structure and sequencing), the participation domain (e.g., turn-taking, inclusion or exclusion of participants, back-channeling), the stylistic domain (e.g., choice of tone, formality level, register), and the non-verbal domain (e.g., gaze, posture, gestures). By considering rapport on a bi-polar dimension, the model accommodates not only the (non)verbal "polite" behavior used to create or maintain a pleasant working relationship but also the challenging behavior in conflictive settings, such as negotiations. As such, it is of interest to researchers who want to account for different aspects of relational talk, from politeness and accommodation strategies to contentious and conflictive strategies, as well as for manifestations of power and the motivations that might underlie such behaviors. From a pedagogical perspective, we suggest the model can also provide a useful starting point for ESBP teaching geared to skills training in spoken business interactions, in that it can help raise awareness of the domains of interaction that can play a role and need to be taken into account in relationship building. In addition, as it provides an overview of discrete areas of interaction that teaching (materials) might center on, it suggests that various aspects of these domains can be dealt with in a systematic—and comprehensive—manner in ESBP courses.

In her study of rapport building across cultures, Planken focused on two aspects in her BELF interactions: the use of "safe talk" to build rapport (the discourse content domain of rapport management), and the use of personal pronouns as indicators of the negotiator relationship (the participation domain of rapport management). Her study included the use of *you* as an indicator of other-orientedness and inclusive *we* as an indicator of cooperativeness, versus the use of exclusive, institutional *we* as an indicator of professional distance, and the use of *I* as an indicator of self-orientedness (Planken, 2005, pp. 383–384). Her analyses reveal that, overall, the professional negotiators initiated a significantly higher number of safe talk topics in their BELF than the aspiring negotiators and used safe talk in all three phases of their negotiations—that is, in the Opening, Bargaining, and Closing phases, whereas the students used safe talk only in the Opening and Closing phases. An interesting characteristic in both corpora was that the negotiators made relatively little use of the "non-business" category of safe talk, such that Planken concludes that "the safe talk topics initiated . . . , by the professionals in particular, largely constituted business-related content. . . . [These sequences] could be seen as further instances of professional talk" (2005, p. 389). Interestingly, the majority of the "non-business" category sequences that were initiated, particularly in the professional corpus, were related to the intercultural context of the negotiations. For example, they involved brief discussions about (foreign) language difficulties, experience with the other's culture, cultural idiosyncrasies (of the speaker's own or the other speaker's culture), and cultural comparisons. Thus, cultural difference became a resource for safe talk and a means to build the relationship.

With regard to the degree of solidarity and involvement, as reflected in the negotiators' use of first and second person pronouns (*I* and *you*) and inclusive versus exclusive or institutional *we*, Planken found both similarities and differences. The most interesting differences were that the inexperienced negotiators underused institutional *we* in comparison to their experienced counterparts and that, unlike the experienced negotiators, they also used non-inclusive pronouns (*I* and *you*) in the Bargaining phase of the negotiation. This created "highly subjective discourse in potentially the most conflictive and face-threatening negotiation phase, . . . suggesting hostility rather than reflecting the no-nonsense, businesslike approach that they might have been aiming for" (2005, p. 396).

Planken's study is useful in that it provides insight into the way in which real negotiators who use BELF on a day-to-day basis build rapport in intercultural negotiations, as well as suggesting areas of concern for the BELF classroom. With respect to the use of small talk, for instance, the findings indicate that this resource for rapport building was underused by the pre-experience BELF speakers, in comparison to the professional BELF speakers. Also, the findings suggest that by underusing institutional *we* and formulating potentially face-threatening discourse (i.e., bargaining sequences) from a largely subjective perspective, the aspiring negotiators were unsuccessful at maintaining professional distance and thus at creating a professional identity within the negotiation event. These findings are a clear indication of how rapport management can be used to underpin the development of research-based ESBP teaching materials. As the world continues to globalize, and multilingual, intercultural encounters increase as a result, nowhere will the analysis of intercultural discourse be more pertinent than in the business arena. Rapport management offers an inherently positive perspective on business, not just as a competitive transactional activity but also as a collaborative, and ultimately relational, human undertaking. The final section of this chapter, while maintaining the focus on BELF, turns attention to two studies that have specifically considered the multicultural and multilingual perspective of intercultural business communication by investigating multiparty, international business meetings.

BELF in Multiparty, Multicultural Business Meetings

Gina Poncini (2004) and Pamela Rogerson-Revell (2007) have both considered multiparty meetings in European multinational organizations (Italian and French respectively) in which BELF was the shared language. We consider each investigation in turn, outlining the insights they provide on the nature of BELF (communication) and its impact on users, and where possible, the potential implications of the findings for BELF teaching.

In her longitudinal study of an Italian company, and more specifically the company's meetings with its international distributors, Poncini concentrates on business discourse in BELF in multilingual settings, and the management of cross-company communication in large interactions, involving as many as three dozen participants at a time from fourteen different cultures. She deliberately avoids the "problem approach" to intercultural communication, and concentrates instead on three salient linguistic aspects of BELF: the use of personal pronouns, the use of specialized lexis, and the use of evaluative lexis. Poncini draws the notion of "business relationship" from the business marketing literature, and applies it to her longitudinal analysis of the company-distributors relationship, as expressed during a series of meetings.

This analysis is combined with a pragmatic approach to the issue of how to define culture in corporate, multinational contexts: here, Poncini introduces the perspective of meetings as having their own culture, or *groupness*. What emerges overall is that "groupness" helps overcome potentially "disruptive behavior" such as monologues or side conversations among participants, and overrides difficulties caused by variations in information level among participants, and their varying degrees of BELF competence. Poncini shows how "groupness" is maintained in particular through the hard work and listening skills of those participants (main company speakers) who facilitate, moderate, interpret, and summarize for the benefit of all the parties at the table (see also the preceding discussion of Louhiala-Salminen, 2005, on the importance of listening skills for the interpretation of BELF speakers' cues).

With regard to the patterns of use of personal pronouns in the meetings, Poncini's analysis shows how individual BELF speakers use pronouns to switch roles, build identities, and shift allegiance during the meetings and within the company. As such, personal pronoun use appears to be central to "groupness." With respect to lexis too, the analysis shows that specialized lexis works to reflect and construct the social roles participants play in the company and at meetings, to frame the business activities undertaken, and therefore, again, to support and (re)create "groupness." Evaluative lexis, on the other hand, is used in meetings to strategically accomplish tasks such as image-building, pre-empting criticism, building positive connotations, managing participation, and construing roles. Evaluative lexis in BELF, then, would seem to be especially relevant in interpersonal (meeting) tasks and in fostering relationships. Interestingly, Poncini also notes that BELF speakers use lexical chains in their meeting discourse that are far more sophisticated than mere technical jargon.

Poncini's approach to the company that is the subject of her study has several advantages over the prescriptive knowledge that is generally administered to business students and students of ESBP through texts that are not based on real-life practices. For example, it privileges situational factors rather than (assumed) cultural differences, focusing on what actually happens when a group of business people from various cultures have to work together on common issues, how conflicts are averted or mediated by the main company representative, and the different strategies that are used to build common ground among the multilingual, multicultural contributors. As such, it avoids the pitfall of the one speaker–one culture perspective, and questions the idea of the "homogeneous cultural group," as well as the role of cultural differences in multicultural encounters. Also, like Planken's study, Poncini's analyses throw light on how English as a common language is used to establish and maintain business relationships in an intercultural setting, and highlights some of the aspects of (BELF) discourse that contribute to creating the situated "groupness" that would seem to be a prerequisite for establishing a conducive working relationship in the multiparty, multicultural encounters she studied.

Pamela Rogerson-Revell's 2007 publication reports on a preliminary study aimed at exploring the use of and difficulties with BELF in business meetings in a European professional organization, based on documentary evidence from an internal company report, together with the findings of a written survey among meeting participants (native English speakers and BELF users). The study is part of a larger, ongoing project that investigates the nature and role of BELF, focusing specifically on its use in multiparty, multicultural business meetings, and aims to build on earlier research in the field (e.g., Bargiela-Chiappini & Harris, 1997; Firth, 1996; Planken, 2005; Poncini, 2004; Rogerson-Revell, 1998, 1999) and to develop relevant, research-based training materials to facilitate international professional communication (see also, e.g., Charles & Marschan-Piekkari, 2002; Rogerson-Revell, 1999, 2003; St. John, 1996).

The research was conducted at the Groupe Consultatif Actuariel Europeen (GCAE), a consultative and advisory group of actuarial associations from 30 European countries, which aims to facilitate discussion with European Union institutions on legislation relevant to the actuarial profession, and which meets regularly to discuss current issues. According to Rogerson-Revell, "GCAE has a variety of meeting types," held across Europe, "from small internal and informal gatherings of a few local staff to large formal meetings held externally" (2007, p. 110). Her survey data were collected during the GCAE's annual meeting, at which the whole group discusses key issues and reviews the previous year's business. This particular event consisted of formal sub-group meetings (eight to twenty participants) and culminated in a meeting at which the entire group was present (approximately 50 participants). The initial impetus for Rogerson-Revell's research on this particular organization was the fact that the group itself had been concerned about the "unequal participation of members in meetings," and had produced an internal report outlining some of the concerns felt by members and illustrating some of the difficulties encountered by non–native English speakers in GCAE meetings. The report provided the basis for the written questionnaire, which aimed to gather data about participants' BELF use, their first language, the number of other languages spoken, etc. In addition, interviews with group members aimed to tap their views on the use of English in GCAE meetings and on perceived communication issues in general in such encounters. The discussion here is restricted to the findings regarding BELF users.

The majority of BELF speakers (67 percent) reported attending meetings in English very often or quite regularly. How comfortable they felt in such encounters was seen to be related to the size of the meetings: fewer BELF speakers felt "very comfortable" in large business meetings than in small meetings and, in turn, fewer felt comfortable in small meetings than in one-to-one conversations. However, 56 percent reported feeling "quite comfortable" in small meetings or one-to-one conversations, while only 26 percent reported feeling equally comfortable in large meetings in English. The average BELF user had studied English for six years, and rated his/her English proficiency as lower in speaking skills than in listening, writing, and, particularly, lower than in reading. Just over 40 percent of BELF users stated that they found both native and non-native speakers of English easy to follow, 33 percent stated a preference for native speakers, and 24 percent reported finding BELF speakers easier to understand. With regard to accents, "U.K. English" or "U.S. English" were found to be easy to comprehend, but there were also references to other varieties (e.g., German, Dutch, Scandinavian, French), as well as to general characteristics that promoted comprehensibility, such as speaking slowly or with a "cultured native accent" (Rogerson-Revell, 2007, p. 115). With regard to "difficult" accents, 47 percent indicated difficulty in understanding some native speaker accents (e.g., London English, African, Scottish, Irish) and 36 percent reported difficulties understanding types of BELF accent (including Catalan, Japanese, Far Eastern). Again, there were also general references to, for instance, "heavy regional" or "uneducated" accents, and "non-articulated English." In addition, several BELF users referred to the problem of people speaking too fast or too quietly, while others mentioned the problem of finding the right words or having difficulties when interrupting and expressing opinions or viewpoints appropriately.

Rogerson-Revell concludes that there "seems to be a spectrum of issues" relating to the specific communication difficulties experienced by BELF users in international meetings, ranging from comprehension difficulties through difficulties in both comprehension and production to difficulties in managing interactions appropriately. This last category seems to relate to BELF users who assess their linguistic proficiency relatively highly but feel they have difficulty in high-speed discussions, specifically when trying to interrupt or

express a viewpoint. Finally, she notes that "the difficulty of getting heard
. . . can severely frustrate an individual's or an organization's representation," and that BELF users may have little or no part in the decision-making
process; the latter category includes those who are less competent linguistically or who feel less comfortable in dealing with contention and are more
likely to give in to others as a result. What Rogerson-Revell sees as essential
if true collaboration is to take place in encounters such as those at GCAE,
where most participants "do business" in BELF, is that such events are made
"as equitable as possible" (2007, p. 118). Although the results from this
study are preliminary, they are useful because they shed light on some of the
language issues that play a role in multi-party, intercultural encounters and
because they provide an indication of the reasons for such difficulties and
the frustrations BELF users experience as a result. In addition, they indicate
areas of "meetings discourse" that BELF users find problematic.

The findings from research in the field of business discourse—and more
specifically from research that has incorporated investigations of BE or
BELF as it is used in international business settings—might serve to bridge
the gap between theory and practice. Findings from such studies can provide
an indication of the nature of BELF in use and of the needs and problems
of BELF users in real business; they can therefore help pinpoint areas that
deserve attention in BE(LF) courses and can be used as a starting point for
the development of research-based, directly relevant ESBP materials that
reflect "business talk" in the real world.

*   *   *

BRIGITTE PLANKEN is an Assistant Professor at the Department of International Business Communication, Radboud University, the Netherlands. Her
areas of interest include English as an international business language
and the rhetoric of environmental and social reporting.

CATHERINE NICKERSON is a Visiting Faculty in the Communication Unit
at the Indian Institute of Management Bangalore and an Associate Editor
for the Journal of Business Communication. She has lived in India, the
United States, the Netherlands, and the United Kingdom, and she has
been teaching and researching in business communication and the use of
English as an international business language for the past 15 years. Her
most recent book, *Business Discourse,* was published in 2007 by Palgrave
Macmillan.

REFERENCES

Bargiela-Chiappini, F., & Harris, S. (1997). *The languages of business: An international perspective* (pp. 21–48). Edinburgh, UK: Edinburgh University Press.

Bargiela-Chiappini, F., Nickerson, C., & Planken, B. (2007). *Business discourse.* Basingstoke, UK: Palgrave Macmillan.

Belcher, D. (2004). Trends in teaching English for specific purposes. *Annual Review of Applied Linguistics, 24,* 165–186.

Briguglio, C. (2005). *The use of English in multinational settings and the implication for business education.* Unpublished doctoral dissertation, University of Western Australia—Perth.

Charles, M., & Marschan-Piekkari, R. (2002). Language training for enhanced horizontal communication: A challenge for MNCs. *Business Communication Quarterly, 65*(2), 9–29.

Connor, U., & Upton, T. (2004). *Discourse in the professions: Perspectives from corpus linguistics.* Amsterdam: John Benjamins.

Firth, A. (1996). The discursive accomplishment of normality: On "lingua franca" English and conversation analysis. *Journal of Pragmatics, 26,* 237–259.

Gollin, S., & Hall, D. (2006). *Language for specific purposes.* Basingstoke, UK: Palgrave Macmillan.

Hewings, M., & Nickerson, C. (Eds.). (1999). *Business English: Research into practice.* London: Longman.

Louhiala-Salminen, L., Charles, M., & Kankaanranta, A. (2005). English as a lingua franca in Nordic corporate mergers: Two case companies. *English for Specific Purposes, 24*(4), 401–421.

Nelson, M. (2000a). *The business English lexis site.* Retrieved March 18, 2007, from http://users.utu.fi/micnel/business_english_lexis_site.htm

———. (2000b). *A corpus-based study of business English and business English teaching materials.* Unpublished doctoral dissertation, University of Manchester—UK.

———. (2003, March 20). Worldly experience. *Guardian Weekly.* Retrieved March 19, 2007, from http://education.guardian.co.uk/tefl/story/0,5500,917515,00.html

———. (2006). Semantic associations in business English: A corpus-based analysis. *English for Specific Purposes Journal, 25*(2), 217–234.

Nickerson, C. (2005). English as a lingua franca in international business contexts. *English for Specific Purposes, 24*(4), 367–380.

Planken, B. (2005). Managing rapport in lingua franca sales negotiations: A comparison of professional and aspiring negotiators. *English for Specific Purposes, 24*(4), 381–400.

Poncini, G. (2004). *Discursive strategies in multicultural business meetings.* Bern: Peter Lang.

Rogerson-Revell, P. (1998). *Interactive style and power at work: An analysis of discourse in intercultural business meetings.* Unpublished doctoral dissertation, University of Birmingham—UK.

————. (1999). Meeting talk: A stylistic approach to teaching meeting skills. In M. Hewings & C. Nickerson (Eds.), *Business English: Research into practice* (pp. 55–72). London: Longman.

————. (2003). Developing a cultural syllabus for business language e-learning materials. *ReCALL, 15*(2), 155–169.

————. (2007). Using English for international business: A European case study. *English for Specific Purposes, 26,* 103–120.

Seidlhofer, B. (2002). The shape of things to come? Some basic questions. In K. Knapp & C. Meierkord (Eds.), *Lingua franca communication* (pp. 269–302). Frankfurt am Main: Peter Lang.

————. (2004). Research perspectives on teaching English as a lingua franca. *Annual Review of Applied Linguistics, 24,* 209–239.

Seidlhofer, B., & Jenkins, J. (2003). English as a lingua franca and the politics of property. In C. Mair (Ed.), *The politics of English as a world language* (pp. 139–154). Amsterdam: Rodopi.

Spencer-Oatey, H. (Ed.). (2000a). *Culturally speaking: Managing rapport through talk across cultures.* London: Continuum.

————. (2000b). Rapport management: A framework for analysis. In H. Spencer-Oatey (Ed.), *Culturally speaking: Managing rapport through talk across cultures* (pp. 11–46). London: Continuum.

Spencer-Oatey, H., & Xing, J. (2003). Managing rapport in intercultural business interactions: A comparison of two Chinese-British welcome meetings. *Journal of Intercultural Studies, 24*(1), 33–46.

————. (2005). Managing talk and non-talk in intercultural interactions: Insights from two Chinese-British business meetings. *Multilingua, 24*(1–2), 55–74.

St. John, M. J. (1996). Business is booming: Business English in the 1990s. *English for Specific Purposes, 15,* 3–18.

Swales, J. (2000). Languages for specific purposes. *Annual Review of Applied Linguistics, 20,* 59–76.

Williams, M. (1988). Language taught for meetings and language used in meetings: Is there anything in common? *Applied Linguistics, 9*(1), 45–58.

6

English for Specific Business Purposes: Written Business English and the Increasing Influence of Multimodality

CATHERINE NICKERSON
Indian Institute of Management Bangalore

BRIGITTE PLANKEN
Radboud University, the Netherlands

Abstract

The first part discusses a number of important influences on the research on written Business English (BE), including the work of the genre analyst Vijay Bhatia, the concern with the business letter in much of the research in the 1980s and 1990s, and the continuing dominance of English as an international business language. The second part considers the teaching of written BE, together with a profile of four publications that show evidence of the influence of research in the generation of teaching materials. The third and final sections focus on the theories of multimodality and their recent applications in business discourse research. Examples from outside of the ESBP world are given as is speculation on what multimodality might mean in the future for teaching written BE.

What Is Written Business English?

In 2007 we discussed the history of business discourse and the influence of the work of the genre analyst Vijay Bhatia in particular on researchers interested in writing in organizational contexts (Bargiela-Chiappini, Nickerson, & Planken, 2007). Researchers such as Ulla Connor, Leena Louhiala-Salminen, Didar Akar, and Anna Kankaanranta have all drawn on Bhatia's understanding of the concept of genre in their investigation of written business language. As we observed, Bhatia's book-length study published in 1993 "extends the ESP approach to genre analysis that was pioneered by John Swales for academic writing (e.g. Swales, 1990), and re-applies it to professional discourse, including sales letters and application letters" (Bargiela-Chiappini et al., 2007, p. 10). A decade later in 2004, when he published *Worlds of Written Discourse*, Bhatia expanded the ESP tradition even further, in his investigation of written business discourse and the exploration of the relationship between text and context in particular (see also Bhatia, this volume, for a discussion of legal discourse). These publications and the development of ideas that can be traced within them have shaped both the research that has been carried out to investigate the written forms of BE and the applications of this research in the teaching of English for Specific Business Purposes (ESBP).

In the 1980s and early 1990s, work on written business discourse was concentrated on the investigation of the business letter. Contrastive studies such as the influential 1987 publication by Jenkins and Hinds on the differences between (U.S.) English, French, and Japanese business letters and the book-length publication by Yli-Jokipii (1994) on requests in British, American, and Finnish business correspondence exemplify the work done at that time. A decade later, the collection edited by Gotti and Gillaerts in 2005 shows that the influence of the business letter has remained, although the concern is now more with the way in which the business letter as a genre has been recycled as a part of other genres such as email and annual reports, and rather less with the original genre itself. Apart from the business letter, researchers in the 1980s and 1990s also reported on other types of written business texts that were perhaps less likely to be of interest in the ESBP classroom. These included genres such as specific types of internal reports (e.g., Rogers, 1989, in a study of the reports filed by dealers in the automotive industry), the mission statement (Rogers & Swales, 1990; Swales & Rogers, 1995), invitations for bids (Barbara & Scott, 1999), and the annual general report (Hyland, 1998; Thomas, 1997). Although these studies provided a wealth of information on the ways in which different forms of writing were used in business, there seemed to be little or no apparent connection with the findings of the research and what went on within the ESBP classroom. This is interesting, since the majority of the business discourse researchers previously referred to were also (and still remain) active as ESBP practitioners (see also St. John, 1996; Nickerson, 2002, for further comments on this).

One other characteristic of BE is that many researchers have considered Business English as more or less synonymous with business language, no doubt reflecting the undeniable dominance of English as the language of international business. Of course studies of business languages other than English do exist (e.g., Bargiela-Chiappini, 2005a, 2006), and many researchers have carried out contrastive studies of BE compared to other languages (e.g., Al-Ali, 2004, compares English and Arabic in job application letters; Yeung, 2004, compares Chinese and Australian English in management discourse; Thatcher, 2000, compares written policies and procedures in Spanish and American English), but the majority of studies investigating business language have concentrated on English. English as a lingua franca has become a major focus in the work of business discourse analysts in the past decade, and the acronym BELF, referring to Business English as a Lingua Franca, is increasingly being used by researchers interested in understanding the characteristics of English as an international business language—an acknowledgement that in the majority of cases the interactions that take place do not involve business people for whom English is a first language (see Louhiala-Salminen, Charles & Kankaanranta, 2005, and Planken & Nickerson, this volume, for a discussion on this point). The dominance of English in business settings is also reflected in the extensive number of published teaching materials designed to teach ESBP.

The Emergence of New Media

In the course of the 1990s, there was a gradual move away from the business letter and the more traditional forms of business writing to a concern with the electronic forms of communication that were becoming increasingly important within the contemporary business context. The 1986 paper by Zak and Dudley-Evans on the features of word omission and abbreviation in telexes, published in the journal *English for Specific Purposes,* was perhaps the first to consider the relationship between the use of a particular medium and how this might influence the language used (Zak & Dudley-

Evans, 1986). And outside of the ESBP tradition, this was echoed six years later in the influential paper by Yates and Orlikowski, who considered the relationship between genre and medium in their discussion of electronic forms of communication in organizations (Orlikowski & Yates, 1994; Yates & Orlikowski, 1992).

A number of researchers have investigated email communication in English, and explored its uses and characteristics by and in multinational corporations. The studies by Nickerson (2000), Gains (1999), van Mulken and van der Meer (2005), and Gimenez (2002, 2006), for instance, all focus on email communication in English. Gimenez's work in particular has explored the use of new media in corporate contexts and the embeddedness of email within corporate culture, and the 2005 publication by Van Mulken and Van der Meer explores the (cross-cultural) differences between US and Dutch corporations in their use of email communication in English in correspondence with customers. Of the researchers concerned with electronic forms of communication in business settings, one of the most notable is the Finnish researcher Leena Louhiala-Salminen. From the mid 1990s onward, she has explored the use of electronic media in business contexts, with a particular emphasis on fax and email communication in English in Finland. Louhiala-Salminen's work shows how different methodologies may be used to great effect in investigating written ESBP. For instance, she has referred to survey-based research, corpus-based genre analysis, text analysis, and informant studies (1995, 1996, 1997, 2002). In addition, in collaborative work she has compared the similarities and differences between the English used in fax communication in Turkey and Finland (Akar & Louhiala-Salminen, 1999), and in her most recent work together with her colleagues Mirjaliisa Charles and Anna Kankaanranta at the Helsinki School of Economics, she has explored the integration of written and spoken forms of communication, with specific reference to BELF email, at two major Swedish-Finnish cross-border mergers (Louhiala-Salminen, Charles & Kankaanranta, 2005). In more than a decade of investigating real-life data in business contexts, Louhiala-Salminen's work has highlighted the crucial importance of considering all modes of communication in order to gain a rich understanding of the ways in which international business people communicate in English; in any one transaction, this may involve English being used parallel to one or more other languages (e.g., Swedish and Finnish), it may involve one or more forms of electronic media (e.g., fax and email), and it may involve both spoken and written English (e.g., email and a meeting).

Finally, in the most recent work on Business English and new media, there has been an increasing concern with the application of the construct of multimodality, as exemplified by the work of researchers such as Bargiela-Chiappini (2005b), de Groot, Korzilius, Nickerson, and Gerritsen (2006), and, most recently, the 2007 collection on multimodal discourse edited by Garzone, Poncini, and Catenaccio (2007).

Teaching Written Business English

Business English can perhaps be considered one of the biggest money spinners in terms of global education, again reflecting the dominance of English as an international business language. The Amazon site lists literally thousands of publications of various types in its marketing of materials designed to teach and comment on BE. On December 5, 2006, for instance, these were: books (5,556), software (856), DVDs (622), and electronics (135). However, very few of these publications are based on the type of research discussed in the previous section, and there is a similar scarcity of reports on research-based BE teaching, at least in the published literature (Bargiela-Chiappini et al., 2007; Nickerson, 2002; Nickerson, 2005). Examples of ESBP projects that have included the collection of empirical data in various business contexts for teaching purposes include the 2000 publication by Li So-mui and Mead, which looks at the communication needs of textile and clothing merchandisers in Hong Kong, and the Corpus of International Business Writing (CIBW) teaching project and the Indianapolis Business Learner Corpus (IBLC) research initiative, which were part of a large-scale collaborative project between institutions in the U.S. (Indiana University–Purdue University), Belgium (Handelshogeschool Antwerp), and Finland (Åbo Akademi Finland), involving genre-based research and teaching projects specifically targeting application letters (see Connor, Davis & De Rycker, 1995; Connor, Davis, De Rycker, Phillips & Verckens, 1997; Verckens, De Rycker & Davis, 1998). Other research, such as the EU sponsored survey-based REFLECT Project (www.reflectproject.com), the consultancy work carried out by Charles and Marschan-Piekkari at Kone Elevators in Finland (Charles & Marschan-Piekkari, 2002), and the concordance-based study of politeness strategies in application letters by Upton and Connor (2001), discusses the implications of each respective study's findings for ESP training in business organizations in detail, but the training materials themselves are not included. As previously mentioned, since many of those involved in researching business discourse are also active in teaching ESBP, this remains a curious disconnect. Our own experience as ESPB practitioners and researchers would suggest that many of us do indeed refer to our research in the ESBP classroom and allow it to influence our work, but published accounts of this either in the form of research papers or in textbooks remain few and far between (see Planken & Nickerson, in press, for a discussion on the application of research findings in the teaching of ESPB at the Radboud University in Nijmegen, the Netherlands).

Four publications show evidence of the influence of research in the generation of teaching materials. The first of these is the 2002 consultancy project carried out by City University of Hong Kong to design an ESP/management communication project for the Training Department of the Hong Kong Jockey Club (Baxter, Boswood, & Peirson-Smith, 2002); the second is the project on intercultural communicative competence described by Planken, van Hooft, and Korzilius (2004) at the Radboud University Nijmegen; the third, the project discussed by Nickerson, Gerritsen, and van Meurs (2005), which looked at the use of ESBP in print advertising in several EU countries; and the fourth, the 2004 textbook on business language by Almut Koester (Koester, 2004). All of these provide useful examples of teaching situations and/or teaching materials involving ESBP, where the influence of research findings has been acknowledged and incorporated into the materials.

The 2002 publication by Baxter, Boswood, and Peirson-Smith details an ESP/management communication project that was developed and then implemented by the Department of English at the City University of Hong Kong for the Training Department of the Hong Kong Jockey Club. The researchers—who then also became the trainers—describe the way in which they collected the information they needed to inform their teaching materials, using both primary data collected from the organization and previously published accounts of business writing. Baxter et al. report that the project was intended to develop "the capacity of senior managers to write committee papers, the documents that drive top-level decision making in the organization" (2002, p. 17). In order to provide the Jockey Club with appropriate training, the researchers took a three-pronged approach:

1. An in-depth needs analysis before the course, which involved corpus analysis of the committee papers, a questionnaire with those managers at the Jockey Club who would be taking the course, and a set of interviews with 20 key informants at the organization (see also Li So-Mui & Mead, 2000, for a similar approach)

2. The development of a set of training materials designed to practice the activities carried out by the participants in writing one of the committee papers

3. The development of a set of training materials designed to target the committee paper as a highly specific genre that plays a crucial role within the Jockey Club

The needs analysis was an important part in developing appropriate training materials, since it did not only identify the collaborative writing activities surrounding the writing of the committee paper as an area of concern for the trainers, but also allowed the researchers to analyze and understand the target genre and the role it played in shaping the organization. The Jockey Club informants described problems both with an over-long drafting process and in finding appropriate structure and argumentation, and the researchers were also able to identify problems in understanding the audience, in managing the collaborative writing process, in writing strategically, and in selecting the correct format to be used. As a result, Baxter et al. (2002) developed a set of course materials to address these issues, rather than concentrating on grammar and style—that is, by practicing the activities needed to put the document together, by working with authentic committee papers, and by familiarizing the participants with useful ways of structuring their work, such as Jordan's Situation-Problem-Solution-Evaluation structure and Blicq's Summary-Background-Facts-Outcome model (Blicq, 1993; Jordan, 1984). The Jockey Club project is an excellent example of (discourse-based) research informing an ESBP training project in that the trainers were themselves researchers in the initial stages of the project. Baxter et al. (2002) describe the successful completion of the training course and an evaluation six months later that showed that the Jockey Club executives had made considerable progress in writing the committee papers more effectively.

The 2004 publication by Planken, van Hooft, and Korzilius (2004) describes a set of learning projects (the "business projects") and the tasks needed to complete them (the "communication tasks"). The aim of the projects was to teach English, Spanish, French, or German to Dutch business communication students, with specific reference to the development of their intercultural communicative competence. The authors describe the process through which the course materials were developed. For the ESBP course, this included reference to (a) existing published materials designed to teach Business English that could be incorporated into the projects, and

(b) the findings of business discourse research referring specifically to business genres such as emails, reports, and business letters. The target business genres were then taught within the framework of a simulated business project. In a business project in which students explored the potential for cooperation between a Dutch and an English company, for example, they were required to research publicly available documentation (corporate websites, annual reports, etc.) on real-life joint ventures and to identify factors of failure or success, to create and give a formal oral presentation about one of these joint ventures, and to write a formal business letter in which they present information about one of the companies in the project. They then finalized the project with a role-played, initial joint venture negotiation between the Dutch and English company, and a management summary in which they presented their analysis of the organizational "match" between the Dutch and the English companies, and in which they outlined a proposal for a joint venture between the two. Planken et al. (2004) differentiate between awareness raising tasks and production tasks—that is, in a set of awareness-raising activities, students were first asked to analyze the particular genre they needed to complete, followed by production tasks where a role-play simulation was used to provide a practice situation. In this way, students first become familiar with the important genres that contribute to LSBP in a real-life situation, and are then provided with an opportunity to practice.

In a second Radboud University project report, Nickerson, Gerritsen, and van Meurs (2005) describe a similar attempt to raise student awareness of the genres used in the real business world. In this project, teams of staff and business communication students collaborated together to carry out a study of the use of English in print advertising in magazines aimed at young women in the Netherlands, Germany, and Spain. The teams first carried out a survey of the ways in which English was used across the three countries in print advertising in the glossy magazine *Elle,* and this was followed by an experimental investigation of the attitudes to and comprehension of English, based on data collected from between 40 to 50 respondents in each of the three countries. The project was roughly divided into three parts: a theoretical part in which students became familiar with the relevant literature on the use of English in business genres, particularly advertising; a corpus analysis, where students looked at the lexical items used in the texts they were investigating and made an inventory of the amount and type of English that was used; and an experimental part in which the students designed a questionnaire with test items based on the corpus analysis, to investigate how well the readers of *Elle* for each of the three countries were able to understand the English used in advertising texts and also what their attitude was to that use of English. In all three of the countries investigated there was widespread use of English in print advertising in *Elle*, such that English was used in more than half of all the advertising that appeared. In international print advertising campaigns more English was used in Germany than in Spain, and more in the Netherlands than in Germany. Many campaigns were not translated into Dutch for the Netherlands, whereas they were partly (but not completely) translated for Germany and Spain. In the experiment, there were no significant differences between respondents in the three countries in either their attitudes toward the use of English or their proficiency in comprehending fragments of the advertising texts (e.g., Elizabeth Arden's slogan *Smile with all your senses*). In fact, more than 70 percent of all the respondents were able to give a correct global meaning of the slogans presented to them. This helped to demonstrate to students the value of doing empirical research to prove or disprove theoretical observations on the comprehension of English, given that the literature had (wrongly) predicted that the Dutch respondents would be more proficient than the Germans, who would in turn be more proficient than the Spanish. In their conclusion, Nickerson et al. (2005) discuss a number of important ways in which the project contributed to raising student awareness of written ESBP. First, as a result of the corpus analysis and their background reading, the students participating in the project became familiar with variations in the use of English in general across the three EU states and were able to study an important example of the use of English in a promotional genre used across the different cultures. Second, students became aware of the fact that not all readers of advertising texts in the European context are necessarily able to understand what is presented to them: 30 percent of all respondents could not give a convincing translation or global meaning of the slogans. Finally, in completing the corpus analysis and developing the materials needed to conduct the experiment, the students were developing their English language skills in a practical and motivating way.

The 2004 publication *The Language of Work* by Almut Koester looks specifically at how language is used in business and the workplace, using a data-driven approach (Koester, 2004). Koester refers to real-life data in a variety of different situations, and for written forms of business English, she refers to promotional letters and emails. The commentaries in the book are underpinned with specific reference to the work of discourse analysts such as Hoey (2001) and of genre analysts such as Louhiala-Salminen (1999), Devitt (1991), and particularly Bhatia (1993). Bhatia's work on promotional letters, for instance, is used to construct the unit on sales promotion letters, including a moves analysis in which students are asked to identify the beginnings and endings of moves like *establishing credentials* and *offering incentives*. In this activity in the textbook, the students are first introduced to the analysis of a British sales promotion letter following Bhatia's (1993) moves analysis. They are then asked to replicate this analysis by applying it to a different text that forms an interesting cross-cultural contrast to the first text, in this case a similar US advertiser's letter. In her commentary on the analysis of this second text, Koester refers back to Bhatia's original work and uses this to illustrate the possible difference between a British and American style of writing. The *Language of Work* is intended for UK students at the end of high school or the beginning of tertiary education, so not all of what it contains will be applicable to the global ESBP student body. It is, however, an excellent (and rare) example of how research can be used to underpin published teaching materials.

Theories on Multimodality and Their Applications: The Relationship with Business English

In the past five years, researchers interested in business discourse have begun to refer to theories on multimodality put forward by researchers such as Kress and Van Leeuwen (2001), together with the incorporation of multimodality and hypertextuality, in the theory of hypermodality, which is proposed by Lemke (2002). A detailed discussion of multimodality and hypermodality falls beyond the scope of this chapter, but essentially, Kress and Van Leeuwen (2001) provide a comprehensive framework in their 2001 publication *Multimodal Discourse* that views speech and writing as only two ways of making meaning within a range of other options that may also include other modes of making meaning, such as colors, objects portrayed in photographs, type-face, voice quality, type of recording, etc. Lemke's work extends this concept to include hypertextuality, in a construct he refers to as hypermodality, such that "not only do we have linkages among text units of various scales, but we have linkages among text units, visual elements and sound units" (Lemke, 2002, p. 301; see also Bargiela-Chiappini et al., 2007, for a detailed discussion of these concepts). Several researchers interested in the ways people communicate in business have built on these theories and have extended established approaches to the analysis of written forms of business communication by re-interpreting them from a multimodal perspective. Again, because of its dominance in web-mediated communication, English has been the main focus in this body of work (see the studies by Cyr, Bonanni, Bowes & Ilsever, 2005, and by Hu, Shima, Oehlmann, Zhao, Takemura & Matsumoto, 2004, who look at customer preferences for local versus non-local versions of both English and non-English corporate websites). Examples include Askehave and Nielsen's study of a homepage, which combines multimodal ideas and genre analysis (Askehave & Nielsen, 2005), de Groot, Korzilius, Nickerson and Gerritsen's study of annual general reports (2006), which is a multi-modal corpus and genre analysis that considers both visual and textual themes and the interplay between them (de Groot et al., 2006), and Bargiela-Chiappini's application of Lemke's ideas in the analysis of a UK banking website and the ways in which it "makes meaning" through linguistic, visual and textual (hyper)links (Bargiela-Chiappini, 2005). Finally, the 2007 collection co-edited by Garzone et al (Garzone et al., 2007) provides a series of recent multimodal investigations into different forms of business writing, such as web blogs, corporate websites and press releases posted on the net.

The field of business communication has provided several publications focusing on new media that could be applied equally well in the ESBP context. From around 2001 onwards, the *Business Communication Quarterly* has regularly published examples of how electronic media have been incorporated into teaching business communication students. These provide a wealth of interesting and useful information that could be transferred into different cultural contexts and used with ESBP students around the world. For instance, the articles by Lawrence (2003) and by Wallace and Mundell (2003) both discuss the evaluation of websites, including characteristics such as audience and information design (Lawrence, 2003; Wallace & Mundell, 2003). One recent *BCQ* publication provides an example of the way in which multimodality can be incorporated into the ESBP classroom; in the 2006 publication by Planken and Kreps, the authors discuss how they try to raise student awareness of multimodality and the meaning-making potential of visual and text units in the content design of web pages, within an ESBP context—one of their own Business English courses. In the course, the students are first made familiar with research-based guidelines for website design and usability, and aspects of the theory of multimodality, which they then apply in a critical analysis of an existing English language website. Based on their analysis, students present a written business report in which they present their findings and recommend improvements with regard to design, content, and usability. As a final assignment, the students go on to design and implement a new section (aimed at a new target group) for the existing website they have analyzed, and motivate their choices regarding usability, design, and content (including choices regarding visual and textual information) in an oral presentation and a business report. The authors thus combine the macro theory of multimodality, the principles of web design, and their own knowledge and experience of ESBP in an innovative Business English course. Multimodal (re)applications of established approaches to the analysis of text, as described in Planken and Kreps' publication, are still in their infancy and accounts of their impact on the teaching of ESBP are yet to appear in number. We believe, however, that studies such as this that purposefully draw on a number of different disciplines in a multidisciplinary way may show the way forward for the teaching of ESBP in the future.

* * *

CATHERINE NICKERSON is a Visiting Faculty in the Communication Unit at the Indian Institute of Management Bangalore and an Associate Editor for the *Journal of Business Communication.* She has lived in India, the United States, the Netherlands, and the United Kingdom, and she has been teaching and researching in business communication and the use of English as an international business language for the past 15 years. Her most recent book, *Business Discourse,* was published in 2007 by Palgrave Macmillan.

BRIGITTE PLANKEN is an Assistant Professor at the Department of International Business Communication, Radboud University, the Netherlands. Her areas of interest include English as an international business language and the rhetoric of environmental and social reporting.

REFERENCES

Akar, D., & Louhiala-Salminen, L. (1999). Towards a new genre: A comparative study of business faxes. In F. Bargiela-Chiappini & C. Nickerson (Eds.), *Writing business: Genres, media and discourses* (pp. 227–254). Harlow, UK: Longman.

Al-Ali, M. N. (2004). How to get yourself on the door of a job: A cross-cultural contrastive study of Arabic and English job application letters. *Journal of Multilingual and Multicultural Development, 25*(1), 1–23.

Askehave, I., & Nielsen, A. E. (2005). What are the characteristics of digital genres? Genre theory from a multimodal perspective. *Proceedings of the 38th Hawaii International Conference on System Sciences.* Retrieved April 24, 2006, from http://csdl2.computer.org/comp/proceedings/hicss/2005/2268/04/22680098a.pdf

Barbara, L., & Scott, M. (1999). Homing in on a genre: Invitations for bids. In F. Bargiela-Chiappini & C. Nickerson (Eds.), *Writing business: Genres, media and discourses* (pp. 227–254). London: Longman.

Bargiela-Chiappini, F. (2005a). Asian business discourse(s) [Special issue]. *Journal of Asian Pacific Communication*, Part 1, *15*(2).

———. (2005b). In memory of the business letter: Multimedia, genres and social action in a banking website. In P. Gillaerts & M. Gotti (Eds.), *Genre variation in business letters* (pp. 99–122). Bern, Switzerland: Peter Lang.

———. (2006). Asian business discourse(s). [Special issue]. *Journal of Asian Pacific Communication*, Part 2, *16*(1).

Bargiela-Chiappini, F., Nickerson, C., & Planken, B. (2007). *Business discourse*. Basingstoke, UK: Palgrave Macmillan.

Baxter, R., Boxwood, T., & Peirson-Smith, A. (2002). An ESP program for management in the horse-racing business. In T. Orr (Ed.), *English for Specific Purposes* (pp. 117–146). Alexandria, VA: TESOL.

Bhatia, V. K. (1993). *Analysing genre: Language in professional settings*. London: Longman.

———. (2004). *Worlds of written discourse: A genre-based view*. London: Continuum.

Blicq, R. (1993). *Technically—write! Communicating in a technological era* (4th ed.). Engelwood Cliffs, NJ: Prentice Hall.

Charles, M., & Marschan-Piekkari, R. (2002). Language training for enhanced horizontal communication: A challenge for MNCs. *Business Communication Quarterly, 65*(2), 9–29.

Connor, U., Davis, K., & De Rycker, T. (1995). Correctness and clarity in applying for overseas jobs: A cross-cultural analysis of U.S. and Flemish applications. *Text, 15*(4), 457–476.

Connor, U., Davis, K., De Rycker, T., Phillips, E.M., & Verkens, J. P. (1997). An international course in international business writing: Belgium, Finland, the United States. *Business Communication Quarterly, 60*(4), 63–74.

Cyr, D., Bonanni, C., Bowes, J. & Ilsever, J. (2005). Beyond trust: Website design preferences across cultures. *Journal of Global Information Management, 13*(4), 24–52.

De Groot, E., Korzilius, H., Nickerson C., & Gerritsen, M. (2006). A corpus analysis of text themes and photographic themes in managerial forewords of Dutch-English and British annual general reports. *IEEE Transactions on Professional Communication, 49*(3), 217–235.

Devitt, A. (1991). Intertextuality in tax accounting: Generic, referential and functional. In C. Bazerman & J. Paradis (Eds.), *Textual dynamics of the professions* (pp. 336–357). Madison: University of Wisconsin Press.

Gains, J. (1999). Electronic mail: A new style of communication or just a new medium? An investigation into the text features of e-mail. *English for Specific Purposes, 18*(1), 81–101.

Garzone, G., Poncini, G. & Catenaccio, P. (Eds.). (2007). *Multimodality in corporate communication: Web genres and discursive identity.* Milan: FrancoAngeli.

Gimenez, J. (2002). New media and conflicting realities in multinational corporate communication: A case study. *International Review of Applied Linguistics in Language Teaching, 40*(4), 323–344.

———. (2006). Embedded business emails: Meeting new demands in international business communication. *English for Specific Purposes, 25,* 154–172.

Gotti, M., & Gillaerts, P. (Eds.). (2005). *Genre variation in business letters.* Bern, Switzerland: Peter Lang.

Hoey, M. (2001). *Textual interaction: An introduction to written discourse analysis.* London: Routledge.

Hu, J., Shima, K., Oehlmann, R., Zhao, J., Takemura, Y., & Matsumoto, K. (2004). An empirical study of audience impression of B2C web pages in Japan, China and the UK. *Electronic Commerce Research and Applications, 3,* 176–189.

Hyland, K. (1998). Exploring corporate rhetoric: Metadiscourse in the CEO's letter. *Journal of Business Communication, 35*(2), 224–245.

Jenkins, S., & Hinds, J. (1987). Business letter writing: English, French and Japanese. *TESOL Quarterly, 21*(2), 327–349.

Jordan, M. (1984). *Rhetoric of everyday English texts.* London: Allen & Unwin.

Koester, A. (2004). *The language of work.* London: Routledge.

Kress, G., & Van Leeuwen, T. (2001). *Multimodal discourse: The modes and media of contemporary communication.* London: Arnold.

Lawrence. S. F. (2003). Analysis report project: Audience, e-writing and information design. *Business Communication Quarterly, 66*(1), 47–60.

Lemke, J. L. (2002). Travels in hypermodality. *Visual Communication, 1*(3), 299–325.

Li So-mui, F., & Mead, K. (2000). An analysis of English in the workplace: The communication needs of textile and clothing merchandisers. *English for Specific Purposes, 19,* 351–368.

Louhiala-Salminen, L. (1995). *'Drop me a fax, will you?': A study of written business communication.* Jyväskylä, Finland: University of Jyväskylä.

———. (1996). The business communication classroom vs reality: What should we teach today? *English for Specific Purposes, 15*(1), 37–51.

———. (1997). Investigating the genre of a business fax: A Finnish case study. *Journal of Business Communication, 34*(3), 316–333.

———. (1999). 'Was there life before them?' Fax and email in business communication. *Journal of Language for International Business, 10*(1), 24–42.

———. (2002). The fly's perspective: Discourse in the daily routine of a business manager. *English for Specific Purposes, 21*, 211–231.

Louhiala-Salminen, L., Charles, M., & Kankaanranta, A. (2005). English as a lingua franca in Nordic corporate mergers: Two case companies. *English for Specific Purposes, 24*(4), 401–421.

Nickerson, C. (2000). *Playing the corporate language game: An investigation of the genres and discourse strategies in English used by Dutch writers working in multinational corporations.* Amsterdam: Rodopi.

———. (2002). Endnote: Business discourse and language teaching. *International Review of Applied Linguistics in Language Teaching, 40*, 375–381.

———. (2005). English as a lingua franca in international business contexts. *English for Specific Purposes, 24*(4), 367–380.

Nickerson, C., Gerritsen, M., & van Meurs, F. (2005). Raising student awareness of the use of English for specific business purposes in the European context: A staff-student project. *English for Specific Purposes, 24*(3), 333–346.

Orlikowski, W., & Yates, J. (1994). Genre repertoire: The structuring of communicative practices in organizations. *Administrative Science Quarterly, 39*, 541–574.

Planken, B., & Kreps, A. (2006). Raising students' awareness of the implications of multimodality for content design and usability: The web site project. *Business Communication Quarterly, 69*(4), 421–425.

Planken, B., & Nickerson, C. (2008). Business English and the Bologna Declaration in the Netherlands: Integrating business communication practice, content and research. In I. Fortanet & Ch. Räisänen (Eds.), *ESP in higher European education: Integrating language and content* (pp. 165–179). London: John Benjamins.

Planken, B., van Hooft, A., & Korzilius, H. (2004). Promoting intercultural communicative competence through foreign language courses. *Business Communication Quarterly, 67*, 308–315.

Reflect Project. www.reflectproject.com

Rogers, P. S. (1989). Choice-based writing in managerial contexts: The case of the dealer contact report. *Journal of Business Communication, 26*(3), 197–216.

Rogers, P. S., & Swales, J. M. (1990). "We the people?" An analysis of the Dana Corporation policies document. *Journal of Business Communication, 27*(3), 293–314.

St. John, M. J. (1996). Business is booming: Business English in the 1990s. *English for Specific Purposes, 15*(1), 3–18.

Swales, J. M. (1990). *Genre analysis: English in academic and research settings.* Cambridge, UK: Cambridge University Press.

Swales, J. M., & Rogers, P. S. (1995). Discourse and the projection of corporate culture: The mission statement. *Discourse and Society, 6*(2), 223–242.

Thatcher, B. L. (2000). Writing policies and procedures in a U.S. and South American Context. *Technical Communication Quarterly, 94,* 365–400.

Thomas, J. (1997). Discourse in the marketplace: The making of meaning in annual general reports. *Journal of Business Communication, 34*(1), 47–66.

Upton, T. A., & Connor, U. (2001). Using computerized analysis to investigate the text linguistic discourse moves of a genre. *English for Specific Purposes, 20,* 313–329.

Van Mulken, M., & van der Meer, W. (2005). Are you being served? A genre analysis of American and Dutch company replies to customer enquiries. *English for Specific Purposes, 24,* 93–109.

Verckens, J. P., De Rycker, T., & Davis, K. (1998). The experience of sameness in differences: A course in international business writing. In S. Niemeier, C. P. Campbell & R. Dirven (Eds.), *The cultural context in business communication* (pp. 247–261). Amsterdam: John Benjamins.

Wallace, C., & Mundell, D. (2003). Crafting a cyber assignment: The first cut. *Business Communication Quarterly, 66*(4), 102–106.

Yates, J., & Orlikowski, W. (1992). Genres and organizational communication: A structurational approach to studying communication and media. *Academy of Management Review, 17*(2), 299–326.

Yeung, L. (2004). The paradox of control in participative decision-making: Facilitative discourse in banks. *Text, 24*(1), 113–146.

Yli-Jokipii, H. (1994). Requests in professional discourse: A cross-cultural study of British, American and Finnish business writing. *Annales Academiae Scientiarum Finnicae Dissertationes Humnarum Litterarum, 71.* Helsinki, Finland: Suomalainen Tiedeakatemia.

Zak, H., & Dudley-Evans, A. (1986). Features of word-omission and abbreviation in telexes. *English for Specific Purposes, 5*(1), 59–71.

7

Call Center Communication: Measurement Processes in Non–English Speaking Contexts

JANE LOCKWOOD
Hong Kong Institute of Education

GAIL FOREY
Hong Kong Polytechnic University

NEIL ELIAS
Logica, Inc., the Philippines

Abstract

This chapter looks at the English language communication problems that U.S. companies are experiencing when off-shoring their call center operations to non–English speaking destinations such as India and the Philippines. Specifically, the use of the quality assurance (QA) scorecard measurement by outsourcing companies of Customer Service Representative (CSR) English language communication skills when talking to native speaker customers in the U.S. is explored.

While companies claim great success with this scorecard at home in America, they are now complaining that it does not appear to work in countries where English is not the mother tongue. Specifically, companies report that despite high scores achieved on the scorecard by offshore outsourced CSRs, there are many complaints from U.S. customers related to language communication breakdown on the phones from these outsourced destinations.

This chapter first investigates the language and content of a typical scorecard and then outlines an analysis of lexico-grammatical features found in the scorecard and compares these items used for assessment in QA procedures with what sometimes happens in reality, drawing on systemic functional linguistics (SFL) as well as current approaches to communicative language assessment practice. It is argued that in a workplace environment when the CSR is operating in a second language, the scorecard measurement suffers from an incomplete set of criteria for English language communicative competence. In other words, the QA measures in operation need to be developed through research-based tools, drawing on the field of applied linguistics.

Background

The offshore and outsourcing of business is a recent and expanding development in the business sector. It is estimated that the addressable market for global offshoring exceeds US$300 billion, and in the NASSCOM McKinsey Report (2005) it is estimated that by 2010 this business could be worth US$110 billion. In that report, it is suggested that only 10 percent of business that could be offshored has been realized so far. Thus the potential for growth and the impact on language and business communication is immense (see Graddol, 2006, for a review of global trends in English). Asia is the leading offshore destination (Graddol, 2006; NASSCOM McKinsey, 2005), and thus the implications for English language use in this fast-growing business sector need to be addressed.

The business process outsourcing (BPO) industry, which includes offshoring and outsourcing business, affects many languages. For example, a number of Spanish-speaking call centers have been established in Mexico and Brazil, Japanese and Korean call centers in the northern parts of China such as Dalian, and English-speaking outlets in India and the Philippines for destinations such as the USA, UK, Australia, and New Zealand (Vashistha, 2006). The focus of this chapter is on English-speaking call centers in Asia, and specifically, ESP research carried out in the Philippines, where the growth of call centers is phenomenal.

The two most popular destinations, India and the Philippines, now have between them over 350,000 customer service representatives (CSRs), mostly servicing the United States (BPAP, 2007; NASSCOM McKinsey, 2005). The majority of these CSRs are college graduates, and outsourcing companies report improved quality of customer service due to the combination of graduate employees and a strong service culture in Asia (NASSCOM McKinsey, 2005). The Philippines alone is expanding call center employment at a rate of over 60 percent per year (Vashistha, 2006) and is set to continue. However, this rapid growth has exposed concerns that many offshore destinations may not have the necessary talent to support this growth. Sanez (2006, p. 11), the CEO of the Business Processing Association of the Philippines (BPAP), talks of "serious supply side constraints" and an "insufficient quantity of 'suitable and willing talent to fuel growth'." The lack of confidence in the country's ability to provide the necessary manpower is the major hurdle to the rapid development of call centers. Recruitment levels in the Philippines are running at 3 percent of applicants. A study conducted by recruitment company John Clements and Associates, which tested 2,524 graduating students, found that only 3 percent had the required skills for the call center industry, and the biggest problem identified was their level of oral English proficiency (Dominguez, 2006, p. 19). One large third-party call center provider has on average 400 applicants a week; only 1 percent of these would have the language skills required and another 3–5 percent are what are referred to in the industry as "near hires"—that is, with some training they would be at the level required for hiring (Greenleaf & Ferrer, 2007).

From a political, economic, and social perspective, the call center industry is crucial to the development of a strong economy in the Philippines, and providing useful training founded on ESP research to future employees of this industry is essential. It is this emphasis on training within the context of the call center that has motivated the present study to focus on the Quality Assurance (QA) techniques used. QA measures within the industry are used for performance and diagnostic purposes; they also act as a model for recruitment and training. By investigating the QA measures adopted, we are able to understand specific features in the nature of the call and the way in which the organization chooses to interpret such assessment tools. Typically, companies have simply transferred training and QA material from the home country to the offshore destination, and are now finding that training materials developed for domestic employees in the US and UK may not be appropriate for these offshore destinations.

The QA tools are particularly important in call centers that provide customer service. While the performance of call centers specializing in sales (outbound call centers) can be measured by objective numbers, servicing centers (inbound call centers) are typically assessed through Service Level Agreements (SLAs), which specify efficiency measures such as average speed to answer the call, average handling time (AHT), and also quality measures, such as CSATS (customer satisfaction surveys) and local scorecard use for internal QA. The scorecard attempts to measure the "customer experience" through an assessment of a real call, or a series of calls, by a local QA assessor. A scorecard is a common form of measurement used in different organizations to assess the level of performance (Amaratunga, Haigh, Sarshar, & Baldry, 2002; Porter & Tanner, 2004). As noted, the scorecard is used to assess the individual CSR's performance and to provide diagnostic information (Staples, Dalrymple, & Bryar, n.d.). It is important therefore to know whether the QA measures probed in this scorecard are valid and reliable. However, little research has been carried out in the BPO industry, and specifically on the use of scorecards in the call centers. To date the studies focusing on language in call centers tend to be undertaken in a context where the CSR and customer both reside in the same country (Adolphs, Brown, Carter, Crawford, & Sahota, 2004; Cameron, 2000a, 2000b). Only recently in ESP have studies been carried out in these new offshore destinations (Cowie, 2007; Forey & Lockwood, 2007; Friginal, 2007; Hood & Forey, 2008). The focus in these recent studies is on language, genre, and lexicogrammatical features (Forey & Lockwood, 2007; Hood & Forey, 2008; Lockwood, Forey, & Price, 2009) and accent and training (Cowie, 2007; Friginal, 2007). Studies have yet to discuss QA measures and their impact on language.

The Problem

U.S. companies are finding that simply lifting their domestic training programs and QA processes and dropping them into offshore non–native English speaking (NNES) locations does not appear to work. One of the main reasons that companies are experiencing training and QA difficulties with scorecards in the outsourced environment is because the measures needed for an NNES CSR are fundamentally different from those needed for a native-speaking CSR. There are two questions connected to this:

1. What are the scorecards assessing with regard to communication?
2. How can QA scorecard processes be improved to meet the specific needs of the NNES call centers?

The Philippine Context

In the Philippines, English is taught as a second language in most schools and universities. While the students' *knowledge of grammar* may be excellent (and often much better than their U.S. counterparts), their knowledge of *how* this grammar and language is activated in real-life exchanges is quite a different story. The range of registers the NNESs have experience with will probably be quite limited. In the classroom situation and many second language contexts, the demands on the speaker are quite different from the language experience of dealing with frustrated customers. Rather than personal and social contexts related to customer inquiries, the teaching of English in the classroom tends to focus on educational genres (see Macken-Horarik, 2002, for an outline of genres found in education). For example, within an insurance call center context, the CSR is dealing with health-related issues, bereavement, and financial queries. Such real-life interaction has been under-researched, and the US NES customer's register and language choices in such contexts are probably beyond the experience of many Filipino CSRs. Thus it would be extremely difficult, even though the Filipino agents may have passed all their English language exams, to deal with such registers where the language and cultural experience of the customer is markedly different. Knowing *about* language does not mean one is able to use it in a complex functional setting such as a call center (Young & He, 1998).

Why is it that NNESs find real-life interaction with NES so difficult even though they have been receiving English language instruction from an early age at school? Put simply, this often relates to an approach to instruction in English through school and university where heavy classroom emphasis is put on the *form* of the language rather than the *function*. The context of teaching English in a developing country where resources are limited means that there is a higher dependency on written language and grammar rules than on how language makes meaning in specific contexts—that is, the goal and purpose of language as a socially constructed resource (see Christie &

Martin, 1997). Traditional language teachers too have the mistaken notion that grammatical accuracy is the cornerstone of good language use, whereas far more emphasis should be given to understanding how language changes depending on who is talking to whom, what reality is being constructed, and what channel of communication is chosen (Martin, 2001, and Painter, 2001, offer a more detailed description of these register variables, i.e., field, tenor, and mode). The outsourced call center industry has become a victim of inappropriate English language teaching methodologies that have been prevalent in the school system in Asia for many decades now. Our research in the Philippines suggests that much of the English language training for the call center industry is inappropriately focused on discrete grammar rules and accent neutralization, which has little to do with the customer service interaction.

Call center interaction, which relies heavily on understanding the goal and purpose of the call, being able to answer the customers' query clearly and accurately, and a dynamic interaction with the customer in the desired manner via a telephone conversation, is an occluded genre. Success relies on CSRs knowing how to use language, understanding that language is a system of choices, and making the appropriate choices that will satisfy the customer's demands and also fit the assessment criteria used in the scorecards.

This chapter outlines recent trends in assessment in the workplace and presents and examines one example of a scorecard measurement tool. The scorecard is critically evaluated through a deconstruction of the language, goal, and purpose of the assessment measure. Current research (Forey & Lockwood, 2007) illustrates some of the weaknesses of the scorecard as a diagnostic tool for the call center transaction, and a systemic functional linguistic (SFL) theoretical position is incorporated in our understanding of language and the meanings language choices make. Forey and Lockwood (2007) and Hood and Forey (2008), when outlining the genre of the call center interaction, provide an understanding of the text and the choices within the call center interaction, which are then seen to be at odds with the reductionist and structural paradigm reflected in the scorecard. Finally, an alternative model of assessment that has been developed against the background of well-known applied linguistic frameworks is offered (Canale & Swain, 1980; Savignon, 2007). We briefly outline how this alternative model, Business Processing Language Assessment (BUPLAS), can be used for defining and assessing communicative competence. However, a detailed discussion of the development, design, and testing of the BUPLAS assessment tool will not be addressed due to limitations of space.

What Is a Scorecard?

The scorecard is a form of Quality Assurance (QA) process frequently used in the workplace. Quality Assurance measurements have been researched and discussed in the business and management literature (see Amaratunga et al., 2002). In this particular context, where the CSRs are all using English as a second language and the interaction is on the telephone, the talk (the text) is pivotal to the success of the call. Understanding the role of language and assessing this communication is a key component in ascertaining the effectiveness, the training needs, and the future requirements of the workforce.

The scorecard aims to assess product or service knowledge and communication skills during the telephone service interaction. It is administered on a regular basis by team leaders and QA personnel (e.g., trainers and coaches) by listening to live calls or recordings. Commonly, in call centers people work in teams of 10–15 with one "coach," and that coach will be expected to listen to an average of 3–4 calls for each team member a month. The scorecard is used to provide judgmental data about the CSR performance, which is then related to financial rewards, incentives, and/or bonuses, and also used for the business to determine whether the SLAs (Service Level Agreements) are being met. If a situation were to arise where individuals consistently performed poorly, they could lose their job or the provider could face penalties from the customer organization.

Methodology: Language and Assessment in the Call Center Industry

Although language proficiency has been a major factor in the development of the industry, the assessment of the call does not necessarily seem to include an assessment of the key language components that are essential for successful customer service satisfaction. As suggested by Douglas (2000, p. 1), assessment should be "based on a theoretical construct of contextualized communicative language ability." To date, research on language and assessment has tended to focus on educational assessment (see Bachman, 2000; Hamp-Lyons & Condon, 2000; McNamara & Roever, 2006), or assessment and policy, for example in the work of Shohamy (2006) and McNamara and Roever (2006), who discuss government immigration policy in relation to language assessment. Assessment within the workplace tends to focus on the correlation between standard language proficiency exams, such as TOEFL or TOEIC, and the role of attainment levels in these exams (Taylor, 2003). In addition, a limited number of studies have assessed raters' behavior in proficiency assessments (Brown, 1995; Lumley, 1998). In countries such as the Philippines the expense of such standardized exams is prohibitive, and even then the results of such language assessment may not be what the industry needs.

In our discussion of the scorecard as an assessment tool we apply insights from language assessment and also understanding of language as a meaning making system that is socially constructed. In recent years, studies in assessment have developed in ways that have made language assessment a more objective and a more communicative process. Common language assessment practices try to make the process more objective through the design of scales and descriptors against which a number of assessors can objectively mark and calibrate. The absence of such tools opens up the process to personal judgments and results in assessment being potentially subjective.

In the call center industry in the Philippines at present, recruiters in Human Resource (HR) Management have great difficulty in developing language assessment tools. HR personnel have reported that many language assessment practices have little correlation with the work expected of the candidate (Forey & Lockwood, 2007). Some recruiters administer grammar tests, which may give information about what a candidate knows about language but not provide information on whether it can be effectively used. Others judge how American the accent sounds. As outlined by Bachman (1990), good language assessment practice dictates three fundamental principles:

1. **Validity:** The assessment tests what is relevant to the candidate in the target communication situation and its communicative needs.
2. **Reliability:** The test result remains the same across time and raters.
3. **Practicality:** The assessment is easy to administer and mark.

Language assessments that do not meet these fundamental principles fail to address their purpose. The scorecard, as part of the larger QA process, is a "high stakes" assessment, and as an assessment tool in the NNES context, it needs to meet the following criteria:

1. It is a *complete set* of all communicative functions and stages present in call center transactions; that is, it has **validity.**
2. It is a balanced reflection of the relative value (or weighting) that a scorer may give to different components and criteria of the call; that is, it has **validity.**

3. It provides, in a washback sense (see Alderson & Banerjee, 2002; Bachman, 2000; and Weir, 2005, for a discussion of washback), prescriptions of what a good quality call is; that is, it has **validity.**

4. It can be completed quickly and simply; that is, it is **practical.**

5. It is an objective rather than a subjective measure, so that different scorers arrive at the same result; that is, it is **reliable.**

The 35 Golden Points assessment scorecard (the Scorecard discussed here in detail) is a typical call center QA scorecard used by an American company in the Philippines, and it is analyzed in order to ascertain whether it effectively measures and diagnoses the language and communication output of NNES agents. It should be noted that the QA scorecard typically assesses not only for language and communication, but also for attitude and behavior, and product or service knowledge. This discussion focuses specifically on the language and communication scoring aspects.

The Scorecard: The Deconstruction of the QA Scorecard

The Scorecard used in this article is one example of many that have proven adequate in a domestic call center context, but which are problematic in an NNES environment. The scorecard items are divided into five stages:

1. Make a connection: Create a professional image. (7 items)

2. Act positively: Tell them you will help. (6 items)

3. Get to the heart of the matter: Listen and ask questions. (6 items)

4. Interpret the fact: Highlight what you will do. (7 items)

5. Close with agreement. (9 items)

Each item is expressed as a competency statement to which the rater assigns the scale 1–Exhibited, 0–Not exhibited, or NA–Not applicable. Each section in the scorecard is presented in Tables 1–5. At the end of the assessment, the number of "exhibited" items is totalled up, and the result of x (no. of correct items)/35 is given to represent the assessment.

It will be shown that the scorecard does not reflect the issues confronting an NNES speaker and also that the point weighting is poorly distributed since not all stages in a call are equally important. The two stages of **purpose** (3) and **servicing** (4), as outlined by Forey and Lockwood (2007) and illustrated in Figure 7.1, are the most important and complex stages in a call, and it is in these stages where communication breakdown more frequently occurs. Thus the weighting of assessment should reflect the complexity of the call.

Stage 1: The Opening (Make a connection: Create a professional image)

While this stage is crucial to establishing relationship (Hood & Forey, 2005), there is very little risk of communication breakdown at this early stage of the transaction. The only important issue is to sound friendly and professional. This is not difficult for the NNES agent and can be learned. As shown in Table 7.1, Item 1, one of these opening statements would be seen as effective (1) while the other would not (2):

---

(1) *Customer services, this is Carlos, how may I help you?*

(2) *Hi Customer services, Carlos speaking, how can I help you?*

Example 2 would not be given a score as it includes *hi* and *can,* which have been identified as inappropriate. This is problematic. They both fulfil the function of opening the call effectively, and either may be appropriate depending on the customer. Such prescriptive restraints are flawed and also likely to be misunderstood by the NNES CSR, who would believe such language choices are simply wrong.

TABLE 7.1
Greeting

	Components	Criteria for Scoring
1	Greeting—offer welcoming words	No "hi," "hello," "can," "speaking"
2	Greeting—maintain upbeat tone	Does not drop in tone at end, ends in an upbeat (form of a question)
3	Greeting—use unhurried pace	
4	Really listen—don't interrupt	Let caller vent
5	Express empathy through words	Can't have without #6
6	Express empathy through tone	Can't have without #5
7	Use caller's name as soon as you hear it	First opportunity to use name—ask for it if not given

Items 5 and 6, *Express empathy through words* and *tone,* both relate to either the optional purpose moves before gathering information and/or the mandatory purpose move after the gathering of information. Item 5 is problematic insofar as phonology and words together achieve the meaning desired. To deliver an empathetic response in a monotone and or with falling intonation would be understood by the native English speaker as being insincere or at best, formulaic.

Item 7 asks the agent to use the customer's name. In the right context, this may be appropriate (usually when the call is going smoothly) but there are many contexts in which using the customer's name can be inappropriate. The instruction may be misunderstood by the NNES as a substitute for other important areas of functional interaction language, such as reassuring the customers, asking if they require further information, probing, and so forth. Using the customer's name is not a panacea. It is rewarded three times: later in Item 18—*After hold—use name, pause and say thank you*—and in Item 28 on the Scorecard. Thus, if the CSR uses the customer's name at the three specific stages, then it is assumed that the call is successful, which may not be the case.

Stage 2: Gathering Information (Act positively: Tell them you will help)

In this second stage of the call center transaction, assuming the caller is not angry, the interaction is routine. Therefore, like the opening, this part should not be weighted heavily.

TABLE 7.2

Gathering Information (Act Positively: Tell Them You Will Help)

	Components	Criteria for Scoring
8	Tell caller you will help	Must have "I," "you," and a verb—must be clear statement
9	Ask permission to gain more information	Must be clear question (when 3 or more questions are to be asked)
10	Use "I" not "we" when appropriate	"We" used in reference to next steps, ownership
11	Be courteous, use please and thank you	Be polite and friendly
12	Express sincere, helpful attitude with tone	86%—majority of the call
13	Remain calm	Not defensive in words or tone

The important functional language that emerged from the linguistic analysis (Forey & Lockwood, 2007) was the ability to probe for full information if required. Item 9 may be valid, although the criterion statement is mystifying: *Must be clear question (when 3 or more questions are to be asked).* Are we to assume that two questions can be asked without permission?

Other items are either behavioral (e.g., "remain calm"), or items that may or may not be applicable to the interaction. How one measures Item 12— *Express sincere, helpful attitude with tone (86%—majority of the call)*—is very unclear. Vague language is unhelpful to the NNES agent. For example, in Items 10, 22, and 24, the words *appropriate* and *proper* without further definition are, in the end, nothing but subjective judgments. This may not be a problem for an NES agent.

Stage 3: The Purpose of the Call (Act positively: Tell them you will help / Get to the heart of the matter: Listen and ask questions)

There are constant complaints from U.S. raters regarding their call centers in the Philippines that NNES CSRs do not listen effectively. Understanding the problem the customer has lies at the very heart of effective servicing. Here the score weighting should be high.

In the scorecard, Item 14 is extremely important: *Ask questions to find the main point: Issue/purpose of the call.* This requires very good interactive

TABLE 7.3

Get to the Heart of the Matter: Listen and Probe

	Components	Criteria for Scoring
14	Ask questions to find the main point	Issue/purpose of the call
15	Repeat numbers	
16	Avoid jargon and dramatic phrases	Don't distance yourself from caller
17	Before hold or transfer—explain and ask permission	Hold might also be break in conversation
18	After hold—use name, pause and say thank you	
19	Work with, not against the customer	Proactively initiate solutions—do more than just what you are you supposed to do

discourse and language skills as well as an ability to predict and synthesize information quickly in English as it is given. However, the other components in this category could be labelled as routine: Item 15: *Repeat numbers,* and Items 17 and 18: *Before hold or transfer—explain and ask permission; After hold—use name, pause and say thank you.* Item 16 is unclear and Item 19 is, like Item 14, fundamental to the language and communication work of an agent. Item 19 states *Work with, not against the customer.* What this actually means is unclear. When a customer is shouting at you and expressing frustration, how should the CSR "work with this"? This item needs to be a clear and accurate descriptor, explicit to both the CSR and coach.

Stage 4: The Servicing (Act positively: Tell them you will help / Get to the heart of the matter: Listen and ask questions / Interpret the facts: Highlight what you will do)

This stage is another critical phase in the call center transaction. In the Philippines, the NNES CSR has difficulty in this phase of the call center transaction because of the requirement to explain clearly (**discourse** capability) and the ability to **interact**. This is the part of the transaction that is most likely to go wrong. This suggests a need for extra weighting on this part of the

TABLE 7.4
Interpret the Facts: Highlight What You Will Do

	Components	Criteria for Scoring
20	Give security—use specific phrases	Personal, specific, empathic
21	Be knowledgeable and accurate	Technical / process oriented. Tell correct information to caller.
22	Keep call to appropriate length	Concerns that go acknowledged—too much or too little information
23	Be proactive—set a deadline	Don't wait for caller to ask when something will happen
24	Speak clearly with proper volume	
25	Maintain appropriate pace	Don't speak too quickly or too slowly; interruptions
26	Summarize the next step	Doesn't have to be everything, just what is next

call. The scorecard only assesses the product component of the explanation in Item 21: *Be knowledgeable and accurate*. Crucially, the ability to interact and explain extensively (discourse capability) that NNES CSRs exhibit at this stage of the call are not listed in the scorecard. The result is that these are not being measured or diagnosed as problems for training and coaching.

Generally in Stage 4 of the scorecard, the items for scoring are ambiguous and incomplete. Item 20: *Give security—use specific phrases* is unhelpful and imprecise in an NNES context.

There is no attempt in Stage 4 to assess and diagnose the functional language used within those moves such as *empathy, apology, sympathy, reassuring*, and *transitioning*.

Agents are given a score based on whether they summarize the next step, but not what has come before. Further, items such as *keep the call to appropriate length* and *maintain appropriate pace* are general statements of desired behaviors that will vary depending on context.

Stage 5: The Closing (Close with agreement)

The final part of the call center transaction, like the opening phase, is mostly formulaic and takes place when the issues have been resolved. Again the weighting in this part of the scorecard should be minimal. It is therefore interesting to note that there are as many items in this section as in the servicing section and more than in the purpose section. If the score of the opening and closing sections were totalled up, they would be more than the purpose and servicing sections. This kind of weighting will not give accurate and valid QA scores for NNES agents.

As shown in Table 7.5, it is suggested that the closing components are similarly bedevilled with ambiguity (Item 29: *End with a golden phrase*), impracticality (Item 31: *Let caller hang up first*), prescription (Item 28: *Use customer's name*), and very general competency statements (Item 32: *Did you control the call professionally?*).

Discussion

The problems with the set of communicative functions included in the Scorecard are threefold. First, the items are expressed as either very general, all-encompassing statements or else as small, minor, discrete instructions. Second, the items are prescriptive. And third, they are incomplete from a

TABLE 7.5

Close with Agreement

	Components	Criteria for Scoring
27	Get agreement on next steps	Ask for agreement—do not get by default. "Is there anything else?"
28	Use customer's name	
29	End with a golden phrase	Give security in closing
30	Use sincere tone	Trailing off, dropping, flat, sarcastic, defensive
31	Let caller hang up first	
32	Did you control the call professionally?	Must get 8, 9, and if so, will get 32
33		Is the customer closer to a solution as result of your interaction?
34		Was the call within the AHT?
35		Was the customer completely satisfied with your servicing?

language and communication standpoint. All constitute major problems when dealing with NNESs, as these recipients need to exercise choices and judgments when using functional language. Additionally, and most importantly in the context of service level agreements, what is not included as a QA measure will be seen as unimportant. Some striking absences in the Scorecard, for example, are the functions of apology, explaining clearly, and a demonstration of the ability to positively and professionally assert oneself to take control of the servicing within a call.

The incomplete approach in the Scorecard toward defining and scoring functional language will adversely affect the way NNESs are diagnosed for language and communications training. It neither fairly judges nor diagnoses the problems facing NNES agents in an outsourced context. Something more comprehensive and grounded in an understanding of the linguistic stages of a service telephone interaction and the functional and communicative language features of the call center transaction will ensure more validity in the scorecard and therefore more useful analysis that can lead to improvement.

The Deconstruction of the QA Scorecard against Communicative Assessment Principles

This QA Scorecard is based on U.S. perceptions and experiences about what could and does go wrong in an NES call center agent interaction. It focuses on behavioral and attitudinal issues of NES agents that are reflected in their communication. However, the important point is that it only addresses attitude and product knowledge, while ignoring both language skills and how insufficient language skills can present as behavioral and attitudinal problems. A completely different approach needs to be taken in a situation where CSRs are not operating in their mother tongue and are dealing with customers from a different culture. NNES agents may also have attitudinal and product problems, but the components in the Scorecard for NNESs must also be based on an analysis of the English language communication and sociocultural issues that NNES agents experience.

Relative Values and Weightings Assigned in the Scorecard

Some features of the call center transaction are more critical than others in achieving customer satisfaction. For example, Item 21, *Be knowledgeable and accurate,* is more important in call center servicing than Item 31, *Let caller hang up first;* and Item 12, *Express sincere, helpful attitude with tone,* is more important in building trust than Item 7, *Use caller's name as soon as you hear it.* Clearly different stages should not carry equal weighting in assessing the quality of a call. Thus the Scorecard is not a reliable tool for assessing quality in an NNES environment.

Washback of the Scorecard

The QA process Scorecard has a direct impact on the way the CSR learns how to take calls and modify his or her behavior on the phone. This is a phenomenon called "washback" (Alderson & Banerjee, 2002; Bachman, 2000; Weir, 2005). What is tested will be taught and learned. The Scorecard provides negative washback into judgments and diagnoses for NNES CSRs because, from a language and communication point of view, it attempts to be prescriptive and not contextual.

The Practicality of Using the Scorecard as a Language and Communication Assessment Tool

A discrete item-ticking exercise of a complex exchange does not constitute good language assessment practice. Good communication assessment practice first defines the fundamental criteria and then scores around a scale linked to descriptors of what is heard (Douglas, 2000). It would be unusual when developing a language and communication assessment to be able to say that a single partial transaction is either a yes or a no. A concern with the Scorecard is that it requires a yes or no response with no scales and no descriptors to score against. This makes scoring subjective and a poor reflection of the interaction.

In summary, the components are random, the criteria are idiosyncratic, and the points marking system is inconsistent with best practice in language and communication assessment. For NNES agents it will yield poor analysis of what is going wrong in the call center transaction from a language and communication point of view.

The Validity and Reliability of the Process of Scorecard Assessment

In any scoring of language, assessment should be based on comprehensive criteria and a scale that plots proficiency and competency ability and detailed descriptions of criteria for each step on the scale. This minimizes ambiguity in the interpretation of the criteria. The Scorecard here has no scale and no detailed and clear criteria. Its poorly constructed descriptions of language and communication render its assessment invalid and unreliable.

Together with ambiguity, lack of definition is also a problem in the Scorecard. Vague statements like Item 25: *Maintain appropriate pace;* Item 24: *Speak clearly with proper volume;* and Item 22: *Keep call to appropriate length* are all open to interpretation. Such words as *proper* and *appropriate* need rigorous definition if they are to be meaningful in language and communication scoring.

Suggested Model: Based on Communicative Competence

"Communicative competence" (Canale, 1983; Canale & Swain, 1980; Savignon, 1983) comprises a number of elements. These components provide a rich interpretation of what is present in good communication and go far beyond the limited view that good grammar is all that is required. Canale (1983) writes of the nature of linguistic communication as:

a. a form of social interaction and therefore normally acquired and used in social interaction

b. involving a high degree of unpredictability and creativity in form and message

c. taking place in discourse and sociocultural contexts which provide constraints on appropriate language use and also cues as to correct interpretations of utterances

d. carried out under limiting psychological and other conditions such as memory constraints, fatigue and other distractions

e. always having a purpose (for example to establish social relationships, to persuade or to promise)

f. involving authentic, as opposed to textbook-contrived, language

g. judged as successful or not on the basis of actual outcomes

(Canale, 1983, pp. 3–4)

In successful spoken communication, or in successful communicative competence, therefore, the following features need to be evident:

Language competence (ability to use grammar, vocabulary, and the phonological features of the language)

Discourse competence (ability to recognize and construct the flow of a spoken or written text)

Sociolinguistic competence (ability to understand the intercultural nuances)

Interactive competence (ability to make appropriate interpersonal choices)

Strategic competence (ability to repair language breakdown, particularly in spoken language)

Specifically in the call center context, these competencies will mean the CSR has the ability to:

1. interact well and build relationships with customers

2. make appropriate language choices

3. construct text in a way that is understandable to overseas customers

4. use phonological features that are easily understood by the customer

5. maintain control of the call

6. understand the nuances in what the caller says in order to gauge how best to serve the caller

Native English speakers generally have these language and communication skills, but for NNES speakers these communicative competencies will need to be identified, explained, and taught.

There are important issues for English servicing call centers to consider when they outsource their operations to NNES destinations such as the Philippines, India, and China. In the Philippines, the kind of scorecard examined here does not work because there is no proper accounting for the fundamental English language and communication problems being experienced by the NNES CSR force. It is crucial in the development of effective ESP material to invest both in research and the development of material based on detailed needs analysis and addressing the specific context of the work undertaken. As is evident in the case of call centers, how workplace language use is viewed and understood not only has implications for individual language learners but can also have organizational and global consequences.

*   *   *

JANE LOCKWOOD has had 30 years of teaching, teacher education, educational management, and TESOL curriculum and language assessment experience in Australia and different parts of Asia. Her area of special interest and expertise is business and professional English. She completed her Ph.D. in this area in 2003 and has published widely. She has developed English for Specific Purposes (ESP) programs, teacher education programs, and assessment processes for the Information Technology Enabled Services (ITES) in the Philippines and India. She currently is Head of the Centre for Language in Education at the Hong Kong Institute of Education and is Director of Education of FuturePerfect Business English Specialists based in the Philippines.

GAIL FOREY is an Associate Professor and Associate Director for the Research Centre for Professional Communication at the Hong Kong Polytechnic University. She has carried out research and published in the areas of written and spoken workplace discourse, language education, and teaching development. Currently, Gail is working on a project titled *Call Centre Communication Research*; more information can be found at www. engl.polyu.edu.hk/call_centre/default.html.

NEIL ELIAS is a business manager with extensive experience in offshoring, outsourcing, and BPOs in Asia. Since 2007 he has been the Country Manager setting up the Philippines BPO and ITO for Logica PIC serving customers in Europe and Asia. For the three years up to March 2006, Neil started and headed a Business Process Outsourcing operation for the AIG financial group, based in Manila, providing call center and customer service for AIG life insurance business in the United States. Before that he ran a global business practice for an Indian-based outsourcer. Neil has been elected to the Board of Trustees of the Business Processing Association of the Philippines and has been a keynote speaker at many conferences and seminars.

REFERENCES

Adolphs, S., Brown, B., Carter, R., Crawford, P., & Sahota, O. (2004). Applying corpus linguistics in a health care context. *Journal of Applied Linguistics, 1*(1), 9–28.

Alderson, J. C. & Banerjee, J. (2002). State of the art review: Language testing and assessment (Part 2). *Language Teaching, 35,* 79–113.

Amaratunga, D., Haigh, R., Sarshar, M., & Baldry, D. (2002). Application of the balanced score-card concept to develop a conceptual framework to measure facilities management performance within NHS facilities. *International Journal of Health Care Quality Assurance, 15*(4), 141–151.

Bachman, L. (1990). *Fundamental considerations in language testing.* Oxford, UK: Oxford University Press.

————. (2000). Modern language testing at the turn of the century: Assuring that what we count counts. *Language Testing, 17*(1), 1–42.

BPAP (Business Processing Association Philippines). (2007). *Back office outsourcing in the Philippines.* Retrieved October 26, 2008, from http://www.bpap.org

Brown, A. (1995). The effect of rater variables in the development of an occupation-specific language performance test. *Language Testing, 12*(1), 1–15.

Cameron, D. (2000a). *Good to talk? Living and working in a communication culture.* London: Sage.

————. (2000b). Styling the worker: Gender and the commodification of language in the globalized service economy. *Journal of Sociolinguistics, 4*(3), 323–347.

Canale, M. (1983). From communicative competence to communicative language pedagogy. In J. Richards & R. Schmidt (Eds.), *Language and communication* (pp. 2–27). New York: Longman.

Canale, M., & Swain, M. (1980). Theoretical bases of communicative approaches to second-language teaching and testing. *Applied Linguistics, 1,* 1–47.

Christie, F., & Martin, J. R. (1997). *Genre and institutions: Social processes in the workplace and school.* London: Cassell.

Cowie, C. (2007). The accent of outsourcing: The meanings of "neutral" in the Indian call centre industry. *World Englishes, 26*(3), 316–330.

Dominguez, C. (2006, February). *Bridging the gap.* Paper presented at BPA/P General Assembly, Manila. Retrieved June 10, 2006, from www.bpap.org/bpap/industry/21.%20Bridging%20the%20Gap%20022806.pdf

Douglas, D. (2000). *Assessing languages for specific purposes.* Cambridge, UK: Cambridge University Press.

Forey, G., & Lockwood, J. (2007). "I'd love to put someone in jail for this": An initial investigation of English in the business processing outsourcing (BPO) industry. *English for Specific Purposes. 26*(3), 308–326.

Friginal, E. (2007). Outsourced call centers and English in the Philippines. *World Englishes, 26*(3), 331–345.

Graddol, D. (2006). *English next: Why global English may mean the end of "English as a foreign language."* London: British Council.

Greenleaf, R., & Ferrer, J. (2007, February). *English language acquisition and assessment in call centre environments.* Paper presented at Talking across the World: English Communication Skills for the ITES Industry Inaugural Conference. AIM, Manila, Philippines.

Hamp-Lyons, L., & Condon, W. (2000). *Assessing the portfolio: Principles for practice, theory, and research.* Cresskill, NJ: Hampton Press.

Hood, S., &. Forey, G. (2005). Presenting a conference paper: Getting interpersonal with your audience. *Journal of English for Academic Purposes, 24,* 291–306.

———. (2008). The interpersonal dynamics of call-centre interactions: Co-constructing the rise and fall of emotion. *Discourse and Communication, 2*(4), 389–409.

Lockwood, J., Forey, G., & Price, H. (2009). Englishes in the Philippine business processing outsourcing industry: Issues, opportunities and research. In M. L. S. Bautista & K. Bolton (Eds.), *Philippine English: Linguistic and literary perspectives* (pp. 219–241). Hong Kong: Hong Kong University Press.

Lumley, T. (1998). Perceptions of language-trained raters and occupational experts in a test of occupational English language proficiency. *English for Specific Purposes, 17*(4), 347–367.

Macken-Horarik, M. (2002). "Something to shoot for": A systemic functional approach to teaching genre in secondary school science. In A. Johns (Ed.), *Genre in the classroom: Multiple perspectives* (pp. 17–42). Mahwah, NJ: Lawrence Erlbaum.

Martin, J. R. (2001). Language, register and genre. In A. Burns & C. Coffin (Eds.), *Analysing English in a global context* (pp. 149–166). London: Routledge.

McNamara, T., & Roever, C. (2006). *Language testing: The social dimension.* Malden, MA: Blackwell.

NASSCOM McKinsey. (2005). *The NASSCOM McKinsey Study 2005.* Retrieved June 17, 2007, from www.nasscom.in/Nasscom/templates/NormalPage.aspx?id=2599

Painter, C. 2001. Understanding genre and register: Implications for language teachers. In A. Burns & C. Coffin (Eds.), *Analysing English in a global context* (pp. 167–180). London: Routledge.

Porter, L. J., & Tanner, S. J. (2004). *Assessing business excellence.* Amsterdam: Elsevier.

Sanez, O. (2006). *Driving breakthrough growth in BPO/IT-services.* Retrieved June 17, 2007, from www.bpap.org/bpap/publications/Feb2607%20Driving%20Breakthrough%20Growth%20in%20BPO-IT.pdf

Savignon, S. (1983). *Communicative competence: Theory and classroom practice.* Reading, MA: Addison-Wesley.

———. (2007). Beyond communicative language teaching: What's ahead? *Journal of Pragmatics, 39*(1), 207–220.

Shohamy, E. G. (2006). *Language policy: Hidden agendas and new approaches.* London: Routledge.

Staples, W. J. S., Dalrymple, J. F., & Bryar, R. M. (no date). *Assessing call centre quality using the SERVQUAL model.* Retrieved June 14, 2007, from http://scholar.google.com/scholar?hl=zh-TW&lr=&q=Staples+et+al+Quality+using+SERVQUAL+Model&lr.

Taylor, L. (2003). *The Cambridge approach to speaking assessment: Research Notes 13* (August), 2–4. University of Cambridge Local Examination Syndicate.

Vashistha, A. (2006). *e-Services Philippines/C-Level Summit: Country competitiveness and centres of excellence.* Tholons Inc. Retrieved June 17, 2007, from www.bpap.com

Weir, C. (2005). *Language testing and validation: An evidence-based approach.* Basingstoke, UK: Palgrave Macmillan.

Young, R., & He, A. W. (Eds). (1998). *Talking and testing: Discourse approaches to the assessment of oral proficiency.* Amsterdam: John Benjamins.

8

Teaching Legal English: Contexts and Cases

JILL NORTHCOTT

Institute for Applied Language Studies, University of Edinburgh, Scotland

Abstract

This chapter provides an overview of Legal English teaching for second language English speakers adopting a primarily pedagogical perspective. As specificity of context is as crucial as specificity of content, the chapter considers different categories of learners grouped according to their professional or academic purposes and contexts of learning and legal language use. Consideration is also given to the different teaching backgrounds of ESP practitioners involved in teaching English for law. The major contribution made by genre analysis to pedagogical practice especially in the teaching of legal reading and writing skills is acknowledged. Ethnographically oriented research can illuminate specific learning contexts as well as target situations and provide useful information for language educators in designing and implementing courses. Highly specialized legal English teaching contexts require equal partnership between ESP practitioners and legal specialists.

In the process of putting up signs on classroom doors in the School of Law to indicate that an English for Lawyers course would be occupying those rooms in the subsequent weeks, I encountered a member of the university maintenance staff whose comment "About time!" appears to encapsulate the layperson's opinion of the relationship between law and language. As much of this article relates to English language provision for L2 speakers, the anecdote serves to make the point that even for L1 speakers of English the language of the law is still viewed as esoteric and foreign, requiring translation into comprehensible English. This is in spite of the efforts of the Plain English movement whose proponents have laboured untiringly to encourage law professionals to write in language that is both accessible and comprehensible. There is evidence backing their claim for greatly improved intelligibility. Clumps (1996), for example, working with Dutch law undergraduates, reports that although only under half of his sample actually preferred the Plain English versions of short samples of legal text, those who translated these versions into their L1 produced superior translations to those who worked with the original legalese.

The need for English language education to enable L2 law professionals to operate in academic and professional legal contexts requiring the use of English is now well established. This chapter is intended to provide an overview of this area, addressing some of the key questions related to English language provision for law professionals: lawyers, law students, judges, law lecturers, legal translators, and interpreters. The perspective is primarily pedagogical with a focus on teaching and learning.

Implications of the Characteristics of Law as a Discipline

In the field of language education, law has often been regarded as uniquely different from other areas of ESP such as English for Medicine or IT. This is partly in response to the position adopted by legal professionals who cite the large number of books on legal method and guides to the study of law published (e.g., Bradney, Cownie, Masson, Neal, & Newell, 1995; Hanson, 1999) to support this view. There is, it is maintained, no other academic subject that requires such a radical induction to specialized language and ways of thought. Strong (2003), for example, asserts that "students (in the UK) come unprepared to the study of law since it is qualitatively different from the study of other subjects" (p. 1). The close interplay of content and language in law (Gibbons, 2003; Tiersma, 1999) result in unique difficulties for ESP teaching.

This issue has been partially explored within the general versus specific debate. Dudley-Evans and St. John (1998) extended Blue's (1988) distinction between common-core EGAP (English for General Academic Purposes) and specific ESAP (English for Specific Academic Purposes) to ESP generally. In their ELT cline, moving from general to specific, Legal English appears at Position Four with other "courses for broad disciplinary or professional areas" (Dudley-Evans & St. John, 1998, p. 9). However, law is just one among many instances of specialized professional areas ESP teachers may encounter. Dudley-Evans (2001) concludes that the research evidence from discourse and genre analysis has strengthened the case for specificity in EAP teaching. Using academic writing as an example, Hyland (2002) has revisited the specificity debate and makes the case for increasing teacher awareness of discipline and profession-specific variation in order to enable learners to use the conventions of their disciplines appropriately. Bhatia (2002) describes how genres play different roles in different disciplines and gives the example of cases, which are used extensively in both business and legal education. On the surface, business and legal cases share some common features but they play radically different roles in business and law. In common law systems a legal case will begin with the facts followed by the reasoning of the judges supporting their decision. This portion of the judgment, known as the ratio decidendi, may contain a new and binding principle of law that courts must apply in subsequent cases. Legal professionals read cases to find and understand the judges' reasoning in order to identify the principle of law to be applied. White (1981) and Swales (1990) both give accounts of how they were misled by the surface structure of the texts into devising reading skills development tasks for law students focusing on understanding the narrative or the facts of the case:

> the comprehension tasks I invited the students to undertake were misconceived because they were designed to help the students to understand the *stories*. It was only when I attended classes given by a Criminal law professor that I belatedly came to realize that the reading strategy required in legal education was not to understand—and retain the gist of—a narrative, but to spot the crucial fact on which the decision (rightly or wrongly) rested. (Swales, 1990, p. 73)

This is a beginning, certainly, but there are more profound difficulties involved in understanding legal texts of this kind. As Mertz (1996) maintains:

> even were all the technical vocabulary to be transformed somehow into more accessible language the meaning for which lawyers read the text would remain elusive to those reading for referential content. (p. 236)

The nature of law as a discipline results in problems for translators as well as ESP teachers. One school of thought (Harvey, 2002) views legal language as one instance of specialized language and therefore to be approached by translators in a similar way to other types of specialized discourse. The other (Šarčević, 1997, 2001) maintains that only legally trained translators are fully competent to translate legal texts. Northcott and Brown (2006) provide a fuller account of common issues for legal translators and legal English teachers based on an analysis of legal seminar discourse, stressing the need for a high degree of subject specialist and ELP (English for Legal Purposes) teacher cooperation in specialist legal English teaching and training contexts. This has important implications for the knowledge base needed by teachers of legal English, an issue that will be explored in the third section of this chapter.

Legal English Contexts

It is contended in this chapter that specificity of context is at least as crucial a concern as specificity of content. In order to ground the discussion in the practical realm, a data sample collected from one legal English teaching context is referred to. Edinburgh University's Institute for Applied Language Studies has offered Legal English courses for L2 legal professionals for the past twenty years. Currently, apart from tailored courses to meet the specific needs of individuals and closed groups (e.g., Legislative translators from countries preparing for EU accession) and a one-week course for teachers of legal English, three short open courses are on offer:

English for Legal Studies. This is aimed primarily at law undergraduates and recent graduates from civil law countries.

English for Lawyers. This is a course, attracting mainly European commercial lawyers, for legal professionals with a minimum of two years' legal practice.

English for the LLM. A course in English for Academic Legal Purposes (EALP) for those about to begin a post-graduate law degree in English.

Data on learners' needs is routinely collected by means of a questionnaire completed at the beginning of the course and an evaluation questionnaire at the end. Comments here relate to data collected over the five-year period 2000–2005 from participants in the English for Legal Studies (LS) and English for Lawyers (Law) courses. For the LS data, responses from a total of 262 students were considered and a detailed analysis made of the responses from one year's intake (41) as this appeared to be reasonably representative of student views generally. The Law responses totaled 82 for the five-year period. The same year's intake (2004) as for LS was analyzed for comparative purposes. There were 16 responses.

Both groups were asked why they had decided to take the course. Responses from the law students (LS) relate to their future careers and are consistent in the assumption of the necessity of having a good command of legal English in order to get a job. Interestingly, this is not a view expressed just by those who aim to work in the international context for large cross-border firms where most of the work is done in English. Even those who expect to have a career with local law firms perceive the importance of English competence. As one commented: "There is no future for a lawyer who does not know accurately legal English and the English legal system, especially in branches like commercial law where English colonization is very deep, regarding both legal terms and substantive issues."

The lawyers' responses, while similar, were more focused on their current needs and tended to specify particular skills such as the need to write legal documents such as contracts. Asked to complete the sentence "I'd like to learn how to . . ." these responses were given (LS):

- Write (a legal brief, emails to colleagues discussing cases, a contract in English, legal documents)
- Read (legal documents, textbooks)
- Speak fluently (have a legal conversation with someone, speak with clients on the phone, explain legal contents in English, talk about law matters, the equivalents of Spanish company forms and taxes, use the appropriate legal register)
- Understand how the English legal system works

The lawyers (Law) wanted to:

• Understand better English
• Write letters about legal matters
• Make a presentation in English
• Understand legal documents
• Write a claim
• Conduct a consultation with a client in English
• Negotiate on legal issues
• Draft contracts in English

A third course, English for the LLM, ran for the first time in 2004. Questionnaires were distributed to students who had attended the course halfway through their LLM degree courses to obtain data on the efficacy of the pre-sessional course. Apart from comments about the importance of reading and essay writing skills, the main area highlighted was the need for a stronger focus on the common law background and reading and understanding law reports in the light of the function of the ratio decidendi in decided cases as a binding source of UK law. As one respondent commented: "For students from the Civil Law System the method of studying the Common Law is quite different from their previous experience."

This brief snapshot illustrates the need to distinguish the purposes different groups of learners might have for learning legal English. There are obvious differences between students and professionals. Practicing lawyers, for example, focus on work-related genres such as writing claims. However, there are also differences within the student population related to the degree of influence Anglo-American law has in current and future legal study and work environments. Of particular interest is the interrelationship of law and language issues in participant responses. Students, for example, cannot learn how to write a legal essay without understanding how to read law reports. This in turn presupposes understanding the socio-legal context within which these texts are interpreted, hence the need for learners to become familiar with aspects of the UK legal system.

The following sections categorize the different potential groups of learners of legal English according to the study context and discuss some of the particular issues pertinent to each of these categories. Northcott (2008) presents a model focusing on the interrelatedness of three of these variables: study context, teaching and learning methodology, and teacher background.

English for Academic Legal Purposes

Undergraduates Studying in Common Law–Influenced Legal Systems

Students from common law legal systems that have historical or current links with the legal systems of the UK or the U.S. but where the L1 is not English study Legal English in their own law schools. It may be explicitly taught as a separate subject or implicitly learned, as in many UK undergraduate law programs, along with the study of the substantive law. Reading appears to be the most essential skill in these contexts. Deutch (2003) gives an account of a needs analysis for Israeli law students, indicating that the ties between the Israeli and U.S. legal systems are growing, with U.S. court decisions having persuasive authority in Israel, overtaking the historical ties with English law. In South Africa and in Zimbabwe, English is still the dominant language of the law (de Klerk, 2003; Northcott, 1997). In Hong Kong, undergraduate law students need to grapple with English law reports and write problem question essays just as English law undergraduates do.

A genre-based approach has proved an effective way of catering for the language education needs of these students (Bhatia, 1993; Langton, 2002; Weber, 2001). Key genres identified are case reports and statutes. As these written genres are very fixed, it is a relatively straightforward task to develop genre analysis materials to develop students' abilities to comprehend these types of texts once a clear analytical framework has been established. Bhatia (1993); Maley, Candlin, Crichton, & Koster (1995); and Bowles (1995) all provide accounts of the text structure of law reports. Increasingly sophisticated materials have been produced both for classroom and self-study use. Badger (2003) proposes techniques for using newspaper law reports in the legal English classroom as a more accessible option for students than the long texts that constitute the official versions. He attempts also to identify lexico-grammatical features of the ratio decidendi by focusing on the distinction between the features of general as opposed to specific statements. An individual court decision will be specific to the parties. If the judge is framing principles of law, then these will be generalizable and characterized by signals of generality such as use of the present tense and use of indefinite determiners for previously occurring nouns. Badger (2003) emphasizes, however, that "not all rationes decidendi are statements of law and, further, that not all statements of law are rationes decidendi . . . the link between the internal lexico-grammar and the ratio is not direct" (p. 258). Reinhart (2007) has produced genre-based materials for US LL.M students incorporating an analysis of the structure of legal holdings.

As genre analysis of legal text is not confined to ESP, potential pedagogical sources are growing. There is an increasing amount of research done in fields such as computational linguistics, designed to develop tools for the analysis of legal text. Grover, Hachey, Hughson, and Korycinski (2003) describe the development of tools and methods for the automatic linguistic annotation of House of Lords judgments, based on initial genre analysis, in order to provide summaries. Corpus-based methods would appear to be a promising way forward in legal education. However, these need to be approached with caution. Because of the diversity of language that may come under the umbrella of legal English, useful corpora must be highly specific. Moreover, consideration must be given to the ways in which legal disciplinary practices impact the way students approach corpora consultation. Hafner and Candlin (2007) give an account of student use of online corpus tools to improve legal writing in a professional legal training course in Hong Kong, concluding that, as lawyers draft from precedents, they are more likely to look for model documents than search for specific legal phrases. Moreover the detailed linguistic analysis envisaged appeared to be over and above the needs of the legal practitioners. It is important to adopt an ESP perspective that understands that the disciplinary practices of linguists are often not the preferred practices of the professions.

Much of the focus in the undergraduate law context is on developing writing skills. Candlin, Bhatia, Jensen, and Langton (2002) reviewed the available resources for legal writing, concluding that as most of the books were intended for L1 students, there was a dearth of suitable material for use in EALP writing contexts. Most of the legal writing materials on the market are produced for U.S. law students. These are often very extensive and include advice on good writing in general as well as detailed analysis of specific legal writing genres contextualized in the U.S. legal system (e.g., Shapo, Walter & Fajans, 1999). The assumption made in the UK is that law students already know how to write or else will pick up the skill by a process of osmosis:

> On the whole, in England and many Commonwealth countries legal draft-ing is not taught at universities or in the law schools. Students are not exposed to the techniques of clear, precise drafting. For the most part, drafting is learnt on the job, picked up piecemeal in chambers by the pupil barrister or in the office by the solicitor's trainee. Little guidance is given. (Butt & Castle, 2001, p. 19)

There is now some evidence of a change in this trend in the UK, with the acknowledgment that legal English teaching approaches and materials used with L2 law students may also be of relevance to L1 students. For example, McKay and Charlton (2005) have produced a legal English coursebook specifically intended for both audiences: "to assist those interested in law and wishing to become more conversant in English within a legal context, whether as a native English speaker or someone using English as a second or foreign language" (p.1).

The problem question essay, in which students demonstrate their legal reasoning abilities and knowledge of the law by applying existing case law to the solution of a different legal problem, has received attention from ESP researcher-practitioners (Bhatia, 1989; Bruce, 2002; Harris, 1997). Vari-ous models have been developed to aid (mainly L1) students in their ability to construct these essays. Strong (2003), for example, presents the CLEO (Claim Law Evaluation Outcome) method to tackle essay writing. These methods are clearly adaptable to meet the needs of L2 students.

UK Law Undergraduates

Second, there are L2 students in undergraduate law programs in English-speaking countries. In addition to improvement of general Academic Eng-lish skills there is a need for specific legal English skills improvement. In fact, for these students, with marginal English language proficiency, it is even more imperative that language education is specifically related to the demands of the law course as they have no time for extra activities. The methods used predominantly in the non-UK environment are clearly appli-cable in this context too. However, in UK universities the numbers of non–

English speaking undergraduate law students are not generally high enough to permit specialist language improvement classes. It is often left to the non-specialist EAP teacher to cater for the writing needs of law students in a class of mixed academic specialisms. Smyth (1997, 1999) has developed language materials and approaches adapted to the demands of the students' specific law courses that can be used by non-specialist teachers of legal English.

LL.M Sudents

A third category, which has seen growth in recent years, is that of LL.M students studying in the U.S. and the UK and, increasingly, in LL.M programs taught in English in other European countries. These courses are attended both by analyzing lawyers and recent law graduates from civil law jurisdictions both in Europe and Asia, in particular China.

Feak and Reinhart (2002) give an account of a pre-sessional program for LL.M students in the US. Northcott (2006) has an account of the development of a four-week English for the LL.M course designed primarily for students at Edinburgh University. Although the students in question already have an undergraduate law degree, the requirements of study in a common law jurisdiction are often completely new to them. Clearly, the more legal systems students have to contend with, the more challenging understanding and participating in an LL.M will be. As well as English or Scots law, a good understanding of EU law is frequently necessary in order for the students to begin to understand their LL.M materials. This background knowledge may be assumed by UK law lecturers.

For LL.M students a major area of difficulty is found in seminar participation. Overseas students from Asian countries, in particular China and Japan, find the Socratic methods employed in post-graduate law seminars stressful. The emphasis on individual participation and contribution is unfamiliar and the legal English teacher's task will include developing student confidence for this demanding learning environment.

Diploma of Law Courses

In addition to L2 students attending LL.M courses there is some evidence of a beginning trend toward attendance, by Chinese students in particular, on Diploma of Law courses, traditionally the route for English non-law graduates intending to enter the English legal profession. An LL.M from a UK or

U.S. university was seen as a route to a legal job. As more and more Chinese students return to China with this qualification, it is becoming clear that the qualification (essentially evidence of specialist knowledge of a specific legal area rather than a vocational qualification) will not necessarily lead to employment as a lawyer. Diploma of Law courses teach the substantive English law and an EALP course for students preparing to attend them will need to focus on the same areas as for undergraduate law students.

Law Undergraduates from Civil Law Countries

These students may also attend Legal English courses although they are not studying English or American law and their legal systems are not directly influenced by the common law. In Europe these courses are taught increasingly in university law schools as some understanding of Anglo-American legal systems becomes a prerequisite for lawyers, particularly commercial lawyers, across Europe. Moreover, the use of English has increased in the enlarged European Union and new legislation is frequently drafted in English. Legal English programs are active in many of the universities of central and Eastern Europe. These courses are offered both within the law schools and faculties where they may be either part of the legal studies curriculum or provided by the language support units alongside more general ESP courses. The language departments where there is a tradition of materials writing have proved to be a source of well-written legal English textbooks and materials, designed specifically for local needs (e.g., Bardi, 2001; Kossakowska-Pisarek & Niepytalska, 2004). Some of the legal English coursebooks most widely available from UK publishers originated as courses taught to European law undergraduates (Chartrand, Millar & Wiltshire, 2003; Riley, 1994).

In some ways the more difficult decisions about course content are reserved for the EGLP (English for General Legal Purposes) course. Participants are often law students or recent graduates who are not studying English law or working in an English speaking context although they might possibly do this in the future. Typically, such a course will be topic-based, mirroring the syllabus of an undergraduate law degree. The language and concepts of the law are not often separable because legal terms derive their meaning from a particular legal system. This means that legal terminology needs to be presented within the context of the common law legal system from which it originated. The difficulty is to be found in developing language skills and providing legal terms that will be useful in the specific, but as yet unspecified, legal contexts in which participants will use their legal English. To illustrate the dilemma, let us consider the terms used for the parties in civil proceedings. In England, a *claimant* sues a *defendant* whereas in Scotland a *pursuer* sues a *defender*. The term *plaintiff*, although still used in the U.S., is no longer used in England. While familiarizing students with the variants, for productive purposes perhaps the U.S. terms would be the most useful in international contexts. Generally speaking, students in this group are more interested in aspects of legal English of most use in the international environment, such as English for international commercial and contract law. The concept of international legal English in any specific legal field is, however, controversial, and it is only possible to tackle this area by reference to sociocultural contexts—that is, specific legal systems. A typical method employed is to look at, for example, the essential elements of a contract under English law and then to ask students to use the language they have learned in order to compare their own country's contract law (Chartrand, Millar & Wiltshire, 2003).

U.S. Law Schools

In the US, where law is not taught at undergraduate level, there is a much stronger graduate school emphasis on skills-based courses. Here legal English courses may be run in tandem with introduction to American law courses for both L1 and L2 speakers of English and may be taught by either law lecturers or language teachers, using specially prepared introductory materials. These are often very extensive and come with instructors' notes. They are however, very context-specific and do not lend themselves easily to adaptation for non-U.S. contexts.

English for Lawyers

Globalization has resulted in English becoming the lingua franca of international legal practice as well as the international business language. Commercial lawyers representing international clients need to understand and even draft contracts in English. Cross-border mergers of law firms necessitate an understanding of legal English for meetings and negotiations and overall liaison with colleagues in offices in different countries. Even in countries such as Romania, where one might expect French to be a more natural lingua franca, Romanian and French lawyers communicate through English.

In dealing with clients, English may also be the language of choice although it is not the first language of either the lawyer or the client.

Within the European context, in addition to the commercial law firms, smaller private firms increasingly need English in their dealings with individual clients. As movement between the countries of Europe continues to increase, everyday life takes on increasingly international dimensions: buying and letting property, entering into employment contracts, divorce, and adoption are just a few examples. In dealing with British clients, Spanish lawyers, for example, need to be able to explain Spanish legal concepts and procedures in English. As legal translation is essentially about translating systems, this requires the ability to give good explanations but also necessitates an understanding of the differences in the ways the two legal systems operate. Lack of proficiency in English is seen by many lawyers as a barrier to career progression and the reason given for attending a legal English course is often the desire to widen career options.

An English language course for lawyers will inevitably share features of Business English courses. Giving presentations, telephoning, participating in meetings and negotiations, writing letters and reports are all communication skills required by both business and legal professionals. In addition lawyers need to interview and advise clients. Of the specifically legal genres with which lawyers will need to work, either receptively or productively, the priorities are legal documents, in particular contracts and legal letters. Haigh (2004) provides a useful syllabus for a course in English for legal communication for lawyers.

This increasing globalization of legal practice has been recognized in the creation of legal English qualifications available through the examination boards. The TOLES (Test of Legal English Skills) test, which targets lawyers intending to practice in the UK, has been available for a number of years. The new Cambridge ILEC (International Legal English Certificate) gives certification of ability to operate in English in international legal working environments. Although the test is highly rated for its face validity, in terms of the authenticity of topics, texts, and language (Thighe, 2006) it raises the question of what exactly constitutes international English in an area that has always been very closely tied to specific contexts and cultures. This is an area in which it is very difficult to isolate the variables in testing and merits much more research. The effect of prior background knowledge on reading performance, for example, is a crucial issue. The very fact that the texts lawyers need to be proficient in reading are operative legal texts rather than texts about the law raises many questions. For example, a lawyer with commercial experience will find it much easier to read contractual language than a lawyer without this background, regardless of English proficiency level.

Judges and Prosecutor

In the European civilian legal systems there is an increasing requirement for legal English for public legal officials. In the Czech Republic, for example, judges and prosecutors are required to improve their legal English as part of the CPD (Continuing Professional Development) requirement. The need to participate in conferences and meetings at a European level is usually the motivating factor.

Legal English Education Provision

In the UK, providers of language education for legal professionals can be found in both the public and private sectors. In university-based language schools within the TEFL world, influenced by Applied Linguistics, English for Legal Purposes (both EAP and EPP) has been largely considered as a type of ESP, taught by English language teachers with a background in Applied Linguistics or with Cambridge DELTA (Diploma in English Language Teaching to Adults) qualifications. Many of these teachers, working with learners from disciplines such as law in which they have little or no background, quickly analyze that they cannot approach the task as experts in the law and seek collaboration with experts (Bruce, 2002; Candlin et al., 2002; Howe, 1993; Morrison & Tshuma, 1993; Northcott & Brown, 2006; Smyth, 1997). Of all ESP fields, English for law is a field widely acknowledged as presenting particular difficulties for the ESP teacher and there is a clear need for the teacher to have some subject-specific knowledge, whether this is obtained by the traditional route of the undergraduate law degree or by other means.

What "knowledge" is needed depends on the specific contexts of the learners. The ESP teacher with a post-graduate Applied Linguistics qualification, experienced in the theory and practice of both needs and language analysis, can effectively analyze the language learning needs of specific groups of learners in this as in other SP fields and develop a course program based on learner needs. There are, increasingly, published materials available from which a selection can be made or coursebook chosen and adapted to suit the learners' needs. On the other hand a legal professional such as an English solicitor, for example, whose qualifications may have been obtained through old-fashioned "cramming" and who has worked with clients in particular areas of the law, operating mainly at the level of problem-solving, often with little recourse to the law books and no knowledge of legal systems other than his/her own does not, arguably, have the requisite knowledge for this kind of ESP teaching. Deutch (2003, p. 141) expresses the dilemma similarly.

While legal English teachers have to deal with highly professional material, most of them have never had a legal education. Various solutions have been offered to overcome this serious obstacle that results in both the production of unprofessional materials and the students' negative attitude to the course due to their language teachers' deficiency. Several law schools employ lawyers for teaching legal English to overcome the negative effects of unprofessional language courses. However, lawyers lack the pedagogical background for teaching a language course.

Nevertheless, the commercial sector has tended to favor lawyers over language teaching professionals to work with their clients, usually on a one-to-one or small group basis, where pedagogic concerns are perhaps not so significant. There is increasingly a demand for dual qualified teachers to work with lawyers. UK-based private language schools attract a high premium for courses that are tailored to the needs of individuals and taught by lawyers with TEFL qualifications.

Teacher Education for Legal English

There are many teaching situations in which teachers may at different times be required to work with learners from different professional and disciplinary contexts. Few have the luxury of focusing entirely on Legal English teaching and it is therefore impractical to require teachers to have a substantial background in law. The question then arises, how can teachers develop their skills for specialist legal English teaching? Maclean (1997) and Northcott (1997) are both advocates of a reflective "thinking-in-action" approach (Maclean, 1997, p. 173) for teachers transferring from general to specific language teaching. Northcott gives an account of an unusual legal English teaching context—a training program for interpreters in the courts in Zimbabwe, concluding that the demands of a new teaching assignment can act as a catalyst for teacher education.

Short courses in Teaching English for Law based on the more prevalent Teaching English for Business courses are offered by some of the university-based language schools in the UK and also in the private sector schools specializing in legal English. These courses will usually focus on issues such as language analysis and course design, available published materials, and using authentic source material as the basis for materials design. Those teachers for whom legal English is likely to form a major part of their teaching will often seek out opportunities to develop their legal knowledge base. Attendance at law lectures, reading introductory books on core subjects, keeping up to date with developments in the law through reading newspaper articles and subscribing to email lists (e.g., Jurist) are all common strategies. For the legal professional intending to teach legal English, CELTA (Certificate in English Language Teaching to Adults) and other introductory TEFL courses will provide an introduction to methodology and classroom management skills.

Centrality of Needs Analysis

It will by now be apparent that there is no prescriptive list of items that form the basis of a legal English course. Decisions about course content will be based first and foremost on learners' needs and purposes. Purposes in turn depend upon contexts of use. There is a large and still relevant body of literature on needs analysis in ESP (e.g., West, 1994). An analysis of the target situation (TSA) forms only part of the prerequisite for course design; learning needs and the present situation of the learners in terms of their current level of English and pre-existing legal content knowledge must also be established (Hutchinson & Waters, 1987). Bhatia (2002) outlines the different stages in analyses of linguistic data for pedagogical applications. There has been a movement from descriptions of lexico-grammar through studies of discourse structure, with the focus currently on the contexts in which the language is used. Ethnographic needs analyses of specific professional and academic settings provide a good starting point for identifying the contexts in which the learners will need to use the language and those communicative events that place most stress on the learners' language abilities (Northcott, 2001). As in other areas of ESP, less work has been done to analyze oral academic than written legal genres and an ethnographic approach lends itself to this further exploration of "the complex realities of the world of institutionalized communities" (Bhatia, 2002, p. 3).

In designing a course for LL.M students for example, attendance at LL.M seminars confirmed for me the demands made upon the language competence of L2 speakers, particularly when there are the additional factors of inadequate background knowledge and the necessity of coping with new learning styles. In preparation for each seminar, students are expected to read, on average, 100 pages of text. This is often a combination of texts about the law (textbooks, journal articles) and operative legal texts (e.g., treaties, statutes, EC directives, regulations, judgments). In the seminar itself they may then be expected to participate in debate and argument involving taking and expressing a particular stance and citing legal authority for that stance.

In addition to information about the learning context (What do the students need to do in English? What skills do they need to develop?), these seminars provided very useful data relevant to the language students might need in order to participate. Although the subject specialist's role involves developing understanding of specialist terminology in the course of increasing understanding of the area, in law much is taken for granted about what the students already know. The English for the LL.M course designer needs to identify the general legal English, general academic English, and language for participation in discussion and debate necessary for the students to understand or produce.

A considerable amount of progress has been made in the analysis of written legal genres and discourse contributing to pedagogic description that can be used in language education for legal professionals. There is still much to be done in the area of identifying and analyzing spoken academic legal genres. The complexity of the field requires those involved in language education to have an awareness of the specific needs and contexts of use in which their learners operate as well as an awareness of different legal genres. Ethnographic skills are particularly valuable for those needing to develop language programs for students attending specific legal academic courses. For highly specialized legal English teaching situations, development of equal partnerships between legal specialists and language educators would appear to offer the best way forward.

* * *

JILL NORTHCOTT is a Lecturer and Head of English for Business and Law at Edinburgh University's Institute for Applied Language Studies. She designs and teaches English courses for undergraduate law students, LL.M students, and lawyers. In the field of English for Law she has worked with teachers in Hungary and the Baltic Republics, court interpreters in

Zimbabwe, trainee judges in Lebanon, and Legal English teachers and text-book writers in Romania. She writes and publishes occasionally on Business and Legal English issues and has recently joined the editorial board of the *Journal of English for Academic Purposes*.

REFERENCES

Badger, R. (2003). Legal and general: Towards a genre analysis of newspaper law reports. *English for Specific Purposes, 22,* 249–263.

Bardi, M. (Project Coordinator). (2001). *English for legal purposes* [Prosper with English]. Bucharest: British Council.

Bhatia, V. K. (1989). Legislative writing: A case of neglect in EA/OLP courses. *English for Specific Purposes, 8,* 223–238

———. (1993). *Analysing genre: Language use in professional settings.* London: Longman.

———. (2002). A generic view of academic discourse. In J. Flowerdew (Ed.), *Academic discourse* (pp. 21–39). London: Pearson Education.

Blue, G. (1988). Individualising academic writing tuition. In P. Robinson (Ed.), *Academic writing: Process and product* (pp. 95–99). Oxford, UK: Macmillan Education. (ELT Documents 129)

Bowles, H. (1995). Why are newspaper law reports so hard to understand? *English for Specific Purposes, 14,* 201–222.

Bradney, A., Cownie, F., Masson, J., Neal, A., & Newell, D. (1995). *How to study law* (3rd ed.). London: Sweet & Maxwell.

Bruce, N. (2002). Dovetailing language and content: Teaching balanced argument in legal problem answer writing. *English for Specific Purposes, 21,* 321–345.

Butt, P., & Castle, R. (2001). *Modern legal drafting: A guide to using clearer language.* Cambridge, UK: Cambridge University Press.

Candlin, C., Bhatia, V.K , Jensen, C., & Langton, N. (2002). Developing legal writing materials for English second language learners: Problems and perspectives. *English for Specific Purposes, 21,* 299–320.

Chartrand, M., Millar, C., & Wiltshire, E. (2003). *English for contract and company law* (2nd ed.). London: Sweet & Maxwell.

Clumps, J. (1996). Language preferences of undergraduate law students and the effect on translation. *Translation and Meaning, 4,* 365–376.

De Clerk, V. (2003). Language and the law: Who has the upper hand? *AILA Review, 16,* 89–103.

Deutch, Y. (2003). Needs analysis for academic legal English courses in Israel: A model of setting priorities. *English for Academic Purposes, 3*, 123–146.

Dudley-Evans, T. (2001). Team-teaching in EAP: Changes and adaptations in the Birmingham approach. In J. Flowerdew and M. Peacock (Eds.), *Research perspectives on English for academic purposes* (pp. 225–238). Cambridge, UK: Cambridge University Press.

Dudley-Evans, T., & St. John, M. J. (1998). *Developments in English for specific purposes*. Cambridge, UK: Cambridge University Press.

Feak, C., & Reinhart, S. (2002). An ESP program for students of law. In T. Orr (Ed.), *English for specific purposes* (pp. 7–24). Alexandria, VA: TESOL.

Gibbons, J.(2003). *Forensic linguistics*. Oxford, UK: Blackwell.

Grover, C., Hachey, B., Hughson, I. , & Korycinski, C. (2003). Automatic summarisation of legal documents. *Proceedings of the 9th International Conference on Artificial Intelligence and Law (ICAIL 2003)*, Edinburgh, Scotland.

Hafner, C., & Candlin, C. (2007). Corpus tools as an affordance to learning in professional legal education. *Journal of English for Academic Purposes, 6*, 303–318.

Haigh, R. (2004). *Legal English*. London: Cavendish.

Hanson, S. (1999). *Legal method*. London: Cavendish.

Harris, S. (1997). Procedural vocabulary in law case reports. *English for Specific Purposes, 16*, 289–308.

Harvey, M. (2002). What's so special about legal translation? *Meta, 47*, 177–185.

Howe, P. (1993). Planning a pre-sessional course in English for academic legal purposes. In G. Blue (Ed.), *Language learning and success: Studying through English* (pp. 148–157). London: MacMillan.

Hutchinson, T., & Waters, A. (1987). *English for specific purposes: A learning-centered approach*. Cambridge, UK: Cambridge University Press.

Hyland, K. (2002). Specificity revisited: How far should we go now? *English for Specific Purposes, 21*, 385–395.

Kossakowska-Pisarek, S., & Niepytalska, B. (2004). *Key legal words*. Warsaw, Poland: Leon Koźmiński Academy of Entrepreneurship and Management.

Langton, N. (2002). Hedging argument in legal writing. *Perspectives, 14*(1), 16–52.

Maclean, J. (1997). Professional participation: A technique for LSP teacher education, 158–175. In R. Howard & G. Brown (Eds.), *Teacher education for LSP* (pp. 186–201). Clevedon, UK: Multilingual Matters.

Maley, Y., Candlin, N., Crichton, J., & Koster, P. (1995). Orientations in lawyer-client interviews. *Forensic Linguistics, 2*(1), 42–55.

McKay, W., & Charlton, H. (2005). *Legal English: How to understand and master the language of the law*. Harlow, UK: Pearson Education.

Mertz, E. (1996). Recontextualisation as socialization: Text and pragmatics in the law school classroom. In M. Silverstein & G. Urban (Eds.), *Natural histories of discourse* (pp. 229–252). Chicago, IL: University of Chicago Press.

Morrison, A., & Tshuma, L. (1993). Consensus ad idem: English for academic legal purposes at the University of Zimbabwe. In C. Rubagumya (Ed.), *Teaching and researching language in African classrooms* (pp. 50–62). Clevedon, UK: Multilingual Matters.

Northcott, J. (1997). EFL teacher involvement in a training programme for court interpreters in Zimbabwe. In R. Howard & G. Brown (Eds.), *Teacher education for LSP* (pp. 186–201). Clevedon, UK: Multilingual Matters.

———. (2001). Towards an ethnography of the MBA classroom: A consideration of the role of interactive lecturing styles within the context of one MBA programme. *English for Specific Purposes, 20*, 15–37.

———. (2006). Law and language or language and law? In D. Bartol, A. Duszuk, H. Izdebski & J. Pierrel (Eds.), *Langue, droit, société* [Cahiers du DNPS]. Nancy-Université.

———. (2008). Language education for law professionals. In J. Gibbons & M. T. Turell (Eds.), *Dimensions of forensic linguistics* (pp. 27–45). Amsterdam: John Benjamins.

Northcott, J., & Brown, G. (2006). Legal translator training: Partnership between teachers of English for legal purposes and legal specialists. *English for Specific Purposes, 25*, 358–375.

Reinhart, S. (2007). *Strategies for legal case reading and vocabulary development*. Ann Arbor: University of Michigan Press.

Riley, A. (1994). *English for law* (2nd ed.). Macmillan: London.

Šarčević, S. (1997). *New approach to legal translation*. The Hague: Kluwer Law International.

———. (Ed.) (2001) *Legal translation: Preparation for accession to the European Union*. Faculty of Law, University of Rijeka, Croatia.

Shapo, H., Walter, M., & Fajans, E. (1999). *Writing and analysis in the law* (4th ed.). New York: Foundation.

Smyth, S. (1997). Sentence first verdict later: Courting the law on a university insessional English language course. *ESP SIG Newsletter, 10*, 15–20.

———. (1999). Communicating in legal English or taking the law into our own hands? *ESP SIG Newsletter, 15*, 6–15.

Strong, S. I. (2003). *How to write law essays and exams*. London: LexisNexis.

Swales, J. (1990). *Genre analysis*. Cambridge, UK: Cambridge University Press.

Thighe, D. (2006). Placing the International Legal English Certificate on the CEFR. *Research Notes, 24,* 5–7. University of Cambridge ESOL Examinations.

Tiersma, P. (1999). *Legal language*. Chicago, IL: University of Chicago Press.

Weber, J. J. (2001). A concordance- and genre-informed approach to ESP essay writing. *ELT Journal, 55*(1), 14–20.

West, R. (1994). Needs analysis in language teaching. *Language Teaching, 27,* 1–19.

White, G. (1981). The subject specialist and the ESP teacher. *Lexden Papers* [Essays on teaching English for specific purposes by the staff of the Colchester and Bedford Study Centres], 2, 9–14. Oxford: Lexden Centre.

9

Intertextual Patterns in English Legal Discourse

VIJAY K. BHATIA
City University of Hong Kong

Abstract

Lexico-syntactic complexities in most forms of legal discourse are so overwhelmingly obvious that they have managed to attract maximum attention from ESP practitioners, often at the cost of a number of other characteristic rhetorical and discoursal aspects of legal genres. Without undervaluing the importance of lexico-syntactic features of legal discourse, this chapter brings into focus some of the important intertextual patterns that play a key role in the construction and interpretation of legal genres, especially focusing on their form and function, thus highlighting the role they play in the construction, interpretation, and use of a range of legal genres in ESP.

Of all the professional and disciplinary discourses, legal discourse offers the most complex range of intertextual relationships, which often create problems of interpretation for both the specialists as well as the non-specialists. Unfortunately, however, this important aspect of legal discourse has not been given adequate attention in English for Academic Legal Purposes literature. Legal specialists, with their extensive training, often manage to cope with such complexities; however, non-specialists, particularly those functioning in today's world of contesting and overlapping disciplinary concerns, find them inaccessible. This problem of inaccessibility of legal genres has become even more acute in English for Academic Legal Purposes because of the recent introduction of multidisciplinary and interdisciplinary programs in most of the major universities globally, where the integrity of academic disciplines is becoming increasingly complex and offers new challenges to learners and teachers alike. The situation has become critical due to the pressures from the corporate world, both on the part of firms, organizations, and institutions looking for interdisciplinary expertise, on the one hand, and on the part of potential employees looking for corporate jobs across contesting and overlapping disciplinary boundaries, on the other. A necessary consequence of this blurring of boundaries across disciplinary cultures in the world of academics is that in almost all professional contexts discourses are becoming increasingly interdisciplinary, complex, and dynamic (Bhatia, 2004). The main purpose of this chapter is to investigate the extent to which the accessibility of a set of disciplinary genres from legal contexts is dependent on intertextual links across several texts and genres within the same discipline. To do so it analyzes intertextual patterning within "systems of genres" (Bazerman, 1994) typically used in legal contexts. Such intertextual links serve not simply a general function of textual coherence but also a more specific disciplinary function of making legal discourse clear, precise, unambiguous, all-inclusive, and explanatory, on the one hand, and legal reasoning and arguments supported by judicial authority and precedents within the broader context of shared legal culture on the other hand (Bhatia, 1993, 2004). Applications and implications of some of these intertextual complexities for the teaching and learning of legal English are also considered.

Intertextuality

In order to give some substance to what I mean by intertextuality, I would like to begin with Foucault (1969), who points out that there is no statement that does not presuppose others. He views discourse as constituting social knowledge, emphasizing that any discursive practice is defined by its relations with others, and draws upon others in complex ways, thus highlighting the importance of intertextual relations across different texts or forms of discourse. In a similar manner, Bakhtin (1981) proposes the concepts of dialogue and ambivalence to suggest interdependence of texts and utterances. For him, the "linguistic significance of a given utterance is understood against the background of language, while its actual meaning is understood against the background of other concrete utterances on the same theme, a background made up of contradictory opinion, points of view, and value judgments" (Bakhtin, 1981, p. 281, quoted in Lemke, 1995, p. 23). However Kristeva (1980) was perhaps the first one to use the term *intertextuality* to point out that every text displays some pattern of interactions by appropriating other texts. Intertextuality is thus viewed as texts or voices embedded within other texts, which may be interpreted as appropriation of words, phrases, or sentences from one text by another. Similarly, Lemke (1995, p. 23) also points out that "We make sense of every word, utterance, or act against the background of (some) other words, utterances, acts of a similar kind." He goes on to add, "This implies . . . that it is very important to understand just *which* other texts a particular community considers relevant to the interpretation of any given text." Taking the notion of interrelatedness of texts further, Devitt (1991) mentions a three-dimensional concept of intertextuality: referential, functional, and generic. Referential intertextuality refers to the use of or reference to other texts, for instance, a letter making a reference to an earlier letter. Functional intertextuality describes how a network of texts is formed within a community, such that past texts create the need for future texts and also influence their form and content. Generic intertextuality refers to the types of texts available to the profession, their evolution into genres from recurrent rhetorical situations, and the subsequent formation of these genres into a set of established genres that are recognized as germane by the profession in question.

Fairclough (1992) also makes a useful distinction between "manifest intertextuality" and "constitutive intertextuality." Manifest intertextuality he sub-categorizes into "discourse representation," "presupposition," "metadiscourse," and "irony," all of which are influenced by the text in one way or another. "Constitutive intertextuality" he later identifies as interdiscursivity constituting genres and styles. In a similar fashion, Candlin and Maley (1997) claim:

> Discourses are made internally viable by the incorporation of such *inter-textual* and *interdiscursive* elements. Such evolving discourses are thus intertextual in that they manifest a plurality of text sources. However, in so far as any characteristic text evokes a particular discoursal value, in that it is associated with some institutional and social meaning, such evolving discourses are at the same time interdiscursive. (Candlin & Maley, 1997, p. 203)

Both intertextuality and interdiscursivity are useful resources used in rather conventionalized ways to make meanings clear, specific, unambiguous, and often all-inclusive by incorporating prior texts and genres. I would like to characterize intertextuality as appropriation of text-internal resources, whereas interdiscursivity, on the other hand, focuses on more innovative attempts to create hybrid constructs by appropriating or exploiting established conventions or available generic resources, thus accounting for a variety of discursive processes to appropriate text-external generic resources (for details see Bhatia, 2004, 2007). Although the two concepts of intertextuality and interdiscursivity are closely related and are often co-present in many legal genres, this chapter will focus centrally on intertextuality, and only marginally refer to interdiscursivity.

Intertextuality in Legislative Provisions

Legislative provisions display a variety and depth of intertextual links rarely noticed in any other form of disciplinary or professional discourse. Intertextuality in this genre serves not simply the function of making textual connections with preceding and preceded legislation, but it is also used to signal a variety of specific legal relationships between various aspects of the legislative provisions in which they occur and those of others either in the same document or in some other, which may have some legal bearing on its interpretation or application. As Caldwell, an experienced parliamentary counsel, put it,

> very very rarely is a new legislative provision entirely free-standing . . . it is part of a jigsaw puzzle . . . in passing a new provision you are merely bringing one more piece and so you have to acknowledge that what you are about to do may affect some other bit of the massive statute book. (Quoted in Bhatia, 1982, p. 172)

In a corpus of legislative discourse based on the UK Housing Act 1980, I have found four major kinds of intertextual devices, which seem to serve these functions:

- Signalling textual authority
- Providing terminological explanation
- Facilitating textual mapping
- Defining legal scope

Signalling Textual Authority

Textual authority is signalled in the form of a typical use of complex prepositional phrases, which may appear to be almost formulaic to a large extent. A very typical example of this kind of signalling is the following provision from the British Housing Act 1980.

110.5   The applicable local average rate is whichever of the two rates for the time being declared by the local authority in accordance with subsection (6a) below is applicable.

110.6   A local authority shall for such period not exceeding six months and beginning at the commencement of subsection (1) above as it may determine and for every subsequent period of six months declare, on the date falling within the month immediately preceding that period, a rate applicable to the advances and transfers . . . and a rate applicable to the sums left outstanding . . . ; and

(a) the rate applicable . . . shall be a rate exceeding by ¼ per cent that which the authority estimates it has to charge . . .

(b) the rate applicable to the sums left outstanding shall be a rate exceeding by ¼ per cent the average . . . of the rates . . .

In Section 110.5 the use of the complex prepositional phrase *in accordance with subsection (6a) below* signals not only a purely textual link with the following subsection, but also indicates the nature of legal relationship that one must expect there. *In accordance with* raises an expectation of obligation in whatever one may find in the subsection being referred to. This obligation is also confirmed by the use of legally binding *shall* in Subsection 110.6. On the other hand, in Section 13.4, the use of *in pursuance of section 4(2)* raises an expectation of right depending on the individual's choice, which is further confirmed in Section 4.2 in the use of *may*, which is often used to express rights rather than obligation.

13.4   The preceding provisions of this section do not confer any right on a person required in pursuance of section 4(2) to share the right to buy . . .

4.2   A secure tenant may . . . require that not more than three members of his family . . . should have the right to buy with him . . .

TABLE 9.1
Signalling Textual Authority

under		*subsection . . .*	*of the . . . Act*
in accordance with	*(the provisions of)*	*chapter . . .*	*of the schedule*
in pursuance of		*section . . .*	*of . . . instrument*
by virtue of		*paragraph . . .*	

The use of *under* or *by virtue of,* on the other hand, is more neutral; however, many legal writers do not always tend to use these expressions so explicitly, often causing difficulties of interpretation, especially for those who have only an outside or peripheral interest in the language of legislation. The signalling of textual authority can be summarized in the form of Table 9.1.

Providing Terminological Explanation

Terminological explanation is so central to legal writing that even the most common and ordinary expressions can take on special values in the context of law. *House, flat, residence,* and many expressions of this kind may claim specialist interpretation in the context of the Housing Act 1980. Similarly, expressions such as *injury, hand, defame, reputation,* etc., assume exclusive or legally significant meaning in legal contexts. One of the main functions of legal writing thus is to provide terminological explanation wherever such expressions are supposed to have assumed ordinarily deviant but legally significant meaning. The term *charity,* for instance, has an ordinary meaning, which may be accessible to most of us as a result of our being socialized in the society we live in; however, in the context of a specific legislative statement, the meaning of *charity* needs to be explicitly codified rather than assumed to be known. It is often the case that common understandings of such terms are vague, flexible, and less precise. Legal interpretation needs a more precisely available definition, as in this section from Housing Act 1980.

    2.1 The right to buy does not arise if the landlord is a housing trust which is a charity <u>within the meaning of the Charities Act, 1960</u>.

Facilitating Textual Mapping

The third major function of intertextuality in legal discourse is to signal textual coherence, as a reminder, as it were, to the reader that whatever is being stated or legislated here must be interpreted in the context of something else expressed elsewhere. This is often signalled by the use of -en participle clauses, as in another section from Housing Act 1980.

> 54.3   The continuous period mentioned in subsection . . . (2) above is the period beginning with the grant of the protected shorthold tenancy and continuing until either . . .
>
>   (a) no person is in possession of the dwelling-house as a protected or statutory tenant; or . . .

If we compare the last two functions of intertextuality in legislative expressions, we may find quite a bit of overlap between the two, so much so that at some point they become almost indistinguishable. Typical realizations of these two functions include expressions like *falling within the meaning of,* at one end, which is clearly text-claritive in nature, to *referred to in subsection* . . . , at the other end, which is clearly text-cohering in kind, with a number of others somewhere in the middle, such as *specified in section* . . . , *set out in subsection* . . . or *described in section* . . . and *mentioned in subsection.* . . . The overlap can be summed up in the diagram (Figure 9.1).

Defining Legal Scope

The final category of intertextual links often used in legislative statements are what I have elsewhere referred to as those defining legal scope of the provi-

FIGURE 9.1
Signalling Textual Coherence

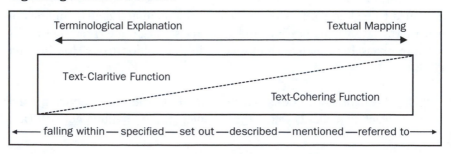

sion in question. Since every single legislative statement within a particular legal system is seen as part of the massive statute book, and none of them is likely to be of universal application, it is often necessary to define the scope of each of these legislative expressions, especially when it is anticipated that it is likely to be in conflict with what has already been legislated. In order to signal and wherever possible to resolve such conflicts or tensions, legislative counsels often use appropriate intertextual devices depending on the nature of conflict anticipated and the resolution desired. In the case of Section 16.1 of Housing Act 1980, for instance, the writer simply signals the restricted scope of the provision in the context of paragraph 11(2) of schedule 2 of the act.

16.1 The landlord shall be bound to make to the tenant —

(a) —

(b) . . . a grant of a lease of the dwelling-house for a term not less than 125 years (<u>subject to paragraph 11(2) of Schedule 2 to this Act</u>)

On the other hand, in section 8.6 of the same act, an anticipated conflict has not only been signalled but resolved too by providing that 8.6 will have legislative effect in spite of the conflicting requirements stated in the Land Registration Act of 1925.

8.6 A charge taking effect by virtue of subsection (4) above shall have, notwithstanding subsection (5) of section 59 of the Land Registration Act 1925, a land charge for the purposes of that section.

The following diagram indicates a more complete range of intertextual devices defining the scope of legal provisions:

FIGURE 9.2
Defining Legal Scope in Conflicting or Contradictory Provisions

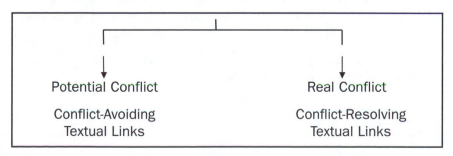

Some of the most commonly used devices to signal conflicting cases are:

- Listing of conditions on the fulfilment of which it operates
- Listing of exceptions under which it ceases to operate
- Explaining/defining circumstances under which it operates
- Extending the scope of the provision
- Restricting the scope of the provision
- Specifying consequences of non-compliance with provision

Most often these legal conflicts are signalled by the somewhat neutral complex prepositional phrase *subject to,* though often it is further specified by the modification of the noun phrase, such as the following:

---

subject to the conditions stated in sub-section . . . below

or

subject to the exception mentioned in section . . .

or

subject to the limits imposed by the provision in section . . .

Conflict-Resolving Textual Links

In the case of real conflicts between preceded or preceding provisions, one often finds two standard devices to signal a resolution of such conflicts. In the case of the new provision taking priority over the other one, the common device used is *notwithstanding the provisions of section . . . ,* which clearly signals that the new provision will operate in spite of the conflicting requirements of some other. In order to signal the opposite effect, one may often find the use of *without prejudice to the generality of section. . . .* Sometimes, we also find somewhat more general expressions to this effect, such as these:

---

in addition to the powers under section . . .

or

instead of complying with the provisions of section . . .

However, such cases are rare. The parliamentary counsels more often than not go for established devices to signal conflicts, whether they are potential or more real.

Intertextuality in Legal Cases

We have so far discussed one of the most significant legal genres providing authority to most legal arguments and decisions, both in common law as well as civil law jurisdictions. We now turn to the second most common legal genre, legal judgments and cases, which provide legal authority for arguments and decisions in law, particularly in common law jurisdictions, where these are often used as precedents for decision-making in the courts. Like legislation, legal judgments also display a complex array of intertextual devices linking to other judgments and cases as well as to legislative provisions; however, they are often more elaborate in their form and functions, integrating several functions at the same time. Thus although they tend to serve similar legal functions, they have somewhat different rhetorical realization.

Providing Judicial Authority

The most common function of intertextuality in judgments is to provide judicial authority, which could be from earlier judgments or legislative provisions. A significant aspect of this kind of intertextuality in legal judgments is that it is an integral part of legal reasoning and is interestingly woven into the argument of the judge. It is not enough to refer to just the case; it is necessary to attribute the authority to the judge, in addition to the conclusion being used to support or dispute the argument in the present case. This is a typical example.

Wellington (R on the application of) v Secretary of State for the Home Department (2007)
[2007] EWHC 1109 (Admin) (Crown Court) Royal Courts of Justice, Strand, London,

LORD JUSTICE LAWS
8.
This appeal raises the question whether the period of imprisonment to be served by a mandatory life sentence prisoner as punishment should be determined by the executive or the judiciary.

It does not concern the question how individual cases should be approached. On the hypothesis, however, that the appeal in *Anderson* succeeds, it is important to guard against misunderstanding in one respect. If the role of the executive in setting the tariff should cease it does not follow that life imprisonment for murder may never, even in the worst cases imaginable, literally mean detention for life. In the Divisional Court in *R v Secretary of State for the Home Department, Ex p Hindley* [1998] QB 751, 769, Lord Bingham of Cornhill CJ observed that he could 'see no reason, *in principle,* why a crime or crimes, if sufficiently heinous, should not be regarded as deserving lifelong incarceration for purposes of pure punishment.' On appeal to the House of Lords, and with the agreement of Lord Browne-Wilkinson, Lord Nicholls of Birkenhead, and Lord Hutton, I expressed myself in similar terms: *R v Secretary of State for the Home Department, Ex p Hindley* [2001] 1 AC 410, 416H.

There are several interesting and crucial aspects of this intertextual pattern. First, the attribution to the judge who gave the judgment is given along with the identification of the case in the beginning. This serves the text-cohering referential function. Second, the relevant section of the judgment that either supports or disputes the legally material facts provides judicial authority for the argument. Finally comes the legal decision, which may or may not be a direct quote, but certainly serves an important function of defining the scope of authority or application. Sometimes these relevant judicial authorities are integrated within relevant legislative provisions, of which the following is a good example.

Wellington (R on the application of) v Secretary of State for the Home Department (2007)
[2007] EWHC 1109 (Admin) (Crown Court) Royal Courts of Justice, Strand, London,
11.

In *Lichniak* [2003] 1 AC 903, in which their Lordships' opinions were delivered on the same day as those in *Anderson* (the cases were heard together before a constitution of seven judges), the

House of Lords had to consider whether the mandatory life sentence for murder imposed by English domestic law pursuant to
s.1 (1) of the Murder (Abolition of Death Penalty) Act 1965 was
compatible with ECHR Article 3 and Article 5. (Article 5(1) pro-
hibits deprivation of liberty save in accordance with a procedure
prescribed by law.) Lord Bingham said (paragraph 2):

"The thrust of the appellants' case can be shortly summarised:
section 1(1) is arbitrary and disproportionate because it requires
the same life sentence to be passed on all convicted murder-
ers, whatever the facts of the case or the circumstances of the
offender, and irrespective of whether they are thought to present
a danger to the public or not."

Their Lordships concluded, however, that there was no incon-
sistency between the mandatory life sentence for murder and
Articles 3 and 5; and it is here that the case most closely touches
the issues before us.

It is interesting to note the depth of intertextuality in this case. The argument is developed on the basis of two somewhat different cases, *Lichniak*
and *Anderson,* on the one hand, and on the other hand, an attempt is made
to resolve the tension between relevant sections of the Murder (Abolition
of Death Penalty) Act 1965 and the ECHR Article 3 and Article 5. Intertextuality deepens further as a consequence of the quote from Lord Bingham. Terminological explanations of the kind we discussed in legislative
provisions are somewhat rare in judgments. Another interesting aspect of
intertextuality in legal judgments is that full references are built into the text
rather than given either in the form of references at the end of the judgment
or in the form of footnotes common in legal textbooks, which we turn to in
the next section.

Intertextuality in Legal Textbooks

Intertextuality in academic legal genres such as textbooks manifests itself
most predominantly in the form of footnotes. Footnotes perform a number
of different rhetorical functions.

Providing Terminological Explanation

One of the prominent functions of footnotes in legal textbooks is to provide terminological explanation, just as in legislative genres. The only difference is that in textbooks the authority for definitions often comes from legislative provisions. Whereas in legislative provisions, terminological explanations take the form of explicit definitions often placed in the beginning of a statutory provision, in textbooks these are invariably inserted as footnotes, sometimes in the form of explicit definitions, as in Footnote 2 given here, but often in the form of implicit explanation, as in Footnotes 1 and 3. Often the footnote will incorporate the exact definition, quoting from authoritative sources with some explication or interpretation from the author of the textbook. This section from a textbook on defamation provides typical examples of such phenomena.

The Defamation Act 1952, s7 (1) provides for a statutory qualified privilege[1] to protect the publication in a newspaper[2] or the broadcasting[3] of certain reports and other matter specified in the Schedule to the Act. The reports and other matter specified in the Schedule fall into two categories—

(a) statements which are privileged without explanation or contradiction; and
(b) statements which are privileged subject to explanation or contradiction.

[1]Defamation Act 1952, s 7(1) is in the following terms: 'Subject to the provisions of this section, the publication in a newspaper of any such report or other matter as is mentioned in the Schedule to this Act shall be privileged unless the publication is proved to be made with malice.' The section has greatly widened the scope of the qualified privilege previously afforded to certain newspaper reports by the Law of Libel Amendment Act 1888, s 4(now repealed by the Defamation Act 1952, s 18 (3)).

[2]'Newspaper is defined for the purposes of this section as meaning 'any paper containing public news or observations thereon, or consisting wholly or mainly of advertisements, which is printed for sale and is published in the United Kingdom either periodically or in parts or numbers at intervals not exceeding thirty-six days'. The intervals 'not exceeding thirty-six days' may be contrasted with the provision for intervals 'not exceeding twenty-six days' in the Newspaper Libel and Registration Act 1881, s 1, which is relevant to a defence under the Law of Libel Amendment Act 1888, s. 3: see appendix 1, post.

[3]Defamation Act 1952, s. 9 provides: '(2) section 7 of this Act . . . shall apply in relation to reports or matters broadcast by means of wireless telegraphy as part of any programme or service provided by means of a broadcasting station within the United Kingdom . . . (3) In this section "broadcasting station" means any station in respect of which a licence granted by the Postmaster General under the enactments relating to wireless telegraphy is in force, being a licence which (by whatever forms of words) authorizes the use of the station for the purpose of providing broadcasting services for general reception.

(Neill & Rampton, 1983, p. 96)

Since this form of footnotes offering terminological explanations consists of not only exact definitions but also incorporates explanations as well as complete referential links to suggest the authorities that provide the definitions, it is hardly surprising that the footnotes are more detailed and extensive than the text itself. Without such terminological explanations, it is very likely that unsuspecting readers, especially the non-specialists, may be tempted to interpret terms such as *privilege, newspaper,* and *broadcasting* in their ordinary everyday meaning. However, not all footnotes have such a text-claritive function. Many times, they simply provide referential text-cohering links.

Text-Cohering References

Legal discourse, particularly in the context of a common law legal system, relies heavily on legal authorities from earlier judgments as they are used as precedents. Considering the number of cases that are decided on a daily basis, it is crucial for legal discourse to signal exact referential links in either the claims or arguments made. Although law is generally considered jurisdictional, cases from other jurisdictions are also often used to discuss or sometimes decide subsequent cases. Legal authority may be incorporated within the text but the exact reference is often relegated to footnotes, which thus serve a very important function in legal discourse. Such references also take a conventionalized and standardized format. Here is a typical example of this rhetorical device.

In every case it is necessary for the plaintiff to prove that the words were published about him. In *Sadgrove v Hole*, A. L. Smith MR put the matter as follows:[1]

> 'The plaintiff to succeed in the action must prove a publication of and
> concerning him of libellous matter, and if he does not satisfy the onus of
> proof which is on him in this respect there is no cause of action.'

[1][1901] 2 KB 1 at 4. See also *Bruce v Odhams Press Ltd* [1936] 1 KB 697
at 708, [1936] 1 All ER at 291, per Slesser LJ: *Morgan v Odhams Press Ltd*
[1971] 2 All ER 1156 at 1165, [1971] 1 WLR 1239 at 1248, per Lord Morris
of Borth-y-Gest.

(Neill & Rampton, 1983, p. 22)

Providing Judicial or Legislative Authority

Legal decisions and arguments are always backed up by legal authorities
that come from three major sources: legislation, legal judgments (often
quoting arguments from judges), or cases, or other leading or established
experts in specific areas of the law in question. Textbooks often make use of
these authorities to support their claims or arguments or dispute alternative
arguments. A footnote on a supporting precedent from a single case can
provide a reference, a summary of the main point, and also a quotation of a
legal authority, as in this case.

A right of action for libel or slander vested in a person who is adjudicated bank-
rupt does not pass to the trustee in bankruptcy although the defamation may
have been the sole cause of bankruptcy.[1]

1. See *Howard v Crowther* (1841) 8 M & W 601 at 604 (an action for the
seduction of a servant), where Alderson B said: 'Assignees can maintain no
action for libel, although the injury occasioned thereby to the man's reputation
may have been the sole cause of his bankruptcy'.

(Neill & Rampton, 1983, p. 48)

On the other hand, it is also common to find a reference to several cases in
support of an argument. The purpose is to give as much explanatory information as necessary on alternative interpretations or possibilities, as in the
following case.

the courts have held that contracts between family members may be denied efficacy on the basis that the parties did not intend to be legally bound,[29] though this may be rebutted by evidence of an express intention to be so bound,[30] or an implied intention from the evidence.[31]

[29]*Balfour v Balfour* [1919] 2 K.B. 571 (agreements between husband and wife are not intended to be legally binding); *Rogers v Smith,* unreported, Supreme Court , July 16, 1970 (promise by a mother that the cost of supporting her would be paid from her estate after her death was not enforceable since the promise was too general and plaintiff would have looked after the mother in any event); *Mackay v Jones* (1959) 93 I.L.T.R. 117 (a promise given in expectation of a legacy was not enforceable since it was an agreement between family members).

[30]*Courtney v Courtney* (1923) 57 I.L.T.R. 42 (a separation agreement between husband and wife is valid when they are living apart); *Hynes v Hynes,* unreported, High Court, December 21, 1984 (an agreement to transfer a business undertaking was held enforceable, despite being between brothers).

[31]*Jones v. Padavatton* [1969] 1 W.L.R. 42 (would a reasonable person looking at the agreement, and its surrounding facts, believe that it should be enforced); *Parker v Clark* [1960] 1 All E. R. 93.

(Friel, 2000, p. 81)

These examples provide only a few of the complicated intertextual patterns in some of the major legal genres. A more detailed and comprehensive study will need more space than this chapter can offer. Let me now turn to some of the applications of these findings, in particular to English for Academic Legal Purposes.

This chapter has analyzed intertextual devices commonly used in some of the legal genres to illustrate that, in addition to their text-cohering function, they also serve a number of typical legal functions, giving expression to shared generic expectations (Swales, 1990) on the part of the members of the legal community. It was also pointed out that intertextuality serves somewhat different legal functions in different genres and is realized through the use of rather different lexico-grammatical and rhetorical resources. Textual coherence in applied linguistics is often viewed as independent of generic considerations and hence treated as a matter of linguistic texture or appropriateness (Halliday & Hasan, 1976) rather than generic effectiveness. With the increase in multidisciplinary and interdisciplinary exposure in academic contexts, it is becoming all the more necessary that such generic variations and discipline-specific discursive devices should be taken more seriously, especially in the context of English for Specific Academic and Professional Legal Purposes. Ignoring such generic characteristics of specialist discourses means not only undervaluing effectiveness in specialist communication but also creating potential obstacles in the acquisition of professional and disciplinary discourse, especially relevant to legal discourse, for academic as well as professional purposes. The complexity of intertextuality and interdiscursivity can be seen in Figure 9.3. As we can clearly see, most of the academic and professional purpose genres that are used in academic and professional contexts are different manifestations of legislative provisions, judgments, and cases, interdiscursively and intertextually realized to serve specific academic or professional communicative purposes in the broader context of legal culture.

In plain legal English literature overwhelming attention has been paid to the use of lexico-syntactic resources in legislative sentences, emphasizing readability and accessibility of legislative intentions; however, the arguments often overlook three important aspects of legislative discourse that

FIGURE 9.3

Intertextual and Interdiscursive Patterns in Legal Discourse

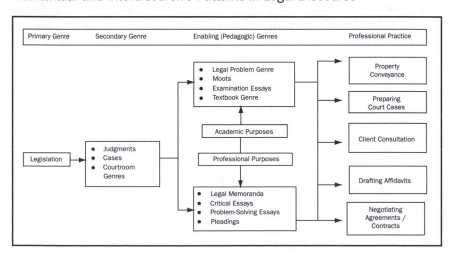

are primarily responsible for making legislative sentences inaccessible to specialists as well as to lay persons. The first one is of course the nature and function of the legal system within which these legislative statements are written and interpreted. There is evidence of disagreement between the plain English reformist lobbies and members of the drafting community. The second aspect is the use of two rather different conceptual worlds: one is the world of real actions and events to which these legislative provisions apply, and the other is the ideal or the desired world, which is indicated in and through legislative provisions. The relationship between these two interactive worlds is important in all legal genres and can be studied as part of what Candlin and Maley (1997) and Bhatia (2004) see as interdiscursivity. There is an urgent need to look into the notion of interdiscursivity in legal discourse, particularly the way in which different conceptual worlds are brought together in the negotiation and implementation of justice. This aspect of legal discourse is more conceptual in nature and hence may not have a direct impact on the issues raised in plain English legislation. However, the notion of intertextuality is crucial to our accessibility and understanding of legal genres, especially the way they all use a complex variety of intertextual links across present and previously legislated provisions and negotiated judgments. These links provide a complex texture to legal genres, which is the very essence of legal discourse, and hence any attempt to ignore this aspect of legal practice and culture can only undermine necessary clarity, precision, unambiguity, and all-inclusiveness, all of which have so far been considered valuable in legal expression.

*   *   *

VIJAY K. BHATIA is a Professor in the Department of English at the City University of Hong Kong. He is best known for his work in ESP and genre analysis of academic and professional discourse, especially in the areas of law, business, and media discourse. He has published in several international journals, some of which are *Applied Linguistics, English for Specific Purposes, World Englishes,* and the *Journal of Pragmatics.* Two of his major contributions to genre theory are *Analysing Genre: Language Use in Professional Settings,* published by Longman, and *Worlds of Written Discourse: A Genre-Based View,* published by Continuum.

REFERENCES

Bakhtin, M. M. (1981). Discourse in the novel. In M. Holquist (Ed.), *The dialogic imagination* (pp. 259–492). Austin: University of Texas Press.

Bazerman, C. (1994). Systems of genres and the enhancement of social intentions. In A. Freedman & P. Medway (Eds.). *Genre and new rhetoric* (pp. 79–101). London: Taylor & Francis.

Bhatia, V. K. (1982). *An investigation into the formal and functional characteristics of qualifications in legislative writing and its application to English for academic legal purposes.* Unpublished doctoral dissertation, University of Aston, Birmingham, UK.

———. (1993). *Analysing genre—Language use in professional settings.* London: Longman.

———. (2004). *Worlds of written discourse: A genre-based view.* London: Continuum.

———. (2007, May). *Interdiscursivity in legal discourse.* Invited paper presented at the Second Roundtable on Discourse Analysis, City University of Hong Kong.

Candlin, C. N., & Maley, Y. (1997). Intertextuality and interdiscursivity in the discourse of alternative dispute resolution. In B-L. Gunnarsson, P. Linnel, B. Nordberg (Eds.), *The construction of professional discourse* (pp. 201–222). London: Longman.

Devitt, A. (1991). Intertextuality in tax accounting. In C. Bazerman & J. Paradis (Eds.), *Textual dynamics of the professions* (pp. 336–357). Madison: University of Wisconsin Press.

Fairclough, N. (1992). *Discourse and social change.* Cambridge, UK: Polity Press.

Foucault, M. (1969). *The archaeology of knowledge.* New York: Random House.

Friel, R. J. (2000). *The law of contract* (2nd ed.). Dublin: Round Hall Sweet & Maxwell.

Halliday, M. A. K., & Hasan, R. (1976). *Cohesion in English.* London: Longman.

Kristeva J. (1980). Word, dialogue and novel. In J. Kristeva (Ed.), *Desire in language.* (pp. 64–91). Oxford: Blackwell.

Lemke, J. L. (1995). *Textual politics: Discourse and social dytnamics.* London: Taylor & Francis.

Neill, B., & Rampton, R. (Eds.) (1983). *Duncan and Neill on defamation.* London: Butterworths.

Swales, J. M. (1990). *Genre analysis: English in academic and research settings.* Cambridge, UK: Cambridge University Press.

10

English for Medical Purposes

LING SHI
University of British Columbia, Canada

Abstract

English for Medical Purposes (EMP) refers to the teaching of English needed by ESL-speaking medical personnel, medical researchers, and professors and students in medical or nursing schools. Since each group of these learners has a different needs profile, EMP is, by nature, a genre-informed pedagogy based on needs assessment of specific groups of learners. A review of relevant research suggests that descriptions of characteristic lexical and syntactic features of medical texts could help develop genre-related teaching materials whereas examinations of spontaneous interactions between doctors/nurses and patients could help physicians and nurses improve their communication skills. However, the fact that each group of EMP students has distinctive needs has pushed some EMP practitioners to conduct their own research or needs analysis to develop courses. To identify the specific needs of their students, these EMP practitioners, apart from using questionnaire surveys, have analyzed target situations through field observations and interviews, identified deficiencies betweens students' current performance

and their desired performance in the target language situations, or conducted ethnographies for an ongoing assessment of students' needs. Further inquires are needed to
address such practical issues in the development and teaching of EMP courses as the role of content knowledge and
assessment of student achievement.

Latin was the lingua franca of Western medical texts for centuries (e.g.,
Taavitsainen, 2006). Since the early twentieth century, along with the leading roles played by Anglo-Americans in political, economic, and scientific
fields, English has replaced Latin and become the international language of
medicine (Maher, 1986a). Nowadays, the world's most widely cited medical
journals are published in English (Ariza & Navarro, 2006). The fact that
"doctors around the world basically communicate in . . . English" in academic
journals (Piqué-Angordans & Posteguillo, 2006, p.651) pushes non-native
English or ESL/EFL-speaking doctors/nurses and medical/nursing students to
learn English, a movement that has led to the emergence of English for Medical Purposes (EMP) as an established area of scholarship. After defining EMP,
the chapter reviews relevant research focusing on two characteristics of EMP:
(a) discourse analyses of written and spoken genres in medical contexts with
potential implications for genre-oriented teaching and (b) needs analyses and
course designs for specific groups of students.

A Definition of EMP

As a type of EOP (English for Occupational Purposes), EMP refers to the
teaching of English needed by ESL-speaking medical personnel such as
doctors, nurses, dentists, pharmacists, paramedical staff, laboratory tech-
nicians, healthcare workers, medical researchers, professors and students
in medical/nursing schools, as well as patients. Since it serves a variety of
learners, EMP is a generic category that can be sub-categorized on both
macro and micro levels. On the macro level, EMP can be identified as either
professional or educational (Bruce, 1992; Maher, 1986b). The former refers
to English required by already qualified medical professionals and the latter refers to English required by those learning to become members of the
profession. For example, medical students, in order to successfully complete
their education, need to master a large number of special medical terms
in a short time (Lucas, Lenstrup, Prinz, Williamson, Yip, & Tipoe, 1997),
develop reading and listening skills (Chia, Johnson, Chia, & Olive, 1999),

practice active participation in class discussion, and improve writing skills for written examinations (Chur-Hansen, 1999, 2000). In comparison, clinical researchers need to learn and practice writing with the appropriate stylistic and rhetorical conventions in order to publish (Fox & Meijer, 1980) and to practice public speaking for international conferences (Fox & Meijer, 1980; Lynch & Maclean, 2003). EMP is thus to facilitate both the practice of the medical profession and the acquisition of medical knowledge.

Further distinctions of EMP can be made at the micro level based on various functional or hierarchical categories related to complex divisions within the medical profession (Maher, 1986b). For example, EMP can be sub-categorized in terms of specialties or subject areas (e.g., English for Anatomy, Surgery, Dentistry, Nursing, Pharmacy), professional skills (e.g., English for health care, medical conference preparation, journal article writing), or roles of the participants (e.g., English for nursing assistants, ESL patients, doctor-patient interaction). These sub-categories suggest different needs profiles of EMP learners. For example, in English speaking countries, overseas physicians need adequate proficiency in spoken English to practice medicine (Boulet, van Zanten, McKinley, & Gary, 2001), medical undergraduates from non–English speaking backgrounds need to learn informal or colloquial English to conduct doctor-patient consultations in local hospitals (Chur-Hansen & Barrett, 1996), and trainee nurses with non–English speaking backgrounds need to learn the special vocabulary and stylistic conventions for chart writing (Marston & Hansen, 1985). In addition, if ESL-speaking nurses need to learn both the technical and everyday registers so as to translate medical information into terms that patients can understand (Marston & Hansen, 1985), immigrant patients need a survival English vocabulary to describe their health concerns (Frank, 2000). These needs profiles highlight two distinct features of EMP: genre-informed pedagogy and needs assessment of specific groups of learners. It is to these features that I turn.

Discourse Analysis of Written and Spoken Genres in Medical Contexts

Genre-Based Analysis of Medical Texts

EMP researchers turn to genre theory in their studies of medical discourses, following Halliday, McIntosh, and Strevens (1964), who believed that detailed analyses of registers or specialized languages would generate teaching implications. The concept of genre is defined by Swales (1990, pp. 45–46) as "a class of communicative events" with "some shared set of communicative purposes" among the participants. In other words, genre theory guides linguistic and discourse approaches to explore how communicative events or texts unfold in similar or different ways. The focus is on not only a description of formal textual features but also an understanding of why genres are shaped the way they are. Such a focus of genre studies suggests a socio-rhetorical perspective on the relationship between text and context.

Two schools of genre work, the Australian Sydney School and the North American New Rhetoric School, highlight the interactive nature of text and context. The Sydney School adopts a systemic functional approach to explore the realization features of different genres by focusing on how speakers and writers make linguistic choices based on situational or contextual dimensions of mode (textuality), tenor (interpersonal context), and field (ideational content) (Halliday, 1985). In comparison, the New Rhetoric School regards genres as "typified rhetorical actions based in recurrent situations" (Miller, 1984, p. 159). The New Rhetoricians also use concepts from activity theory to suggest that texts are produced as tools to shape and reshape genres (Bazerman, 1997). If the Sydney School draws our attention to the systemic links between text and context and, therefore, the typical or generic structures of genres, the New Rhetoric School emphasizes the dynamic relations between text and context and, therefore, highlights the fluid nature of genres. Guided by both schools, EMP applied linguists have explored both the generic structure of medical texts and the rhetorical strategies of individual writers. Most studies, given the role of medical journals in formalizing and shaping medical writing, have examined the stylistic and rhetorical practice in medical texts using journal articles or a corpus of medical publications. The relevant studies can be distinguished as either research on the specific textual conventions as rhetorical devices or research on the nature and patterns of rhetorical organization.

Exploring the lexical and syntactic features of medical text, a number of researchers have illustrated the macro-level rhetorical functions of various linguistic features in medical texts (Baker, 1988; Ferguson, 2001; Salager-Meyer, 1994; Skelton, 1997; Thomas & Hawes, 1994; Varttala, 1999; Williams, 1996; Wingard, 1981). One study conducted by Ferguson (2001) found that *if*-conditionals in the Methods section of research articles are typically in the past tense and semantically course-of-event type, in contrast to those conditionals used in other sections. Another study on medical research articles, conducted by Thomas and Hawes (1994), associated verbs reporting citations with their rhetorical functions of reporting consensus views, generalized conclusions, and specific findings. Also examining the use of verbs, Williams (1996) found that clinical research papers are more assertive than experimental research papers. Skelton (1997), in an effort to further explore the language of certainty and doubt, demonstrated how medical research papers typically use certain reporting verbs or lexical devices to present truth as research tradition versus truth based on statistical or non-statistical evidence. In comparison, other researchers compared genres of case reports and research papers to illustrate how expressions of tentativeness are related to the general structure of the texts. Smith (1984), for example, observed that author-marked comments tend to appear in the Comment sections of case reports but in both the Introduction and Discussion sections of research papers. Salager-Meyer (1994) reported that the Discussion sections in research reports, where researchers try to avoid making conclusive statements, are more hedged than the Comment sections in case reports. If hedging illustrates the precision of language, it is also, as Varttala (1999) illustrated, used rhetorically by specialist authors to adapt medical information in popular scientific articles for a lay or less educated audience. Given the fact that medical information is directly related to human welfare, the language of precision in medical sciences is a sophisticated artifact that has remained at the center of EMP research. The key, in Smith's (1984, p. 25) words, is "to distinguish objective statements of accepted facts from author-marked observations."

Other researchers have explored the nature of discourse development or rhetorical organization of medical texts rather than syntax and vocabulary (Francis & Kramer-Dahl, 1991; Galve, 1998; Nwogu & Bloor, 1991; Webber, 1994). Webber (1994), for example, reported how medical specialists use questions in the organization of medical text to engage the readers especially of journal editorials and letters. With questions that open the possibilities of alternatives, readers are guided through the reasoning process. In another study, Galve (1998) illustrated that medical journal texts, like other scientific English texts, are dynamically and intertextually linked as writers frequently use nominalizations (turning clauses into nouns) to refer to previous text while introducing new text. Also exploring the organization of information but comparing professional and popular genres of medical texts, Nwogu and Bloor (1991) found how the pattern of thematic progression (the ordering of old, i.e., theme, and new, i.e., rheme, information) distinguishes research papers (displaying more constant patterns in which the same theme appears repeatedly) from journalist reports of medical research (exhibiting simpler linear patterns in which each rheme becomes the theme of the next sentence). Another study that compared professional and popular medical text, conducted by Francis and Kramer-Dahl (1991), investigated the metafunctions (ideational, textual, and interpersonal) of lexicogrammatical patterns and found that a clinical report, when popularized, undergoes a genre shift from a professional case report following appropriate procedures of gathering and interpreting evidence to a story based on the actual sequence of a patient's experiences.

Research on the patterns of discourse structures of various types of medical texts has also been informed by move analysis. Using Swales' (1990) approach to chunk texts into moves, each with a distinct orientation and content of discourse-based explicit lexical items, meanings, and illocutionary force, researchers identified a hierarchical order of move or information structures for the entire medical research paper (Kanoksilapatham, 2005; Nwogu, 1997; Skelton, 1994), abstracts of research papers (Salager-Meyer, 1992), and the journalistic version of research articles in science magazines and newspapers (Nwogu, 1991). In their studies of research articles, researchers have identified various moves within the explicitly marked sections of Introduction, Methods, Results, and Discussion. For example, Nwogu (1997) identified an eleven-move schema, with three each occurring in the Introduction (present background information, review related research, and present new research) and Methods section (describe data-collection, experimental procedures, and data analysis), two in the Results section (indicate consistent and non-consistent observations) and three in the Discussion section (highlight overall outcome, explain specified outcome, and state conclusions). In another study, Kanoksilapatham (2005) found a slightly different structure with fifteen rhetorical moves in biochemistry research articles. Although sharing most of the moves with other medical research papers, biochemistry research articles are characterized by certain extra moves such as stating and justifying procedures or methodology in the Results section.

Salager-Meyer (1992), in her analyses of the abstracts of medical journal articles, focused on the form and function relationship. She found that the move structure of abstracts typically contains a statement of the problem in the present or present perfect tense to stress the relevance of the study, a statement of purpose in either the present or past tense as the writer strategically chooses a time location to fit his/her purpose, a description of the methods and results in the past tense, and finally a conclusion and recommendation marked by either the present tense to enhance generalizability or the use of modals to signal author-marked tentativeness and suggestions.

Compared with research papers and abstracts, popularized medical texts have been observed to follow a different move structure. In a study of journalistic reports of medical research in science magazines and newspapers, Nwogu (1991) found nine possible moves clustered into three broad groups of "description, explanation and evaluation," a system that journalists follow in their writing. By providing the readers with vital details of the research in the beginning, the writer persuades the readers to read the whole text.

The description of characteristic linguistic features of medical texts serves as a departure point for developing genre-related teaching materials and activities for the classroom. Following the research findings, EMP teachers could move beyond the traditional teaching of general English to help students deploy various linguistic features in the functions identified in medical texts. The structuring of information captured by move analysis should also facilitate the teaching of communicative purposes in the different sections of the research paper. In addition, by learning to choose appropriate reporting verbs in their writing, students can mediate their claims and differentiate between their comments and observed facts. In adopting a genre-oriented approach, EMP practitioners need to draw students' attention to both the conformity and diversity of genres. Such teaching empowers students with not only the knowledge of the conventions but also strategies to explore differences. By practicing critical reading and exploring the reasoning that shapes the rhetorical choices of individual writers, students can learn to make informed linguistic choices in their own writing in relation to different audiences and purposes.

Medical Interactions as Social Practice

Research on the spoken genres in medical contexts, except for some attention given to the formal genres of medical conference monologue (e.g., Dubois, 1980; Webber, 2005) or collegial talk in hospital settings (see relevant studies in Sarangi & Roberts, 1999), has focused on spontaneous face-to-face encounters involving doctors/nurses and patients in order to identify ways physicians and nurses can improve their essential communication skills when performing clinical tasks (Cameron & Williams, 1997; S. Candlin, 2002; Cicourel, 1981, 1985; Fisher & Groce, 1990; Frankel,

1990; Hein & Wodak, 1987; Ibrahim, 2001; Mishler, 1997; Skelton & Hobbs, 1999; West, 1983). Compared with research on written medical genres, which focuses on the structure of discourse based on analyses of lexical items, semantics, syntax, and rhetorical organization, studies of spoken genres focus on the impact of social, political, and cultural dimensions of medical communication on language use. By focusing on communication as social practice, EMP applied linguists have examined how oral interactions differ and unfold based on the strategic use of language by people marked with status differences, such as doctors, nurses, and patients. The connection between the linguistic features and the stratification system of the society resonates with the Hallidayan perspective of a systematic link between the organization of language components and context variables. Speech genres, indeed, are socially shaped (Bakhtin, 1986). As social identities and status entail power, speakers of various social groups or hierarchies interact or perform speech acts in such a way as to mirror, sustain, or challenge the social structure (van Dijk, 1997). The analysis of a socially based context of speech genres has given the research on medical interactions a critical lens. EMP, with its attention on the interplay between language use and social and culture factors, can be also labeled as English for sociocultural purposes.

Doctor-patient interviews, either in hospitals or family practice clinics, are characterized by doctors soliciting information from patients so as to reach a diagnosis and recommend treatment. Such doctor-centered interaction has been explored by researchers following a conversational analysis approach, focusing on turn-taking sequences. Mishler (1984) pointed out that the dominance of the doctor's voice or the "voice of medicine" is based on a three-part discourse pattern starting with the doctor's question, followed by the patient's response, and then the doctor's assessment and the next question. Such a sequence of questions, as Hydén and Mishler (1999) noted, represents an underlying biomedical model of illness. The "voice of medicine," or the medical conception of illness, suggests a contrast or even conflict between the doctor's voice and the voice of the patients as they story their lived experiences. Illustrating the restricted voice of the patients, Mishler (1997) described how one patient's account was fragmented as she was interrupted and sidetracked by the doctor's questions. Like Mishler (1984, 1997), other EMP applied linguists have explored the interaction between the "voice of medicine" and the "voice of the lifeworld" using video or audio recordings of medical interviews.

Research on the "voice of medicine" indicates the dominance of the doctors and their language of power. From Ibrahim (2001) there is evidence that doctors typically control the discourse by asking closed questions that require brief answers from the patients. Researchers also found that doctors, to maintain their dominance and authority, use language too technical for patients (Korsch & Negrete, 1972), ignore some patient-initiated questions (Frankel, 1990; West, 1983), reject patients' own diagnoses of their health problems (Fisher & Groce, 1990), and do not check patients' understanding of their questions or explanations (Ibrahim, 2001). Further, West (1990) found that men/male physicians, when formulating directives, tend to impose their demands on patients through the use of imperatives and statements stressing their own needs and wants. Such a style, as West (1990) pointed out, maximizes status differences and, therefore, affects the patients' compliance with the directives negatively. The language of the doctors, indeed, reflects their professional and superordinate status vis-à-vis patients.

Juxtaposed with the doctors' voice is the voice of the patients. To seek medical attention, patients present their problems and their own explanations of the problems for confirmation. Speaking in the "voice of the lifeworld," patients "have difficulties inserting their voice into a discussion dominated by the voice of medicine" (Fisher & Groce, 1990, p. 241). If the doctors' language mirrors their superordinate status, the patients' language is associated with inferiority. Skelton and Hobbs (1999) reported that there is a tendency for some patients to use the past tense in making requests and expressing present worries. Also in contrast to the dominant voice of the doctor is the confused voice of the patient. Cicourel (1985) found that an elderly female patient sustained her belief or misconceptions about her illness as she repeatedly misunderstood the doctor's explanations and was confused about the technical information she received. Cicourel (1981) also observed that doctors' questions are especially confusing for patients with low social status, different cultural backgrounds, and limited English. The observation was based on a case of epilepsy involving a low-income family in the U.S. Neither the 15-year-old patient nor the mother could speak English, so the uncle, with limited English, was translating at the interview. Confusion was evident when the doctor's question about the patient's childhood fever and seizures ended up with an extended discussion of the mother's measles during her pregnancy with the patient. These findings illustrate that the way language is used at medical interviews can lead to misunderstandings about the information transmitted.

Alongside the findings of the problems in medical interviews, research has also indicated how doctors and patients collaborate in their talk. The collaboration is evident in Mishler's (1997) observation of how a patient's account could be coherently and interactively shaped when the physician adopts the role of an attentive listener. Active learning, as S. Candlin (2002) stated, helps develop a trusting relationship with patients. In her study of how nurses strategically listen and respond with empathy during therapeutic consultations, Candlin found that more self-disclosure is achieved as the patients keep the conversation floor. The disclosing of personal information from the patients, in turn, empowers the nurses and the institution they represent. Patients have also been reported to have a strong desire for a personal relationship with the attending doctor (Hein & Wodak, 1987), yet other patients associate authoritarianism with competence and, therefore, view the doctor's dominance as reassuring (Ibrahim, 2001). Some patients have been found to take responsibility for establishing the relevance of vague utterances when confronted with non-target-like linguistic performance, as Cameron and Williams (1997) discovered in their study on cross-cultural therapeutic communications involving an ESL student nurse from Thailand. Similarly, when patients provide irrelevant accounts, doctors, as Cicourel (1981) reported, listened selectively based on their expertise to reach a diagnosis. The collaboration between the patients and doctors or nurses suggests that a medical interview is a jointly constructed social practice.

Guided by the theoretical framework of how contextual factors affect and constrain language choices, research on doctor/nurse and patient interactions is indicative of how status and power are enacted and maintained in doctor-patient encounters. Such research has also made the medical interactions visible by focusing on various analytic patterns such as questions and answers, directives, and responses (Maher, 1986b). Relevant findings suggest how teaching of EMP can be facilitated by drawing attention to how language can influence the quality of medical care delivery. Role plays are suggested to help trainees develop appropriate communication skills, such as asking the right questions, listening with empathy so as to develop a trusting relationship with the patients, formulating directives in such a way as to minimize status differences, and checking comprehension in order to avoid misunderstandings. These culturally specific interpersonal skills are a challenge, especially to non–native English speaking students. In addition, research has also drawn our attention to clinical practice involving doctors, with a superordinate position, versus patients, with an inferior status. Following Pennycook's (1997, p. 266) argument against vulgar pragmatism, "a position that is deeply concerned about efforts to maintain the status quo," EMP practitioners need to help students reflect critically on the relevant discourse practice and the way it constructs our understanding of medical practice. Viewing doctor-patient interactions as social practice has put EMP in a position to confront and negotiate the relationship between classroom teaching and social practice.

Needs Analysis and EMP Curriculum Design

While research on the nature of the written and speech genres of medical communication certainly has implications for teaching, the connection between linguistic analysis and classroom teaching envisioned by Halliday et al. (1964) has not turned out to be simple and straightforward. Questions have been raised about how relevant findings can be "transmitted into teaching or study materials" (Swales, 2000, p. 68). One reason for this concern has to do with EMP's preoccupation with the special needs of learners. The fact that each group of EMP students has distinctive needs draws our attention to the limited research on various types of medical discourses. For example, there is a dearth of literature on interactions involving pharmacists, dentists, and care aids. There is also little research on transmediation skills or the methods doctors or nurses use to take notes or complete medical charts in their hospital routines. To meet the needs of special groups of students, EMP practitioners, therefore, have been conducting their own needs analysis to develop courses. The underlying belief is that literacy is situated in specific sociocultural contexts. Since teaching is based on needs analysis research, EMP instructors, as Belcher (2006) stated, are first researchers and then teachers.

Over the years, EMP practitioners have expanded ways of doing needs assessment to identify and weigh the importance of features of the target language situations in which students will be using English (Johns & Dudley-Evans, 1991; West, 1997). EMP practitioners survey the students' background, goals, and attitudes (Chia et al., 1999; Frank, 2000), analyze the target situation through field observations and interviews with medical and nursing faculties or hospital staff (C. Candlin, Leather, & Bruton, 1976; C. Candlin, Bruton, Leather, & Woods, 1981; Marston & Hansen, 1985), identify deficiencies between students' performances and the target needs (Bosher & Smalkoski, 2002; Cameron, 1998; Shi, Corcos, & Storey, 2001), and conduct sophisticated ethnographies for an ongoing assessment of students' needs (Eggly, 2002; Hussin, 2002; Uvin, 1996). All these needs analyses, except for those large-scale questionnaire surveys that aim to generate recommendations for EMP programs, focus on developing EMP courses with specific teaching materials.

Target-Situation Needs Analysis

Among those who conducted target-situation analyses, C. Candlin and his associates (1976, 1981) conducted field observations of language on the job and developed EMP courses for training overseas or non–native English speaking Casualty (or emergency room) doctors. They first followed the work cycles of Casualty doctors in dealing with ambulatory patients and stretcher-borne cases to develop cycles of learning procedures. They then identified pedagogical points by associating language skills and functions with each job-specific operational task. One such example was the affective and meta-communication when the doctor signaled to the patient that he/she was still listening while doing the examination or note taking. Real-time recordings were used as teaching materials. In a later study, Candlin et al. (1981) further illustrated how their analysis of language functions in about 850 Casualty consultations resulted in 27 teaching modules to guide students in discussing the relevant communicative acts, to practice various language functions, such as to greet, take leave, interrogate, and accept, and to exercise skill transfer from speech to writing and vice versa. The language functions were practiced through traditional substitution drills and exercises of identification, sensitivity, production practice, and simulation. Each module also included a test tape with prompts soliciting communicative acts. The advantage of such a module course, as Candlin et al. (1981) stated, was the flexibility that allowed instructors to follow the modules selectively to fit the needs of students and the time available.

Also using target-situation analyses, Graham and Beardsley (1986) developed an EMP course for Pharmacy students, whereas Marston and Hansen (1985) developed an EMP course for Nursing students. These course developers, unlike Candlin et al. (1976, 1981), who did field observations, consulted or interviewed content instructors and practicing pharmacists or nurses. In addition, Graham and Beardsley (1986) made use of professional videotapes and books developed by pharmaceutical companies, and Marston and Hansen (1985) surveyed nursing texts and manuals that students would be using. As a result, Graham and Beardsley (1986) identified a list of speech functions for pharmacists to communicate effectively in professional settings. They then designed teaching materials to illustrate each function with example dialogues (either using videotapes prepared by pharmaceutical companies or demonstration by instructors) followed by a discussion of the function and a role-play simulation. The course was team taught by an ESL specialist and a pharmacist. In contrast, Marston and Hansen (1985) identified the language of nursing that students would be using either in training or on the job. Their curriculum included teaching units such as role plays to practice taking patients' medical history; specialized vocabulary and style for writing medical records, with exercises changing standard prose into chart writing; and description of basic nursing procedures using videotapes without sound track. Unlike Graham and Beardsley (1986), who used a standardized test (Speaking Proficiency English Assessment Kit, by the Educational Testing Service) before and after the course to confirm students' improvement on spoken English, Marston and Hansen (1985) could not find a suitable assessment tool to evaluate what their students had learned. Together with Candlin et al. (1976, 1981), Graham and Beardsley (1986) and Marston and Hansen (1985) highlight how target-situation needs analysis can help develop EMP courses for special groups of students.

Deficiency Needs Analysis

Another group of practitioners, while researching the target situation, have moved a step further to conduct a deficiency analysis to identify gaps between the desired performance and the current level of students. Following such a diagnostic approach, practitioners have observed and analyzed medical students' performance in their junior clerkship (Shi et al., 2001) and nursing students' performance in both class and on-site practice in clinical settings (Bosher & Smalkoski, 2002; Cameron, 1998). Based on their analyses of transcripts of video and audiotapes of ward teaching, Shi et al. (2001) found that students, while guided by the tutors in diagnostic thinking, lacked linguistic skills such as using appropriate colloquial and technical vocabulary in eliciting and reporting case histories, applying correct verb tenses to establish the chronology of case reports, and describing location (or parts of the anatomy) and procedure of the physical examination. They then designed a course for students who were close to the junior clerkship (the first clinical experience) that incorporated episodes of videotapes and transcripts of student performance data in teaching and learning tasks to illustrate and provide practice in the relevant linguistic repertoires.

Similarly, Bosher and Smalkoski (2002) translated the needs analysis of nursing students' difficulties in communicating with clients into course units, such as assertiveness talk, therapeutic communication, information-gathering techniques, and cultural aspects of health-care communication. Unlike Shi et al. (2001), however, who used videotapes of students' performance as teaching resources, Bosher and Smalkoski (2002) selected professional videotapes and textbook chapters on nursing communication to discuss examples of effective communication. Also addressing nursing needs, Cameron (1998) defined deficiencies of a group of ESL nursing students by observation and analysis of recordings of students' language use in class and internships. Based on the analyses, a syllabus was designed to focus on speech production accuracy, academic and clinical performances, diverse patient population with dialect and cultural variations, and inferencing skills, either language- or social-based. Recordings of real-time interactions, like those in Shi et al. (2001), were used as teaching resources for illustration, discussion, and listening activities. Cameron (1998) believed that his extensive deficiency analysis laid a solid foundation for a successful EMP course. Shi et al. (2001) and Bosher and Smalkoski (2002) also reported positive feedback from their students. Together, these exemplar studies demonstrate how EMP courses can be tightly constructed based on the gap between the desired language performance and current learner proficiencies.

Ongoing Ethnographic Needs Analysis

If the deficiency approach helps develop teaching materials for incoming students, ongoing ethnographic needs analysis aims at helping the present students through continuing on-site explorations. Exemplar studies have illustrated how practitioners immersed themselves in the training or working environment as they taught for a workplace program for immigrant health care workers at a nursing home (Uvin, 1996), or residency training for international medical graduates in an urban medical center (Eggly, 2002), or clinical placements for nursing students in a hospital (Hussin, 2002). Needs assessment in these studies was ongoing and often took place at the patient's bedside. In addition, students were involved in analyzing their own needs. The objective needs analysis conducted by the practitioners was, therefore, supplemented by the students' own subjective judgment of their needs (Tudor, 1997). Such learner-centered curricula, as Eggly (2002, p. 115) put it, "are in a constantly evolving, interactive relationship with the communication context and the needs of the learners."

Uvin (1996) illustrated how a workplace English course for health care workers based on exhaustive target situation analysis prior to instruction could still fall short of the current students' needs. Not having participated in the course development, his learners, in Uvin's (1996, p. 44) words, could not "identify with the suggested content and methods." Although Uvin interviewed the supervisors and administrators, there seemed to be a gap between students' own understandings of their needs and the definition of students' needs from the practitioner's perspective and the institutional expectations. Such a gap echoes the critical perspective or definition of students' needs as their rights of participation and resistance (Benesch, 2001). To bridge the gap, Uvin (1996) reoriented his course toward an ongoing needs analysis involving learners investigating their own daily experiences. As an instructor, Uvin observed the working environment and met regularly with the residents, supervisors, nurses, and administrators. He also used a problem-posing approach to work with learners in identifying and sharing issues they were facing in daily work, finding ways to solve the problems, and documenting what they had learned. By analyzing their own needs and the context of language use, students became better language learners and users. The participatory approach described by Uvin (1996) is an example of how an ongoing needs analysis can enhance the learning and teaching activities for an on-site vocational EMP course.

Eggly (2002) also followed an ethnographic approach of needs analysis to develop an EMP program for physician-patient communication skills. The program included, inter alia, videotaping each student conducting interviews with real patients in the outpatient clinic followed up with a review of the tapes. The program also offered individual language tutoring to those who either perceived a need themselves or were poorly evaluated by the faculty on language skills. For each of these students, a short-term EMP program was designed. For example, a series of role plays was designed to help one student develop language skills for interviewing patients and reporting cases to the supervising faculty. During the role plays, Eggly, as the instructor, played the roles of the student's patients and the supervising physician. She took notes on the mistakes made by the student and made suggestions for improvements. The tutorials later expanded as the student identified her needs to perform other tasks, such as discussing diagnostic results with family members and writing abstracts for journal submissions. By tailoring the instruction to individual students' needs, the EMP course evolved "through a constant interaction among the teacher, the students, the language, and the tasks to be performed" (Eggly, 2002, p. 113).

Like Eggly (2002) and Uvin (1996), Hussin (2002) engaged students in an ethnographic analysis of their own needs. In an EMP course team-taught by a language specialist and a nursing instructor during their clinical placements, Hussin guided her students in doing genre analysis of samples of language-in-use (audio- and videotapes and written documents) collected from hospitals and clinics. She also visited students in their placements to check their case notes and discharge summaries, which allowed her to further identify students' needs. Students were also encouraged to suggest learning tasks and provide data of their own language performances. In such a situated immersion, learners practiced the language skills in class and then tried them out immediately in the target situation. At the end of the course, students submitted a language learning log to reflect on and assess their own language performances. Hussin (2002) believed that students' involvement in the ongoing ethnographic analysis of their own language problems prepared them for their future working lives.

Summary of Studies on Needs Analyses

The above review describes how practitioners have developed EMP courses using target-situation analysis, deficiency analysis, and ongoing ethnographic needs analysis. These needs analyses all presuppose research strategies or methods such as surveys of students' attitudes; consultations or interviews with administrators, content instructors, and on-site preceptors who supervise students; observations and audio- or videotaping of real-time interactions; and collection and analysis of written documents in the target situation. However, the needs analyses differ in their focuses: the target situation analysis focuses on the professional performance; the deficiency analysis focuses on students' previous performances; and ethnographic needs analysis focuses on the on-site performance of the current students who are often analysts of their own needs. All these types of needs analyses require a close collaboration between the EMP practitioner and the content specialists. In fact, both practitioners in the Eggly (2002) and Hussin (2002) studies are affiliated with the Nursing or Medical faculty. Not only did they team teach with content specialists, but they were also immersed in the culture of the discipline by attending lectures, department meetings, research forums, and staff room discussions. As Hussin (2002) noted, EMP teachers must get inside the texts and tasks of the specialist language and its purposes in order to exploit learning activities around them, especially when teaching students who are close to or in the target situation.

As we move from the target situation to the deficiency and then the ethnographic needs analysis, there is an increasing learner-centeredness. If the target-situation analysis focuses on the desired performance, the deficiency and ethnographic needs analyses turn attention to the students' own performances. At the far end of the continuum, the ethnographic needs analysis involves learners themselves as needs analysts. Such needs analysis becomes an ongoing process rather than a one-shot data collection and analysis. By assessing their own needs, students invest and participate in the process of curriculum development. The ability to learn by identifying and defining one's own needs, as Dovey (2006) pointed out, is a valued attribute of "new vocationalism," which trains people to deal with workplace genres in a constantly changing environment. The needs analyses conducted by the EMP practitioners through immersion in the target situation is also a response to the concerns of the New Rhetoric School about how genres, which are dynamic and fluid, can be taught in classrooms.

Further Inquiries

Emerging from this review of the genre-based analysis of written and spoken medical discourses and the needs-clarifying research for EMP courses are implications for further inquiries. First of all, more research is needed to investigate the reading, writing, and speaking skills of students as they acculturate into their medical and nursing profession while still in school and also after graduation. Research is also needed to explore written genres such as record keeping or chart writing in hospital routines. In addition, spoken genres such as communications between or among doctors/nurses need to be further explored. While genre-based discourse analysis can inform us about the nature of medical communication, EMP practitioners are also confronted with some practical challenges or issues in developing EMP courses. Among these issues are the role of content knowledge and assessment of students' achievement.

As content-oriented language educators, EMP practitioners need to either be somewhat content-knowledgeable or rely on content specialists. However, questions remain about how much specialist knowledge an EMP practitioner needs to have or how much he or she needs to rely on content specialists. If we define content as specialist knowledge, few EMP practitioners possess either a medical or nursing degree or experiences in the profession (Cameron, 1998), and only a small number have acquired some medical knowledge when immersed in the discipline as part of the medical or nursing faculty (Eggly, 2002; Hussin 2002). Research has suggested that although beginning students might not know more than their EMP teachers (Wood & Head, 2004), advanced students do need the correct content information or professional advice, for example, when doing the role plays (Graham & Beardsley, 1986; Shi et al., 2001). Since team teaching with content specialists is expensive (Graham & Beardsley, 1986), most EMP practitioners have resorted to other methods to compensate for their lack of content knowledge. For example, some choose medical topics such as diet, the elderly, and the disabled that are closely related to the world of everyday experience (Webber, 1995) so that they may feel the "least incompetent and ill-informed" (Allwright & Allwright, 1977, p. 59). Others switch the content responsibility to the students through problem-based learning (Belcher, this volume; Wood & Head, 2004), Internet-based learning (Kimball, 1998), or having learners identify their own needs and ways to learn (Eggly, 2002; Uvin, 1996). Since these approaches require learners to simulate clinical thinking and conduct collaborative inquiry for medical information on their own, EMP instructors can focus on the language skills while learning the relevant content knowledge from and with the learners. If EMP courses are moving in the direction of problem-based and Internet-based learning, research needs to explore how teachers can facilitate learner independence in content learning.

The second issue concerns assessment of students' achievement. According to the present review, EMP courses vary in methods of assessments. Some have used standardized English tests (Graham & Beardsley, 1986) or teacher-made tests based on the specific language functions taught (Candlin et al., 1981). However, since standardized tests do not measure the specific language skills taught in the course, and teacher-made tests may not be valid in the eyes of administrators (Marston & Hansen, 1985), other practitioners have used a combination of tasks, including a structured role play, journal entries, or a learning log prepared by students evaluating and reflecting on their own language performances (Bosher & Smalkoski, 2002; Hussin, 2002). In cases where the practitioners are immersed in the clinical environment and able to shadow the students' clinical performance, language assessment becomes ongoing and incorporated into the formal clinical assessment (Eggly, 2002; Uvin, 1996). The on-site clinical assessment suggests follow-up observation or interviews of graduates working in the target situation in order to identify whether EMP courses have actually met their needs (cf. Duff, Wong, & Early, 2002). The gap between the curriculum and the needs of the students highlights the value of a follow-up evaluation.

The pressure to develop effective EMP programs has increased along with the increasing number of ESL/EFL students attending medical or nursing programs in not only native English speaking countries but also, in Kachru's (1985) terms, the Outer and Expanding Circle countries. This pressure is compounded as many English speaking countries have growing numbers of immigrant medical personnel who need EMP training (Bosher & Smalkoski, 2002; van Naerssen, 1978). In order to help these ESL/EFL students, teacher training programs need to be established to train qualified EMP practitioners with the ability not only to analyze written and spoken genres of medical discourses but also to be responsive to dynamic local situations and needs.

* * *

LING SHI is an associate professor in the Department of Language and Literacy Education at the University of British Columbia. Her research has been published in journals such as *English for Specific Purposes, Journal of English for Academic purposes, TESOL Quarterly, Written Communication,* and *Journal of Second Language Writing.*

REFERENCES

Allwright, J., & Allwright, R. (1977). An approach to the teaching of medical English. In S. Holden (Ed.), *English for specific purposes* (pp. 58–62). London: Modern English Publications.

Ariza, M. Á. A., & Navarro, F. (2006). Medicine: Use of English. In K. Brown (Ed.), *Encyclopedia of language and linguistics* (2nd ed., Vol. 7, pp. 752–759). Oxford, UK: Elsevier.

Baker, M. (1988). Sub-technical vocabulary and the ESP teacher: An analysis of some rhetorical items in medical journal articles. *Reading in a Foreign Language, 4*(2), 91–105.

Bakhtin, M. (1986). *Speech genres and other late essays.* Austin: University of Texas Press.

Bazerman, C. (1997). Discursively structured activities. *Mind, Culture, and Activity, 4,* 296–308.

Belcher, D. D. (2006). English for specific purposes: Teaching to perceived needs and imagined future in worlds of work, study and everyday life. *TESOL Quarterly, 40,* 133–156.

Benesch, S. (2001). *Critical English for academic purposes: Theory, politics, and practice.* Mahwah, NJ: Lawrence Erlbaum.

Bosher, S., & Smalkoski, F. (2002). From needs analysis to curriculum development: Designing a course in health-care communication for immigrant students in the USA. *English for Specific Purposes, 21*, 59–79.

Boulet, J. R., van Zanten, M., McKinley, D. W., & Gary, N. E. (2001). Evaluating the spoken English proficiency of graduates of foreign medical schools. *Medical Education, 35*, 767–773.

Bruce, N. (1992). *Enhancing the status of communication in health science education and professional practice.* Paper presented at the TESOL convention, Vancouver, Canada.

Cameron, R. (1998). A language-focused needs analysis for ESL-speaking nursing students in class and clinic. *Foreign Language Annals, 31*, 203–218.

Cameron, R., & Williams, J. (1997). Sentence to ten cents: A case study of relevance and communicative success in nonnative-native speaker interaction in a medical setting. *Applied Linguistics, 18*(4), 415–445.

Candlin, C. N., Bruton, C. J., Leather, J. H., & Woods, E. G. (1981). Designing modular materials for communicative language learning; an example: Doctor-patient communication skills. In L. Selinker, E. Tarone & V. Hanzeli (Eds.), *English for academic and technical purposes: Studies in honor of Louis Trimble* (pp. 105–133). Rowley, MA: Newbury House.

Candlin, C. N., Leather, J. H., & Bruton, C. J. (1976). Doctors in casualty: Applying communicative competence to components of specialist course design. *International Review of Applied Linguistics*, 245–272.

Candlin, S. (2002). A triple jeopardy: What can discourse analysts offer health professionals? In C. Candlin (Ed.), *Research and practice in professional discourse* (pp. 293–308). Hong Kong: City University of Hong Kong Press.

Chia, H.-U., Johnson, R., Chia, H.-L., & Olive, F. (1999). English for college students in Taiwan: A study of perceptions of English needs in a medical context. *English for Specific Purposes, 18*, 107–119.

Chur-Hansen, A. (1999). Teaching support in the behavioral sciences for non-English speaking background medical undergraduates. *Medical Education, 33*, 404–410.

———. (2000). Medical students' essay-writing skills: Criteria-based self- and tutor-evaluation and the role of language background. *Medical Education, 34*, 194–198.

Chur-Hansen, A., & Barrett, R. J. (1996). Teaching colloquial Australian English to medical students from non-English speaking backgrounds. *Medical Education, 30*, 412–417.

Cicourel, A. V. (1981). Language and medicine. In C. A. Ferguson (Ed.), *Language in the USA* (pp. 407–429). Cambridge, UK: Cambridge University Press.

———. (1985). Doctor-patient discourse. In T. A. van Dijk (Ed.), *Handbook of discourse analysis* (Vol. 4, pp. 193–202). London: Academic Press.

Dovey, T. (2006). What purposes, specifically? Re-thinking purposes and specificity in the context of the 'new vocationalism'. *English for Specific Purposes, 25,* 387–402.

Dubois, B. L. (1980). Genre and structure of biomedical speeches. *Forum Linguisticum, 5,* 140–168.

Duff, P. A., Wong, P., & Early, M. (2002). Learning language for work and life: The linguistic socialization of immigrant Canadians seeking careers in healthcare. *Modern Language Journal, 86,* 397–422.

Eggly, S. (2002). An ESP program for international medical graduates in residency. In T. Orr (Ed.), *English for specific purposes* (pp. 105–115). Alexandria, VA: TESOL.

Ferguson, G. (2001). If you pop over there: A corpus-based study of conditionals in medical discourse. *English for Specific Purposes, 20,* 61–82.

Fisher, S., & Groce, S. B. (1990). Accounting practices in medical interviews. *Language in Society, 19,* 225–250.

Fox, C. H., & Meijer, F. (1980). Teaching medical English to foreign-language doctors. *Medical Education, 14,* 316–319.

Francis, G., & Kramer-Dahl, A. (1991). From clinical report to clinical story: Two ways of writing about a medical case. In E. Ventola (Ed.), *Functional and systemic linguistics: Approaches and uses* (pp. 339–368). Berlin: Mouton de Gruyter.

Frank, R. A. (2000). Medical communication: Non-native English speaking patients and native English speaking professionals. *English for Specific Purposes, 19,* 31–62.

Frankel, R. M. (1990). Talking in interviews: A dispreference for patient-initiated questions in physician-patient encounters. In G. Sathas (Ed.), *Interaction competence* (pp. 231–262). Washington, DC: International Institute for Ethonomethodology and Conversation Analysis and University Press of America.

Galve, I. G. (1998). The textual interplay of grammatical metaphor on the nominalizations occurring in written medical English. *Journal of Pragmatics, 30,* 363–385.

Graham, J. G., & Beardsley, R. S. (1986). English for specific purposes: Content, language, and communication in a pharmacy course model. *TESOL Quarterly, 20,* 227–244.

Halliday, M. A. K. (1985). Context of situation. In M. A. K. Halliday & R. Hasan (Eds.), *Language, context and text* (pp. 3–14). Geelong, Australia: Deakin University Press.

Halliday, M. A. K., McIntosh, A., & Strevens, P. (1964). *The linguistic sciences and language teaching.* London: Longman.

Hein, N., & Wodak, R. (1987). Medical interviews in internal medicine: Some results of an empirical investigation. *Text, 7,* 37–65.

Hussin, B. (2002). An ESP program for students of nursing. In T. Orr (Ed.), *English for specific purposes* (pp. 25–39). Alexandria, VA: TESOL.

Hydén, L.-C., & Mishler, E. G. (1999). Language and medicine. *Annual Review of Applied Linguistics, 19,* 174–192.

Ibrahim, Y. (2001). Doctor and patient questions as a measure of doctor-centredness in UAE hospitals. *English for Specific Purposes, 20,* 331–344.

Johns, A. M., & Dudley-Evans, T. (1991). English for specific purposes: International in scope, specific in purpose. *TESOL Quarterly, 25*(2), 297–311.

Kachru, B. (1985). Standards, codification, and sociolinguistic realism: The English language in the Outer Circle. In R. Quick & H. G. Widdowson (Eds.), *English in the world: Teaching and learning the language and literature* (pp. 11–30). Cambridge, UK: Cambridge University Press.

Kanoksilapatham, B. (2005). Rhetorical structure of biochemistry research articles. *English for Specific Purposes, 25,* 269–292.

Kimball, J. (1998). Task-based medical English: Elements for Internet-assisted language learning. *Computer Assisted Language Learning, 11,* 411–417.

Korsch, B., & Negrete, V. (1972). Doctor patient communication. *Scientific American, 277,* 66–74.

Lynch, T., & Maclean, J. (2003). Effects of feedback on performance: A study of advanced learners on an ESP speaking course. *Edinburgh Working Papers in Applied Linguistics, 12,* 19–44.

Lucas, P., Lenstrup, M., Prinz, J., Williamson, D., Yip, H., & Tipoe, G. (1997). Language as a barrier to the acquisition of anatomical knowledge. *Medical Education, 31,* 81–86.

Maher, J. (1986a). The development of English as an international language of medicine. *Applied Linguistics, 7,* 206–220.

———. (1986b). English for medical purposes. *Language Teaching, 19,* 112–145.

Marston, J., & Hansen, A. G. (1985). Clinically speaking: ESP for refugee nursing students. *MinneTESOL Journal, 5,* 29–52.

Miller, C. (1984). Genre as social action. *Quarterly Journal of Speech, 70,* 151–167.

Mishler, E. G. (1984). *The discourse of medicine: Dialects of medical interviews.* Norwood, NJ: Ablex.

———. (1997). The interactional construction of narratives in medical and life-history interviews. In B.-L. Gunnarsson, P. Linell & B. Nordberg (Eds.), *The construction of professional discourse* (pp. 223–244). London: Longman.

Nwogu, K. N. (1991). Structure of science popularizations: A genre-analysis approach to the schema of popularized medical texts. *English for Specific Purposes, 10,* 111–123.

———. (1997). The medical research paper: Structure and functions. *English for Specific Purposes, 16*, 119–138.

Nwogu, K., & Bloor, T. (1991). Thematic progression in professional and popular medical texts. In E. Ventola (Ed.), *Functional and systemic linguistics: Approaches and uses* (pp. 369–384). Berlin: Mouton de Gruyter.

Pennycook, A. (1997). Vulgar pragmatism, critical pragmatism, and EAP. *English for Specific Purposes, 16*, 253–269.

Piqué-Angordans, J., & Posteguillo, S. (2006). Medical discourse and academic genres. In K. Brown (Ed.), *Encyclopedia of language and linguistics* (2nd ed., Vol. 7, pp. 649–657). Oxford, UK: Elsevier.

Salager-Meyer, F. (1992). A text-type and move analysis study of verb tense and modality distribution in medical English abstracts. *English for Specific Purposes, 11*(2), 93–113.

———. (1994). Hedges and textual communicative function in medical English written discourse. *English for Specific Purposes, 13*, 149–170.

Sarangi, S., & Roberts, C. (1999). *Talk, work and institutional order: Discourse in medical, mediation and management settings.* Berlin: Mouton de Gruyter.

Shi, L., Corcos, R., & Storey, A. (2001). Using student performance data to develop an English course for clinical training. *English for Specific Purposes, 20*, 267–291.

Skelton, J. (1994). Analysis of the structure of original research papers: An aid to writing original papers for publication. *British Journal of General Practice, 44*, 445–459.

———. (1997). The representation of truth in academic medical writing. *Applied Linguistics, 18*, 121–140.

Skelton, J. R., & Hobbs, F. D. R. (1999). Concordancing: Use of language-based research in medical communication. *The Lancet, 353*, 108–111.

Smith, D. E. A. (1984). Medical discourse: Aspects of author's comment. *The ESP Journal, 3*, 25–35.

Swales, J. M. (1990). *Genre analysis: English in academic and research settings.* Cambridge, UK: Cambridge University Press.

———. (2000). Languages for specific purposes. *Annual Review of Applied Linguistics, 20*, 59–76.

Taavitsainen, I. (2006) Medical communication, lingua francas. In K. Brown (Ed.), *Encyclopedia of language and linguistics* (2nd ed., Vol. 7, pp. 643–644). Oxford, UK: Elsevier.

Thomas, S., & Hawes, T. P. (1994). Reporting verbs in medical journal articles. *English for Specific Purposes, 13*, 129–148.

Treichler, P. A. (1992). Medicine and language. In W. Bright (Ed.), *International encyclopedia of linguistics* (pp. 411–413). Oxford, UK: Oxford University Press.

Tudor, I. (1997). LSP or language education? In R. Howard & G. Brown (Eds.), *Teacher education for LSP* (pp. 90–102). Clevedon, UK: Multilingual Matters.

Uvin, J. (1996). Designing workplace ESOL courses for Chinese health-care workers at a Boston nursing home. In K. Graves (Ed.), *Teachers as course developers* (pp. 39–62). Cambridge, UK: Cambridge University Press.

Van Dijk, T. A. (1997). Discourse as interaction in society. In T. A. van Dijk (Ed.), *Discourse as social interaction* (Vol. 2, pp. 1–37). London: SAGE Publications.

Van Naerssen, M. M. (1978). ESL in medicine: A matter of life and death. *TESOL Quarterly, 12*, 193–203.

Varttala, T. (1999). Remarks on the communicative functions of hedging in popular scientific and specialist research articles on medicine. *English for Specific Purposes, 18*, 177–200.

Webber, P. (1994). The function of questions in different medical journal genres. *English for Specific Purposes, 13*, 257–268.

———. (1995). Speaking practice in the medical English classroom: Bridging the gap between medical English and the everyday world. *International Review of Applied Linguistics, 33*, 64–70.

———. (2005). Interactive features in medical conference monologue. *English for Specific Purposes, 24*, 157–181.

West, C. (1983). Ask me no questions . . . An analysis of queries and replies in physician-patient dialogues. In S. Fisher & A. D. Todd (Eds.), *The social organization of doctor-patient communication* (pp. 75–106). Washington, DC: Center for Applied Linguistics.

West, D. (1990). Not just 'doctors' orders': Directive-response sequences in patients' visits to women and men physicians. *Discourse and Society, 1*, 85–112.

West, R. (1997). Needs analysis: State of the art. In R. Howard & G. Brown (Eds.), *Teacher education for LSP* (pp. 68–79). Clevedon, UK: Multilingual Matters.

Williams, I. A. (1996). A contextual study of lexical verbs in two types of medical research report: Clinical and experimental. *English for Specific Purposes, 15*, 175–197.

Wingard, P. (1981). Some verb forms and functions in six medical texts. In L. Selinker, E. Tarone & U. Hanzeli (Eds.), *English for academic and technical purposes: Studies in honor of Louis Trimble*. Rowley, MA: Newbury House Publishers.

Wood, A., & Head, M. (2004). 'Just what the doctor ordered': The application of problem-based learning to EAP. *English for Specific Purposes, 23*, 3–17.

11

Problem-Solving for Nursing Purposes

DIANE BELCHER
Georgia State University

Abstract

Although language teaching and nursing education are obviously quite different fields, some striking parallels can be seen in recent developments in both domains. After a brief overview of significant theoretical developments in contemporary language teaching, a short survey of the evolution of nursing education is presented, with attention given to major trends analogous to those in language education. The focus of this paper then turns to one particular recent development, the philosophy and curricular approach known as *problem-based learning* (PBL), and its implementation in medical and, more specifically, nursing education. A rationale for adopting problem-based learning in the ESP classroom is offered and examples of attempts to develop PBL courses for English for academic and medical purposes described.

At first glance, language teaching and nursing education probably appear to most people to have little in common. Language learning can look like a largely cognitive endeavor, as indeed much second language acquisition theory has suggested it is (see Ellis, 1997), and learning to function as a nurse may seem, at least on the surface, to be mainly a matter of learning the particular social interactional skills needed for medical care taking, albeit scientifically informed. Yet, recent developments suggest that the primary goal of the education of both language learners and nursing students is neither simply cognitive nor social-interactional but, instead, sociocognitive. Indeed, language and nursing education have evolved in ways that exhibit some surprising similarities. Especially noteworthy, this paper will argue, is an increasingly popular pedagogical approach in medical and, more recently, language education known as problem-based learning, an approach that so far has received little attention in a field with combined interests in both language and nursing education, namely English for Nursing Purposes. (For an excellent review of recent ENP literature, see Shi's chapter on English for medical purposes in this volume.)

Developments in English Language Learning and Teaching

Language education has undergone some remarkable theoretical shifts in the past century. The early influence of structuralism, often associated with Saussure, and behaviorist psychology, primarily associated with Skinner, was challenged, some would suggest quite successfully, in the mid-twentieth century by the functionalist and social theories of language advanced by Halliday and Hymes (see Savignon, 2001, and Celce-Murcia, 2001). The pedagogical impact of this shift in conceptualization could be seen in a movement away from a structuralist (or grammar-based) and discrete-skill (or separate linguistic modalities: speaking, listening, reading, and writing) approach toward a more integrated-skill, communicative approach that emphasized language as a means of meaning making in specific real-world contexts. Concomitant with a privileging of communicative competence, Savignon and others have noted, was a focus on language functions and learning processes. The functions that should be taught were seen as best discovered through analysis of learners' specific needs, hence the impetus for the language, or English, for specific purposes (LSP/ESP) movement. The interest in language learning processes led to teaching methods that facilitated classroom interaction and discovery (inductive) learning, thus sociocognitive growth.

This communicatively oriented methodological paradigm shift in language education, labeled communicative language teaching (CLT), has been characterized by Brown (2001) as, in effect, a linking of earlier with more recent language teaching goals. CLT is (or should be) concerned, Brown asserts, with both pragmatic and structuralist aspects of language, promoting both fluency and accuracy among learners, with admittedly, in actual practice, more emphasis on the former. CLT attempts to reach these objectives by engaging learners in authentic, meaningful language use and mindful, self-directed language learning. Rather than directly teaching language (or about language), teachers, as noted above, have been encouraged to facilitate language learning by providing opportunities for interaction and strategies for autonomous learning. Not surprisingly then, the CLT movement urges teachers, as Brown points out, to be learner, not teacher, centered; to facilitate cooperative, collaborative learning (as advocated by Vygotskyan sociocultural theory); to take a whole language approach (with authentic, natural language used for all four skills concurrently); and to employ content and task-based lessons (using real-world subject matter and communication problem-solving activities).

As one might expect, current language teacher training goals closely resemble the educational trends identified with CLT (again see Brown). Like language students, language teachers are advised to become autonomous learners, engaging in lifelong learning, self-inquiry (alone or with the help of peers), and critical reflection about the efficacy of their teaching strategies, often referred to as "action research" (Richards & Lockhart, 1996). Reflecting critically on CLT itself, however, has not necessarily been encouraged in teacher training programs, as suggested by Brown's observation: "No one these days would admit to a disbelief in the principles of CLT; they would be marked as a heretic" (p. 44).

Yet, there are those who have taken seriously the call for critical reflection and begun to question the universal value of CLT. Crookes (2003), for instance, has pointed out that "Holliday . . . documentated the sort of 'tissue rejection' that takes place when there are attempts to transplant CLT . . . to classrooms or education systems that already have a functional (but notably different) organization" (p. 153; Holliday, 1992). Critical applied linguists such as Pennycook (1994) have problematized the assumption that center-based (or Western) theories are appropriate for other contexts. It is interesting to note, though, that two of the most influential supporters of CLT in the English language teaching world, Richards and Nunan (see www.professorjackrichards.com and www.davidnunan.com), have done much of their own teaching and research in East Asia, especially in Hong Kong, a productive site of East/West interaction. Perhaps it is a mistake to see CLT as exclusively a product of the West. It is worth noting too that despite a growing list of critics and well-reasoned concerns, the basic appeal of CLT (with numerous permutations, such as "form-focused" CLT) continues, as Brown has observed, which may be indicative of the depth of dissatisfaction many still feel with more traditional approaches that have not resulted in communicative competence (see, for example, Shantou University's English Language Center's mission statement, with its explicit commitment to communicative competence: http://elc.stu.edu.cn/Home/Home). While the most effective means of language learning may be subject to continued debate and investigation, the goal of enabling language learners to function and flourish as independent language users is not one that many in contemporary language education would be likely to openly object to.

Some Parallel and Non-Parallel Developments in Nursing Education

Like applied linguistics, nursing as a separate profession is relatively new, having been established as a profession largely through the efforts of Florence Nightingale in the nineteenth century. The earliest formal nursing education programs were primarily hospital apprenticeships, but by the mid-twentieth century, nursing was viewed as more science than art, and nursing education, increasingly based on biomedical research, moved into universities (Tompkins, 2001). By the start of the twenty-first century, there had already been much talk of the need for a new model of nursing education. As many became disenchanted, Tompkins remarks, with the status of nursing as a pale reflection of medicine, and as a science—mechanistic, atomistic, and unresponsive to patients as whole persons—there was a felt need to return to the ideals of Nightingale and re-establish the philosophical, ethical, holistic approach to the caring nursing arts that she promoted.

Probably no single factor (or even several) can be pointed to as motivating the need for a new model of nursing, and in turn, nursing education. Tompkins lists a number of challenges in this new century that nursing educators feel compelled to consider. Among these challenges are changing demographics, with more people living longer, often with chronic illnesses, and increasingly culturally diverse populations. What some might call an "information flood" also poses challenges as information rapidly increases in amount, complexity, and availability via technology (hence the new field of health informatics) and more knowledgeable health care consumers become eager to participate in health care decision-making. There is also a perceived need for more pro-active nursing, focused more on public education and health maintenance than in the past and aware of the potential impact of the environment (e.g., global warming) on public health. These, of course, are only some of the challenges facing nursing education in this century.

Tompkins and others (e.g., Valainis, 2000) have persuasively argued that with these new challenges have come new responsibilities, and hence a need for new nursing competencies, many of which resonate with recent thinking in language education. Some of the nursing competencies, naturally, are very specific to the profession, such as the ability to manage care across facility boundaries, provide cost-effective quality care, and promote community health. However, both nurses and language educators are faced with learning to cope with new communication media, not infrequently constrained budgets, and the need to educate the public on various issues. Like both language learners and language teachers, nurses too are now seen as needing to learn to independently evaluate their own performance, identifying their own knowledge gaps and problems in their real-world practice and addressing them with a repertoire of strategies and collaborative interaction with others. In addition, just as language teachers are urged to be learner-centered, nurses are encouraged to be patient-centered: able to assess needs from the patient's point of view, to empower patients to participate in their own care, and even to be patient advocates when necessary.

Tompkins suggests that many of the nursing competencies just mentioned can be enhanced by promoting the type of relational knowing found in Chinese traditional medicine, which is characterized by a view of self as defined through relationships with others, and of care-giving as requiring involvement, mutual sharing, and a sense of community. Hall and Allan (1994) likewise argue that Eastern (or more specifically, Chinese) philosophy can inform competency in mutual participation, "in which practice, power and authority are shared . . . through joint exploration of the patient's experiences through the processes of negotiation and consensus seeking" (p. 114).

In sum, there seems to be agreement among many nursing education specialists that nurses need to become, as Rideout and Carpio (2001) succinctly put it, "critical thinkers, independent decision-makers, lifelong learners, effective team members, and competent users of new information technologies," and "above all . . . reflective practitioners, able to identify their own strengths and take action to overcome limitations" (p. 21). These are all goals of language teacher training as well.

A New Model for Nursing Education

In an effort to meet contemporary educational goals, a new and increasingly popular educational model has been developed for medical (not nursing alone) education, namely, problem-based learning (PBL), which can be viewed as a philosophy, a curriculum, and a learning process (Rideout & Carpio, but see also Maudsley, 1999). Originally developed for the education of physicians at McMaster University in Canada in 1969, PBL is in many respects similar to task-based language teaching, though it is more immediately analogous to, and likely influenced by, the case study approach of business education. The defining characteristics of PBL, Rideout and Carpio note, include the obvious use of a real-world problem, usually a complex situation in need of a solution or explanation. Knowledge is constructed through learners' work on the problem. The learning that takes place with PBL is thus teacher-facilitated but student-directed, with students collaboratively choosing which issues to focus on, identifying their own learning needs, finding resources, synthesizing and presenting research to fellow students, and, finally, self-evaluating their learning. The focus, as Rideout and Carpio point out, is much more on learning how to learn (enhancing metacognition) than on accumulating factual knowledge.

The theoretical foundation of PBL, derived from the work of Dewey, Bruner, and Vygotsky (see Rideout and Carpio), will sound familiar to anyone well read in language education theory. PBL takes from Dewey the notion that learners benefit most from self-directed learning, which entails growing awareness of their own learning processes. From Bruner, PBL has adopted the notion of intrinsic motivation as essential to learning and most likely to arise from inquiry about the real world—that is, discovery-based learning. PBL is also informed by Vygotskyan sociocultural theory, which argues for the value of scaffolding, or interaction with more or equally knowledgeable others, while engaged in relevant and meaningful activity.

In addition to social theories of education, PBL has profited from well-known principles of cognitive psychology, as Rideout and Carpio further observe, citing the work of Schmidt (1993) and Schmidt, Lipkin, deVries, and Greep (1989), though there is an element of the social in these principles too, as will soon be seen. In the PBL process, there is activation of prior knowledge, which arises from learners reviewing what they know in order to address the problem, and as a result, restructuring their prior knowledge. PBL also facilitates elaboration of knowledge, as learners working together formulate and criticize hypotheses, discuss evidence, and present summaries of research, all of which results in redundancy in memory structure, thus strengthening memory use. Medical PBL promotes encoding specificity, enhancing rapid information retrieval, by establishing strong parallels between learning and future application situations. Similarly, contextual dependency of learning occurs in PBL as contextual cues are established, enabling long-term memory activation in analogous contexts—that is, in actual clinical practice. The fifth principle of cognitive psychology that informs PBL is epistemic curiosity, which is heightened as learners have the opportunity to develop their own points of view in interaction with others' perspectives on the same problem.

So far the discussion of medical PBL has been rather abstract. A specific example should help make the process of PBL easier to visualize. As mentioned above, PBL always starts with a problem. Ideally, the problem is ill-structured (see Stepien, Gallagher, & Workman, 1993). In other words, it is a puzzling real-world scenario that requires additional information to understand and offers no immediately clear path to a solution. What follows is the type of problem, based on an actual case, that health science students might be given:

> "I can't see a doggone thing. It started off as a headache, and now I can't see." The middle-aged man was flushed and shiny. . . . Three days ago he was at work at a local animal hospital when his head began to pound. . . . The 58-year-old man had a high fever . . . and the thick optic nerves that connect the eyes to the brain were visibly swollen. . . . The patient had diabetes and high blood pressure, but he took his medicines regularly. . . . He'd had routine blood work, a CT scan, an M.R.I. All were normal. The spinal tap, however, was not. . . . The patient didn't have any H.I.V. risk factors, but when . . . suggested he be tested . . . the patient refused. . . . Finally, the patient [said] . . . he was bitten by a cat. (Sanders, 2009, pp. 19–20)

What do students do when handed such sample problems to address? Biley and Smith (1998), citing Schmidt (1983), enumerate a seven-step process that follows the assignment of a problem. First, students working in small groups are expected to clarify the terms (literally and more figuratively) of the problem and investigate any concepts involved that are not immediately understood. They might, for example, in response to the sample problem given, work to arrive at a clear understanding of what is meant by "H.I.V. risk factors." Second, the students need to reach consensus on a definition of the problem that must be addressed. For the sample, the problem is obviously a type of "mystery ailment" diagnosis dilemma. The third step requires analysis of the problem, and ideally the generation of ideas and working hypotheses about the problem. For instance, the students will begin to speculate on the likelihood of H.I.V. as the cause of vision loss in the sample problem. The fourth step involves a systematic compilation of all the ideas and possible solutions generated through group analysis of the problem, followed by (the fifth step) a listing of what needs to be learned to solve the problem, in other words, a formulation of the group's learning objectives. Having completed these five steps, the group is ready to launch their search for additional information that will support their problem-solving efforts. This might entail library or Internet research or possibly interviews with practicing health professionals. For the final step, the students synthesize all that they have discovered and usually present their findings to a larger cohort of students, followed by a group debriefing, during which the group reflects on what it has learned—not just about the specific problem, but about how to solve similar problems. Clearly, these steps are meant to foster self-directed, discovery-based, collaboratively scaffolded learning, with both social construction of meaning and increased metacognition as likely outcomes.

Medical problem-based learning is not problem-free, however (again see Rideout & Carpio, but also Albanese, 2000; Albanese & Mitchell, 1993; Biley & Smith, 1998; Connolly & Seneque, 1999). PBL Students may not achieve high scores on traditional tests of biomedical knowledge, and some may have difficulty accepting and coping with responsibility for their own learning. Yet in general, PBL students tend to be more satisfied with their educational experience than those in traditional programs—to appreciate the flexibility of the PBL program, the independence experienced and confidence gained, the relationships developed with others, and the relevance to clinical practice. Some research even suggests (e.g., Albanese, 2000) that there are long-term benefits, with PBL graduates more likely to affiliate with others—colleagues and patients—in their careers and engage in direct, hands-on patient care, thus putting into practice the type of relational knowing that Tompkins and others have seen as essential to the provision of improved contemporary health care.

Problem-Based Learning for English Language Teaching

At this point it will probably not come as a surprise that a strong case has already been made for bringing PBL into the language classroom. Barron (2002) offers multiple reasons for adopting PBL in English language teaching (ELT), not least among them being PBL's respect for learners—the polar opposite of a deficit theory of learning. PBL, after all, acknowledges that students have prior knowledge upon which to build. Another source of appeal for ELT is the lack of distinction between carrier and real content in PBL. In other words, in a PBL language classroom, content does not just serve language learning; it serves language users in their efforts to solve problems relevant to their worlds. PBL also "encourages the open-minded, reflective, critical and active learning" valued in language education (Barron, p. 305, citing Margetson, 1991).

Barron openly admits, however, that his own attempt to use PBL with language learners was not entirely successful. Barron gave his second-year EAP science students at the University of Hong Kong the task of addressing real-world science problems situated in Hong Kong and publicly presenting their findings in a poster presentation assessed by both EAP and science faculty. Working in small groups, as is usual in PBL, the students assigned each other tasks and went out into Hong Kong to collect data via questionnaires, interviews, and observation. The content appeared to matter to the students, as they considered such problems as environmental pollution and the dangers of cell phones. The assignment let them see science as more than merely academic. Unfortunately, the students collaborated more successfully than did the science and EAP faculty, who failed to agree on uniform evaluation criteria appropriate for PBL, creating a tension that students were well aware of. Barron makes it quite clear that this problem did not result from any shortcomings in the PBL process or the students' engagement with it but from the differing perspectives of the cross-disciplinary faculty involved in assessing the products of PBL.

Much less problematic was Wood and Head's (2004) attempt to implement a PBL EMP, or English for medical purposes, course. PBL, in fact, became a means of solving a pedagogical problem. Asked to teach an English for biomedical science course for pre-medical students at the University of Brunei Darussalam soon to be sent to study at the University of Queensland, in Australia, the instructors faced the constraints of limited time, a lack of relevant existing materials or curricula in their language program, and few medical resources in their university library. Wood and Head's solution was to design a PBL course to prepare the students for the Australian PBL-based medical program they were headed for. The authors assumed that a medically oriented PBL EAP class would ease the students' transition to medical studies, be relevant to their health-care interests without relying on specialist knowledge, and help build transferable academic competencies such as critical thinking.

The PBL course that Wood and Head describe was designed to simulate medical diagnostic problem-solving. It consisted of small-group presentations of unnamed diseases (i.e., not identified by the presenters), with the listening groups charged with arriving at accurate identification through attentive listening and note-taking, followed by research on the Internet, and culminating in collaboratively written reports offering a diagnosis supported by evidence-based reasoning. Members of the presenting groups responded to and evaluated the work of the reporting groups as well as self-evaluated their own effectiveness as presenters in view of the reports. The benefits of engaging in this process, according to Wood and Head, were many. The students' motivation was apparently high, as they enjoyed collaboratively challenging each other and meeting the challenges posed by fellow student groups. Again from Wood and Head's perspective, PBL enabled them, as instructors, to overcome limitations in specialist knowledge, material resources, and preparation time, and thus to offer the course that they felt the students needed, essentially an EAP class with medical content—a course with all the usual academic communication objectives of EAP but with the added relevance of medical subject matter and added value of problem-solving skill-building.

A final recent attempt at a PBL approach in a language class is notable because of its efforts to move beyond the usual simulated problem-solving of PBL. While Flowerdew (2005) does not use the term PBL in the description of her hybrid EAP and EOP (English for Occupational Purposes) course at Hong Kong University of Science and Technology, which was designed to prepare students for academic and workplace communication demands, her approach has many of the hallmarks of PBL. Like Barron, Flowerdew asked her students to collaboratively analyze real-world problems in Hong Kong by collecting data outside the classroom, forcing the students to interact with people in various settings. When the students wrote their reports, they were urged to envision as audience not their instructor and fellow students but those actually in a position to address the problems, e.g., university authorities or other organizations, such as the Hong Kong Environmental Protection Department. In some cases, Flowerdew notes, letters were actually sent to these officials and some student recommendations for change, at the university level, seriously considered or actually adopted. Students thus were not simply empowered in the usual academic sense, in terms of reaching academic communication goals, or even just in the usual future-oriented PBL sense—that is, with regard to preparation for work beyond the classroom. Flowerdew's students were given the opportunity to see themselves as change agents, able to contribute to the visibility of some issues and even serve as catalysts for small-scale changes. It may be difficult to imagine how such a truly real-world, social action approach could be adopted in an EMP, or ENP, class, but a focus on public health education or advocacy issues might provide the type of issue-oriented foundation upon which to attempt to develop such a PBL course.

Offering a medical English course, especially in an EFL environment with limited English-language resources, as Wood and Head have observed, can pose particular challenges with regard to course development (but see also Bosher & Smalkoski, 2002, on challenges faced by ENP course developers in an ESL, i.e., English-dominant, setting). Yet there is an obvious need, as Chia, Johnson, Chia, and Olive (1999) discovered in their survey of medical language needs at a university in Taiwan, for greater EMP development in order to achieve a number of communicative objectives arguably increasingly relevant in the global context of medical communication. Based on their needs assessment, Chia et al. determined that there was a need for EMP courses with more role playing and problem solving to provide realistic contexts for listening and speaking practice, greater use of authentic reading materials to promote fluent reading without translation, more use of medical research literature as materials for evidence-based writing, and more emphasis on the teaching of medical vocabulary in context, which is valuable for all EIL (English as an International Language) medical language use. PBL could facilitate the meeting of all of these goals.

Considering our current state of knowledge, PBL seems the ideal solution to the problem of meeting the combined objectives of communicative language teaching, English for specific purposes, and contemporary medical, or more specifically, nursing, education, in various local contexts around the world (or "glocal" contexts, in which the global and local interact; see Belcher, 2006, p. 134). Although PBL was originally developed in the West (in Canada), it has now been adopted by nursing education programs in a number of non-Western countries (e.g., for PBL in China see Zhang & Zhang, 2000; in Egypt, Habib, Eshra, Weaver, Newcomer, O'Donnell, & Neff-Smith, 1999; in Korea, Yang, 2006). Publications on the use of PBL in English language courses notably describe courses that have taken place in non-Western settings. In that local PBL course designers can choose the problems most relevant for their students to consider, this approach offers a means of tailoring a curriculum to local needs with materials chosen, adapted, or created by local residents. The collective approach to problem solving at the heart of PBL moves learning away from the individually oriented competitiveness often identified with the West and, in fact, often criticized by many Westerners themselves (on PBL's compatibility with ancient Chinese educational philosophy see Lee, Wong, & Mok, 2004). Of course, it remains an open question just how effective PBL might prove to be for an English for Nursing Purposes (or other ESP) curriculum in any particular context, whether EFL or ESL—a question that those who are themselves immersed in and knowledgeable about their own unique local situations are in the best position to address.

* * *

DIANE BELCHER, Professor of Applied Linguistics at Georgia State University, is former co-editor of the journal *English for Specific Purposes* and incoming co-editor of *TESOL Quarterly*. She co-edits the teacher reference series *Michigan Series on Teaching Multilingual Writers* and has co-edited three special issues of the *Journal of Second Language Writing* as well as four books on advanced academic literacy, the most recent of which is *The Oral-Literate Connection: Perspectives on L2 Speaking, Writing, and Other Media Interactions.*

REFERENCES

Albanese, M. (2000). Problem-based learning: Why curricula are likely to show little effect on knowledge and clinical skills. *Medical Education, 34*, 729–738.

Albanese, M., & Mitchell, S. (1993). Problem-based learning: A review of the literature on its outcomes and implementation issues. *Academic Medicine, 68*, 52–81.

Barron, C. (2002). Problem-solving and EAP: Themes and issues in a collaborative teaching venture. *English for Specific Purposes, 22*, 297–314.

Belcher, D. (2006). English for specific purposes: Teaching to perceived needs and imagined futures in worlds of work, study, and everyday life. *TESOL Quarterly, 40*, 133–156.

Biley, F., & Smith, K. (1998). Exploring the potential of problem-based learning in nurse education. *Nurse Education Today, 18*, 353–361.

Bosher, S., & Smalkoski, K. (2002). From needs analysis to curriculum development: Designing a course in health-care communication for immigrant students in the USA. *English for Specific Purposes, 21*, 59–79.

Brown, H. D. (2001). *Teaching by principles: An interactive approach to language pedagogy* (2nd ed.). White Plains, NY: Longman.

Celce-Murcia, M. (2001). Language teaching approaches: An overview. In M. Celce-Murcia (Ed.), *Teaching English as a second or foreign language* (3rd ed., pp. 3–11). Boston: Heinle & Heinle.

Chia, H., Johnson, R., Chia, H., & Olive, F. (1999). English for college students in Taiwan: A study of perceptions of English needs in a medical context. *English for Specific Purposes, 18,* 107–119.

Connolly, C., & Seneque, M. (1999). Evaluating problem-based learning in a multilingual student population. *Medical Education, 33,* 738–744.

Crookes, G. (2003). *A practicum in TESOL: Professional development through teaching practice.* Cambridge, UK: Cambridge University Press.

Ellis, R. (1997). *Second language acquisition.* New York: Oxford University Press.

Flowerdew, L. (2005). Integrating traditional and critical approaches to syllabus design: The 'what', the 'how' and the 'why?' *Journal of English for Academic Purposes, 4,* 135–147.

Habib, F., Eshra, D. K., Weaver, J., Newcomer, W., O'Donnell, C., & Neff-Smith, M. (1999). Problem-based learning: A new approach for nursing education in Egypt. *Journal of Multicultural Nursing and Health, 5,* 6–11.

Hall, B., & Allan, J. (1994). Self in relation: A prolegomenon for holistic nursing. *Nursing Outlook, 42,* 110–116.

Holliday, A. (1992). Tissue rejection and informal orders in ELT projects: Collecting the right information. *Applied Linguistics, 13*(4), 403–424.

Lee, M. L., Wong, F. K. Y., & Mok, E. S. B. (2004). Problem-based learning: Ancient Chinese educational philosophy reflected in a modern educational methodology. *Nurse Education Today, 24,* 136–144.

Margetson, D. (1991). Why is problem-based learning a challenge? In D. Boud & G. Feletti (Eds.), *The challenge of problem-based learning* (pp. 42–50). London: Kogan Page.

Maudsley, G. (1999) Do we all mean the same thing by "problem-based learning"? A review of the concepts and formulation of the ground rules. *Academic Medicine, 74*(2), 178–185.

Pennycook, A. (1994). *The cultural politics of English as an international language.* London: Longman.

Richards, J., & Lockhart, C. (1996). *Reflective teaching in second language classrooms.* Cambridge, UK: Cambridge University Press.

Rideout, E., & Carpio, B. (2001). The problem-based learning model of nursing education. In E. Rideout (Ed.), *Transforming nursing education through problem-based learning* (pp. 21–49). Sudbury, MA: Jones & Bartlett.

Sanders, L. (2009, April 12). Vision quest. *New York Times Magazine,* pp. 19–20.

Savigon, S. (2001). Communicative language teaching for the twenty-first century. In M. Celce-Murcia (Ed.), *Teaching English as a second or foreign language* (3rd ed., pp. 13–28). Boston: Heinle & Heinle.

Schmidt, H. (1983). Problem-based learning: Rationale and description. *Medical Education, 17,* 11–16.

———. (1993). Foundations of problem-based learning: Some explanatory notes. *Medical Education, 27,* 422–432.

Schmidt, H., Lipkin, M., deVries, M., & Greep, J. (Eds.). (1989). *New directions for medical education: Problem-based learning and community-oriented medical education.* New York: Springer-Verlag.

Stepien, W., Gallagher, S., & Workman, D. (1993). Problem-based learning for traditional and interdisciplinary classrooms. *Journal for the Education of the Gifted, 16,* 338–357.

Tompkins, C. (2001). Nursing education for the twenty-first century. In E. Rideout (Ed.), *Transforming nursing education through problem-based learning* (pp. 1–19). Sudbury, MA: Jones & Bartlett.

Valainis, B. (2000). Professional nursing practice in an HMO: The future is now. *Journal of Nursing Education, 39,* 13–20.

Wood, A., & Head, M. (2004). 'Just what the doctor ordered': The application of problem-based learning to EAP. *English for Specific Purposes, 23,* 3–17.

Yang, B. S. (2006). A study on the adapting process of nursing students to problem-based learning. *Taehan Kanho Hakhoe Chi, 36,* 25–36 (in Korean).

Zhang, X., & Zhang, X. (2000). To apply problem-based learning teaching model install course of basic skills and tactics for problem solving. *Shanxi Nursing Journal, 14,* 25–26 (in Chinese).

Part 3

ENGLISH FOR
SOCIOCULTURAL
PURPOSES

12

English for Community Membership: Planning for Actual and Potential Needs

HELEN DE SILVA JOYCE
Community and Migrant Education, Australia

SUSAN HOOD
University of Technology, Sydney

It is a commonsense that if any person is going to be a member of any community, he must know the language of that community, because language is only one that can help you a lot in becoming a members of any community—to express your feelings and use you talents for community and yourself.
Sumit, a student in the NSW Adult Migrant English Service, 2006

Abstract

A major tension underlies the design of English language programs for enabling community membership. On the one hand there is a pressure to respond to a diverse range of specific and immediate needs for language use. At the same time there is an imperative to build the potential of learners to use language beyond specific instances. This chapter explores one response to this tension in the form of a large-scale curriculum designed for adult immigrants in Australia. The chapter articulates the underlying theory of the curriculum and illustrates in practical examples how such theory is enacted.

English for Sociocultural Purposes (ESCP) forms a subcategory of ESP in this volume, distinguished here from both EOP and EAP. In this sense ESCP might be interpreted as addressing all purposes for learning English that are neither academic nor occupational in focus. Alternatively ESCP might be considered as all-encompassing. After all, what purposes are there for language interactions that are neither social nor cultural? A focus on English for Community Membership (ECM) hardly reduces the potential scope, although in this chapter we assume a context in which English is widely used in the community (an ESL rather than an EFL context). While necessarily broad in scope, the inclusion of ESCP and ECM as general categories of specific purpose acknowledges that beyond the domains of work and academic pursuit (and in many ways impacting on them) are other realms of interaction that may equally and importantly form the focus for English language study.

Here we interpret English for Community Membership as referring to programs of language learning primarily designed for adult immigrants and refugees, which aim to facilitate entry into and participation in a spectrum of community life other than work or formal study. In whatever ways English is seen as providing access to community membership, such membership can be high stakes for individual learners (Australian Government Publishing Service, 1986; Lo Bianco, 1987). However, it is also high stakes for the community itself in terms of being an inclusive community where capacity for "participatory association" (Somers, 1993, p. 587) is available to all. The potential social and cultural gains for the individual and for the community as a whole become more critical in a global context in which increased migration can be met with surges in excluding nationalism (Hage, 2003).

Programs that focus on English for community membership present very considerable challenges for course designers. The umbrella descriptor of *community membership* generalizes across a considerable diversity of social purposes or genres. These genres accommodate an extensive range of fields of activity within which learners will take up a multitude of social roles and interpersonal relations enacted across a complex of multimodal interactions. Locations of community membership are likely to include multiple formal and informal institutional and social sites and activities. The significance of language will of course vary from site to site, from community to community, and in relation to available language support services.

The diversity of contexts is likely to be matched by a diversity of learner profiles, including differences in sociocultural and linguistic backgrounds, in levels of proficiency, in levels of education, and in the extent to which learners are literate in another language. Important too are personal circumstances including family structures, income sources, physical and mental health issues, and the kinds of support resources available in the community. There will also be diversity in the short-term and long-term goals of the learners, with both predictable and less predictable circumstances of immediate concern, as well as evolving expectations and desires.

Issues of Specification and Generalization in Course Design in ECM

When we consider the design of ECM courses, the diversity of contexts of use, together with the diversity of learner profiles, imposes a pressure to proliferate kinds of specificity. This may mean proliferation in discrete narrowly targeted courses as exemplified, for example, in *English for Parents of Primary-Aged Children* (Cornish, 1983) or *English for Childbirth* (Weston, 2006). Alternatively it may result in a proliferation of contexts within a more generally focused course as teachers aim to accommodate the many individual needs and circumstances of learners. Such a pressure will be exaggerated in a progressive pedagogy that foregrounds individual needs, and less marked under the influence of a traditional structural syllabus that offers a fixed progression of syntactic structures (see Feez, 1998). However, the pressure to attend to immediate community contexts brings with it a number of important challenges. For example, it can result in a lack of structured course content and visible curriculum goals or pathways. This can add to the stress of the unknown so keenly felt by many refugee and immigrant students (Burton, 1991; McPherson, 1997). Moreover, it is important to ensure that a focus on the here-and-now needs of individuals or groups does not function to trap learners in the instance. It is vital that students are able to build their linguistic potential, to generalize in ways that equip them to successfully interact in a wide range of contexts and, with ongoing learning, in their chosen fields of endeavor. In other words the process of recontextualization of real-world interactions into a pedagogic framework imposes a pressure to constrain and sequence potential content in some principled way, enabling pathways to be planned and resources to be developed for cohorts of students. So against a current of specificity and proliferation runs a counter current toward generalization and consolidation. This tension is a major theme explored in this chapter, in the context of a case study of course design in a particular English teaching program for newly arrived adult immigrants and refugees to Australia.[1]

In the program, community membership is one of three curriculum strands that structure pathways of learning for students. The other curriculum strands focus on job seeking and participating in work and further study. These syllabus strands are developed within a five-level curriculum framework: Preliminary Course and Certificates I, II, III, and IV in Spoken and Written English (CSWE) (NSW AMES, 2003) (see Feez, 2002, for a detailed account of the development of this framework). This curriculum framework is intended to provide visible pathways that progressively scaffold language learning while enabling relevant contextualization and flexibility to respond to changing, emerging, and often urgent learner needs. In exploring this particular program, we consider first some of the theoretical concepts that underpin the approach taken. We then look in more depth at how these concepts are built into the curriculum framework and interpreted by individual teachers in the design of courses and the enactment of pedagogic practices.

Some Theoretical Foundations for ECM Course Design

The CSWE curriculum framework draws its theoretical foundation from the systemic functional model of language (SFL) (Halliday, 1994; Martin, 1992; Martin & Rose, 2008). Fundamental to the systemic functional model is a social perspective on language, and so a social perspective on language learning. SFL theory has been a valuable point of reference in building a consistent and theoretically motivated concept of *purpose* in teaching language for specific purposes (e.g., Christie & Martin, 1997; Hasan & Williams, 1996; Ravelli & Ellis, 2004). Two concepts that are most significant are those of *genre* and *register*.

---

[1] The New South Wales Adult Migrant English Service (NSW AMES) delivers the Adult Migrant English Program (AMEP) to immigrants and refugees under contract to the Department of Immigration and Citizenship (DIAC). The AMEP is a nationally funded ESL program that has been delivered since the early 1950s. Migrants arriving in Australia under certain visa categories are entitled to 510 hours of tuition while some refugees have an entitlement of between 610 and 910 hours.

Genre

In functional linguistic terms, "genres are defined as a recurrent configuration of meanings [which] enact the social practices of a given culture" (Martin & Rose, 2008, p. 6). This implies a concern not only with the specific way in which meanings are configured in any one genre, but with "how [genres] relate to one another" (Martin & Rose, 2008, p. 6). This conceptualization of genre has important implications for the design of programs for learning English.

From an interpretation of culture as a meaning potential and of genres as evolved systematizations of this meaning potential, relations between genres can then be described in terms of kinds of meanings. Distinctions can be made, for example, between genres that function to represent a factual world and genres that function to tell stories. Factual genres can be distinguished between those that function to instruct and those that function to inform. Genres that instruct might also be distinguished in terms of whether they enable action, in which case we label them *procedure*, or whether they restrict action, in which case we label them *protocol* (Martin & Rose, 2008, p. 6). Such a perspective on genre can be represented as a partial system network, as in Figure 12.1, adapted from Martin and Rose (2008, p. 7).

Alternatively, we can consider relationships from a more topological perspective where we map them as similar or different against more than one semantic feature. This is represented at a basic level in Figure 12.2, adapted

FIGURE 12.1

A Partial System Network of Genres

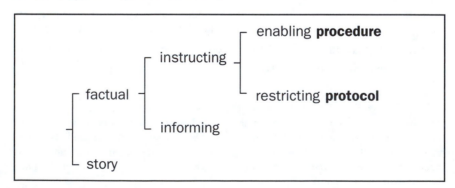

Source: Adapted from Martin & Rose (2008, p. 7).

FIGURE 12.2

Mapping Genres against Semantic Features

	– GENERALIZED	+ GENERALIZED
– Activity structured	description	report
+ Activity structured	recount	procedure

Source: Adapted from Martin (1992, p. 563).

from Martin (1992, p. 563). This matrix of just two semantic features, +/– generalization and +/– activity structured, configures four genres (in small caps).

Working from the mapping of similarities and differences in genres, as illustrated in Figure 12.2, a range of potential sequences emerges that can inform program design. Beginning, for example, with a focus on *description*—that is, on factual accounts of the features and characteristics of specific phenomena—a program of learning might then shift to retelling specific events as "recounts." Alternatively the focus might shift from describing specific entities as descriptions to describing generalized categories of entities as factual reports. Certain kinds of meanings and language thus retain a focus while other meanings and new language are introduced. Activity structured genres such as recounts and procedures afford texts in which action processes are dominant. Other kinds of genres such as descriptions and reports focus on entities rather than activities and so afford more **being** and **having** processes.

Applying Genre as a Curriculum Framing Resource in CSWE

The CSWE is a genre-based curriculum and at each level of the curriculum the scope of genres build a repertoire of meaning-making resources to enable diverse kinds of interaction in the community.

The sequencing of genres across levels of the curriculum, as well as within levels, takes into consideration the relationships between genres. For example, outcomes for learners at Level 1 of the curriculum include the genre of description in spoken and written modes and descriptions of specific entities—*Can write a short description.* At Level 2, the outcomes shift to the genre of information reports and generalized phenomena—*Can write a short information report.* We can also see that the resources developed at Level 1, e.g., *Can conduct a short telephone conversation,* may become foundational for genres at higher levels of the curriculum, e.g., *Can negotiate a spoken transaction to obtain information.* Elemental genres, e.g., *Can tell a short recount,* can build into more complex macro-genres, e.g., *Can participate in a short conversation involving a recount.*

Other considerations in sequencing outcomes across levels of the curriculum include the amount of discourse that students need to produce or comprehend, as illustrated in these genres across different curriculum levels.

CSWE I	CSWE II	CSWE III
Can write a short recount (about 50 words)	Can write a recount (about 100 words)	
Can complete a short application form	Can complete a (longer) formatted text	
	Can write a short report (about 100 words)	Can write a report (about 150 words)

Genres enable the potential expanse of cultural meanings to be mapped so that considerations of purpose for language learning can be made at a high level of generality. These general statements of purpose can then be sequenced in the curriculum in principled, purposeful ways. Genres provide a means by which connections can be made from one instance of interaction to other interactions. So it is one key means for managing the tension between the specific and the general in a pedagogic context. However, as we have seen, the configurations of purposes for language learning in the CSWE framework extend beyond the selection and sequencing of genres to include consideration of other contextual variables such as register.

Register

The idea of contextualizing language use has been a characteristic of most language teaching pedagogies since the emergence of communicative language teaching in the late 1970s and early 1980s. In some cases, this amounted to no more than an artificial placement of syntactic structures in an imagined dialogue, in which any sense that language varied with context was absent. In other cases a genuine topic focus might generate examples of real world texts. In a progressive pedagogy, the opportunity to engage was foregrounded over knowledge of language as system. In a traditional pedagogy, topic or text choice remained largely unconnected to syntactic structures, with the latter remaining the dominant strand in course sequencing. In either case the language-context connection was little more than arbitrary.

From an SFL perspective, the relationship of language to context is theorized as varying in systematic and predictable ways. The context or register of an interaction is modelled along three dimensions—field, tenor, and mode. *Field* refers to the social action or the activity that is taking place. In the context of ECM, relevant fields might be finding rental accommodation or catching public transportation. Field implicates the kinds of grammar and discourse systems that construe ideational meanings. *Tenor* refers to the social roles of participants in an interaction, and the relationships of status and solidarity that characterize those relationships. Social roles implicated in an interaction may be as fellow travellers on the public transportation system sharing frustration and a degree of solidarity at the lateness of the train, or as a member of the public seeking assistance from an insurance company. Tenor implicates the kind of grammar and discourse patterns that express interpersonal meanings. *Mode* refers to the part that language plays in the interaction, along with other ways of making meanings, and so has to do with the ways meanings are organized and coordinated in any interaction. Modes of interaction may vary, for example, from a telephone-mediated exchange about transportation options to the reading of a timetable text that includes verbal and visual elements. Mode implicates the kind of grammar and discourse choices that construct textual meanings.

We also need to incorporate the notion of register into curriculum planning at a general system level and to make generalized predictions of pathways in relation to the register variables of field, tenor, and mode. Most relevant here is the work of Macken-Horarik (1996), who represents domains of cultural learning as a generalized pathway from everyday kinds of interactions to specialized encounters to contexts for reflexive interaction. She characterizes a general progression of language learning across these cultural domains, functioning along the three dimensions of register. Field is interpreted as the content or knowledge encoded in a curriculum. Knowledge progresses along a trajectory from commonsense knowledge relevant to everyday life, through more specialized discipline-based knowledge that builds expert status, to critical knowledge that enables reflexive engagement and critique. Learning to express oneself in various roles and relationships (tenor) progresses from everyday familiar community roles through more socially distant and impersonalized relationships afforded by specialized domains, to managing contingencies of diverse roles in reflexive domains. Learning to organize constructions of meaning (mode) progresses from everyday face-to-face interactions in which language is part of the action, to the practices of specialized domains where written texts dominate, to the reflexive domain where we learn "language for challenging reality" and to manage multiple technologies of interaction (Macken-Horarik, 1996, p. 241).

Applying Register in Course Design

The modelling of progression along dimensions of register is evident to some extent in the sequencing of outcomes across levels of the CSWE curriculum. Mode, for example, is implicated in such learning outcomes as *Can tell a short recount* (CSWE I) and *Can read an informal letter* (CSWE II). Field shifts from the more everyday and familiar to more specialist content are evident in learning outcomes such as *Can respond to spoken instructions in the context of learning* (CSWE I) and *Can demonstrate understanding of a spoken information text* (CSWE II). Tenor is implicated in the sequence of learning outcomes *Can express personal viewpoint in a written description* (CSWE I) and *Can write a short opinion text* (CSWE II).

The application of register variables in framing progression is also important in planning sequences within specific syllabuses or courses of learning. The general curriculum framework of the CSWE allows for considerable flexibility in this regard. It becomes the role of the teacher or syllabus designer to contextualize outcome statements in terms of particular register configurations—that is, in terms of specific fields of social activity, social roles, and modes of interaction.

Field

At syllabus level, the dominant choice for planning sequences of learning in register terms is field, expressed as topics or themes. Typically teachers or syllabus designers identify themes from the stated goals of the learners and/or their own knowledge of community contexts. The themes provide a broad categorization of syllabus content, and are likely to include areas such as Health, Transportation, Accommodation, Shopping, The Neighborhood, School, The Media, Friends and Family, Local Services, and Leisure.

Once a theme has been identified, the teacher then needs to specify the content or knowledge to be incorporated in the syllabus under this theme. The principles of progression outlined by Macken-Horarik provide general guidance in terms of a trajectory from commonsense knowledge in fields of frequent participation to more specialist and critical language interactions in the community. However, the syllabus designer also needs to consider the genres and specific kinds of texts within which field knowledge will be enacted. This process is illustrated in Figure 12.3, which presents guidance given to teachers in designing programs of learning around the theme of *Public Transport*.

Depending on the characteristics or goals of the learners, teachers may decide to limit the texts they cover within a theme when designing units of work, focusing on those texts that are most crucial to community participation or that respond to learners' stated interests.

FIGURE 12.3

Steps in Developing Content within a Theme

TOPIC – PUBLIC TRANSPORT	
1. Identify goal	To develop spoken and written language skills required to make effective use of public transport system
2. Outline the sociocultural knowledge that needs to be integrated into the topic	• the transport system • ticketing procedures and the role of ticket inspectors • sources of transport information
3. Consider the situations of language use within the community context	• reading timetables • reading transport route maps • inquiring about schedules/delays • buying a ticket in a face-to-face exchange /by machine • listening to transport announcements
4. List the texts arising from these situations	• timetables • maps • service encounter—inquiry about schedules/delays • service encounter—buying a ticket • procedural text—instructions for ticket machine • platform announcements

Source: Adapted from Burns & Joyce (1997, p. 77). Reproduced by permission of Macmillan Education Australia.

FIGURE 12.4

General Outcomes Integrated into Themes

TRANSPORTATION	HEALTH	AROUND THE HOUSE	LEISURE
• Ticket machine instructions • Asking directions	• Medicine labels • Doctor's instructions • Outpatient surgery instructions • Healthy eating guides	• Food labels • Cleaning product labels • Appliance instructions • Recipes	• Water safety instructions • First aid procedures • Camping instructions

In a syllabus organized around selected fields or themes, key genres can be revisited in different fields of social activity, enabling students to build generalizable knowledge in terms of text structure and language features. They can learn to recognize the distinguishing features of different genres, to appreciate the social purposes, and to manage some of the critical language resources they entail. The aim is therefore to attend to both the specific contexts of most relevance to learners while building generalizable and transferable knowledge about language. Figure 12.4 provides an example of guidance for teachers in how the genre of *procedure* might be integrated into a range of common themes in ECM courses.

Tenor

At each level of the CSWE, attention is also paid to the contextual dimension of tenor. Learners are introduced to a range of tenor relationships from those of solidarity among familiar equals in conversational exchanges to more formal transactional exchanges characterized by differences in power. At lower levels, students undertake tasks such as identifying the relationship between speakers in listening texts. At higher levels, they begin to focus on the way speakers and writers express their opinions and feelings. This is exemplified in Figure 12.5, presenting an extract of teaching materials developed for Level 3.

FIGURE 12.5

Sample Materials from Level 3

Cathy is certain that she returned the missing book. She uses stress to express her certainty.

a. Listen to the excerpts from the conversation again. Repeat what Cathy says.

b.

- *Yes. I looked last night. But I know I returned it. I brought all the books in before the due date. Now I need to borrow some books again but I was told yesterday I had to pay.*

- *But what if it's not my mistake? I'm really careful with the books I borrow. I always return them in time, and if I can't, I renew them over the phone.*

Source: Adapted from NSW AMES learning materials 2005. Reproduced by permission of NSW AMES.

Mode

Mode refers to the role that language plays in the interaction. This includes the mode of communication as spoken or written, but also the role that language plays in relation to other semiotic systems such as visual imaging. Mode also refers to whether the interaction is one-way as in a spoken broadcast or written discourse or whether there is immediate feedback as in face-to-face casual conversation or computer chat-rooms.

To become participating members of the community, immigrants and refugees need to engage with a range of texts in different modes, including spoken, written, visual, and multimodal texts. They also need to know how these texts interrelate in social contexts of language use. The concept of mode as a variable of language register is an important element in course design in the CSWE. Themes are often divided into units of work that follow the sequence of activities within the social domains of the community. These units focus on the different texts that form participation sequences, as seen in Figure 12.6, representing an example from the theme of health.

Integrating Field, Tenor, and Mode

While it is useful to differentiate different dimensions of register to explore the role they play in organizing teaching and learning in ECM, it is also

FIGURE 12.6

A Social Sequence of Texts Related to the Theme of Health

THEME – HEALTH SERVICES								
Participation Sequence								
Make appointment	→	See doctor	→	Make medical claim	→	Fill prescription	→	Read medicine labels
Sequence of Spoken and Written Texts around a Medical Consultation								
Face-to-face service encounter (spoken) Telephone service encounter (spoken: mediated) Appointment card (written)		Doctor's consultation (spoken)		Form (written)		Face-to-face service encounter (spoken) Info text (spoken)		Procedural text (written) Information about medicine (written)

Source: Adapted from Burns & Joyce (1997, p.75). Reproduced by permission of Macmillan Education Australia.

important to be aware that as one dimension of register shifts, so other variables are implicated. So, for example, in a sequence of teaching and learning around the theme of transportation, students might begin with engagement with a field at a commonsense level as they recount everyday personal experiences in catching public transportation. This then becomes the basis for a more specialized level of engagement with issues of transportation as students examine proposed changes to services. Finally they move on to a critical engagement in the joint drafting of a letter to a local member of parliament, arguing for the transportation needs of members of the community. If we revisit this sequence from a tenor perspective, we see a parallel shift from engagement with others as interested co-members of the public, to being the recipient of implicitly persuasive *factual* press releases, to an unequal relationship of individual to bureaucracy. Mode also shifts from face-to-face interaction with accompanying gestures and facial expressions to written or computer-mediated modes.

Importantly, the register variables of field, tenor, and mode provide a multidimensional framework for considering notions of task difficulty and linguistic challenge, and so progression in course design. This progression is illustrated in Figure 12.7, presenting a set of sample materials from ECM courses across three levels of the CSWE. As learners progress, they engage with increasingly challenging interactions within the same general field of the language of tenancy. However, shifts in aspects of this field implicate

---

FIGURE 12.7

A Sample Progression of Reading Texts around the Theme of Tenancy

CSWE I
I live in an old flat but it is very comfortable. The flat is on the second floor. It's got a large living room but it doesn't have a dining room. It's got two bedrooms, a small bathroom and a lovely big sunny kitchen. It also has a garage downstairs and a big sunny garden. I really like this flat because it is near schools, shops and the train station.

CSWE II
Aston $360 pw. Unit 3 bedroom. Spacious 3BR apartment., Air-conditioning, security, built-in wardrobes, internal laundry, lounge, kitchen/dining area, balcony, car space. Quiet location close to transport and amenities.

CSWE III
On 27 March, you inspected the above unit and I pointed out some problems, which required immediate attention. The most pressing problems were: • the shower screen was badly cracked and water was seeping through the screen onto the floor and into the bedroom • the bedroom carpet was starting to rot and there was a damp smell at all times. You assured me that prompt action would be taken on these problems. However six weeks after the inspection no action has occurred. The seepage of water through to the bedroom is worsening and the damp carpet is becoming a health hazard in the bedroom.

Source: NSW AMES learning materials (2005). Reproduced by permission of NSW AMES.

both genres, and other register variables of tenor and mode. As students move from Level 1 to Level 3, they move from a simple first person description of where they live, to an advertisement for accommodation, to describing problems in a letter demanding action from a real estate agent. The increasing linguistic demands may be in terms of more technical and specialized lexis, an expanded repertoire of linguistic systems such as tense, thematization, and modality, and a broader range of evaluative resources.

Sequencing Discourse Semantics and Grammar in Course Design

In the CSWE curriculum framework, each of the learning outcomes is elaborated somewhat to give an indication of the kind of discourse anticipated, and this is exemplified again in actual instances of interaction. The general learning outcomes of the curriculum are then contextualized in ways that are relevant to specific groups of learners. The doctor's consultation, as illustrated in Figure 12.8, is an example of the macro-genre of a doctor's consultation, commonly introduced within a theme of health. The text is sourced from an authentic exchange and is presented as a model for teachers to draw on as fits their program.

Certain genres implicate certain kinds of linguistic systems and these are also generalizable across texts. For example, the imperative mood is critical in the teaching of procedural genres, and is dominant in the examination stage of the doctor-patient consultation. The actualization of genres in specific contexts and texts becomes the basis for identifying more specific language learning objectives.

Authentic texts provide models for teaching, encouraging teachers to attend to the generic structure, discourse semantic, and lexico-grammatical features of texts. In this way, grammar as language choice is explicitly attended to in a context where the social purpose is apparent. Chosen instances of grammatical choice can then be represented as instances within a system of choices, once again bridging between the specific and the general, and providing opportunities for learners to build their linguistic potential and to develop their capacity to participate in community life beyond the instance.

While specific texts afford attention to specific grammatical choices and systems, there are some general notions of progression in grammatical terms associated with the sequencing of genres and registers in the overarching curriculum framework. There is a progression from more everyday and

FIGURE 12.8

Stages and Grammatical Features of a Doctor's Consultation

STAGES	SOME LANGUAGE SYSTEMS FOR SPECIFIC ATTENTION	SCHEMATIC STRUCTURE
Opening Doctor: *Come in and take a seat.* Patient: *Thanks.*	Imperative mood	
Eliciting Symptoms Doctor: *What seems to be the trouble?* Patient: *I've got this rash on my arm.* Doctor: *Has it been itchy?* Patient: *Yes.* Doctor: *When did it first appear?* Patient: *About a week ago.* Doctor: *Any other symptoms? Like sore eyes?* Patient: *Yes my eyes have been stinging a little.* Doctor: *Can you think of anything which may have caused it? Food or anything?* Patient: *Well it started after I'd been gardening on the weekend.*	Wh- interrogatives Declaratives; body/symptom lexis; circumstantial info Polar interrogatives Polar interrogatives Ellipsis in answers; circum-stantial info Ellipsis in questions Symptom lexis Causality Ellipsis in questions Sequencing in time; circumstantial info	Dialogic exchange of information
Examination Doctor: *OK, roll your sleeve up and I'll take a look ... Turn your arm over ... Uh uh ... Open your mouth and I'll look at your throat ...OK, now tilt your head back and I'll have a look at your eyes ... OK, you can roll your sleeve down now.*	Imperative mood; commonsense lexis for body	Monologic procedure
Diagnosis Doctor: *It looks like an allergic reaction to something probably something in the garden.*	Causality; modality	Monologic explanation
Treatment Doctor: *I'll give you some capsules to take and some cream for the arm. Rub the cream in twice a day and it should clear up.*	Semi-technical medical lexis; Imperative mood; modality	Monologic procedure
(Inquiry) Patient: *Do you think I should have allergy tests?*	Polar interrogatives; modality	Dialogic exchange of information
(Response to Inquiry) Doctor: *We might run some tests to check for allergic reactions, if it doesn't clear up in say a week. OK?*	Modality; causality; clause complex; semi-technical lexis	
Closing Patient: *Fine, thanks doctor.* Doctor: *OK, Bye.* Patient: *See ya.*		Formulaic closing

Source: Adapted from Burns & Joyce (1999, p. 95). Reproduced by permission of Macmillan Education Australia.

FIGURE 12.9

An Example of Teaching Materials Drawing Attention to Grammatical Metaphor

16	Read about nominalisation.

Nominalisation is when a verb group is changed into a noun group. We use nominalisation when we write an exposition because it gives our writing authority and makes our opinion sound objective and powerful.

Compare the following sentences.

> *Research shows that older people* **fail to turn up for work less often than younger people do.**
>
> *Research shows that older workers have* **lower levels of absenteeism.**

In the second sentence the action expressed by the verb group has become a thing. This makes the sentence more compact and sound more objective and powerful.

17	Match the parts of the sentence in italics with the nominalised forms the writer uses in the exposition.

a The government needs to provide *opportunities so that people can learn the right skills and knowledge for the job.*

b There will *be insufficient people who can do those jobs that require special skills.*

c *When people are treated unfairly because they are older, it is* a real problem in the work force.

d Older people are a *group who can provide many of the important skills that our country needs.*

e 50 year olds are *the largest number of people who have been unemployed for long periods of time.*

f There are *fewer women who are giving birth* in Australia.

g Older people experience *a stronger feeling that they are fulfilled and rewarded by the work they do* than younger people.

- age discrimination
- the largest group of long term unemployed
- falling fertility rates
- more job satisfaction
- skills shortages
- appropriate training
- valuable resource

<u>Source</u>: Adapted from NSW AMES learning materials (2005). Reproduced by permission of NSW AMES.

congruent to more specialized and abstract kinds of language as learners progress from lower levels of the curriculum to higher levels. Critical to the management of this progression is what is referred to in SFL theory as *grammatical metaphor*. Very briefly, this refers to grammatical choices that skew the commonsense relationships of structure and function. Put simply, it can mean, for example, that rather than processes being realized structurally as verbs *(inspect the property)*, they can be realized as nouns *(property inspection)*, or rather than an attribute being realized as an adjective *(make it clear)* it is realized in a nominal group *(seeking clarification)*. Developing control of resources of grammatical metaphor is critical if students are to engage in the more specialized and abstract kinds of interactions that characterize higher levels of the curriculum, and not surprisingly, considerable attention is given to supporting the teaching of grammar. One example of such focused attention on grammatical metaphor is evident in the extract from teaching materials in Figure 12.9.

This chapter has highlighted a key tension that characterizes the design of all ESP courses to some extent, but one that is especially pronounced in designing courses in English for Community Membership. This tension is the need to focus attention on specific, local, and often urgent language needs while ensuring that learners are not trapped in these instances. By theorizing the kinds of choices curriculum designers, syllabus designers, and materials writers have made, the chapter has attempted to build a bridge between specific instances and examples from one context to a broader potential of possibilities for other contexts. This potential might be taken up in application and/or research in a number of directions. The instance of curriculum design illustrated here may inform teacher education programs by providing grounding for theoretical discussions around principles of selection and sequencing of content. Alternatively, the theoretical constructs explored may offer a generalized potential that can frame further research both in ECM as well as in quite different contexts of English for Specific Purposes.

❋   ❋   ❋

HELEN DE SILVA JOYCE is the Director of Community and Migrant Education in the New South Wales Department of Education and Training. She has been involved in adult language and literacy education for more than 25 years. She has managed the development of nationally accredited curricula, has written and edited a wide range of teaching and learning resources for

adult and secondary education, and continues to lecture in teacher education at post-graduate level. Her research interests are classroom management and the language and literacy demands of different work contexts.

SUSAN HOOD is a Senior Lecturer in Applied Linguistics and TESOL at
the University of Technology, Sydney. Her research interests focus on the
intersection of linguistics and education in a range of contexts including
curriculum design and pedagogic practices. Her doctoral research was on
evaluation in academic writing, and more recently she has been researching the role of gesture in language teaching. She has taught in post-
graduate English language teacher education in Australia and Hong Kong.

REFERENCES

Australian Government Publishing Service (AGPS). (1986). *Towards active voice*:
Report of the Committee of Review of the Adult Migrant Education Program. Canberra: Author.

Burns, A., & Joyce, H. (1997). *Focus on speaking*. Sydney: Macquarie University.

Burton, J. (1991). Perceptions of learning in the AMEP. *Prospect: An Australian
Journal of Teaching/(TESOL)*, 7(1), 57–72.

Christie, F., & Martin, J. R. (Eds.). (1997). *Genres and institutions: Social processes
in the workplace and school*. London: Cassell.

Cornish, S. (1983). *Making contact: Your child's school*. Sydney: New South Wales
Adult Migrant English Service.

De Silva Joyce, H., & Burns, A. (1999). *Focus on grammar*. Sydney: Macquarie
University.

Feez, S. (1998). *Text-based syllabus design*. Sydney: New South Wales Adult Migrant
English Service & Macquarie University.

———. (2002). Heritage and innovation in second language education. In A. M.
Johns (Ed.), *Genre in the classroom*. Mahwah, NJ: Lawrence Erlbaum.

Hage, G. (2003). *Against paranoid nationalism: Searching for hope in a shrinking
society*. Sydney: Pluto Press.

Halliday, M. A. K. (1991). The notion of context in language education. In T. Le
& M. McCausland (Eds.), *Language education: Interaction and development* (pp.
1–26). Proceedings of the International Conference held in Ho Chi Minh City,
Vietnam.

———. (1994). *Introduction to functional grammar* (2nd ed.). London: Edward
Arnold.

Halliday, M. A. K., & Matthiessen, C. (1999). *Construing experience through meaning*. London: Continuum.

Hasan, R., & Williams, G. (Eds.). (1996). *Literacy in society*. London: Longman.

Lo Bianco, J. (1987). *National policy on languages*. Canberra: Australian Government Publishing Service.

Macken-Horarik, M. (1996). Literacy and learning across the curriculum: Towards a model of register for secondary school teachers. In R. Hasan & G. Williams (Eds.), *Literacy in society* (pp. 232–278). London: Longman.

Martin, J. R. (1992). *English text: System and structure*. Philadelphia: John Benjamins.

Martin, J. R., & Rose, D. (2008). *Genre relations: Mapping culture*. London: Equinox.

McPherson, P. (1997). Social and cultural difference in the classroom. In A. Burns and S. Hood (Eds.), *Teachers' voices 2: Teaching disparate learner groups* (pp. 26–36). Sydney: NCELTR Macquarie University.

NSW AMES (New South Wales Adult Migrant English Service). (2003). *Certificates I, II, III and IV in Spoken and Written English*. Sydney: Author.

———. (2005). *Learning materials*. Sydney: Author.

Ravelli, L., & Ellis, R. (Eds.). (2004). *Analysing academic writing: Contextualized frameworks*. London: Continuum.

Somers, M. R. (1993). Citizenship and the place of the public sphere: Law, community and political culture in the transition to democracy. *American Sociological Review, 58*, 587–620.

Weston, F. (2006). *The language of childbirth*. Sydney: New South Wales Adult Migrant English Service.

13

Critical Citizenship Practices in ESP and ESL Programs: Canadian and Global Perspectives

BRIAN MORGAN
York University, Toronto

DOUGLAS FLEMING
University of Ottawa, Canada

Abstract

ESP's focus on the pragmatic demands of language and texts within specific occupational and institutional settings might at first appear incompatible with the theoretical and ideological priorities that have shaped research in critical ESL pedagogies. This chapter, however, explores and advances a notion of complementarity between these two areas of ELT, particularly in respect to promoting a notion of critical citizenship in ESP and ESL classrooms. The chapter begins by drawing on the research literature to define both passive and participatory orientations toward citizenship theory and preparation. The ability of nation-states to promote coherent national

identities is then examined in light of globalization pressures
and the emergence of transnational, diasporic communities
intent on transforming and hybridizing the social spaces into
which they ostensibly assimilate. Such nation-state tensions
are examined in the specific context of Canada through its
provision of the Canadian Language Benchmarks (CLB).
The extent to which CLB serves as a "hidden curriculum" in
respect to normalizing a passive engagement with citizenship
practices is then detailed, particularly in light of the program
restrictions (e.g., funding, continuous intake classes) that
limit practitioners' interpretive responses. The concluding
section suggests a number of exemplary resources, including textbooks, classroom approaches, and two case studies.

This chapter explores two aspects of ESP that are especially relevant to citizenship preparation education in terms of transformative theory development and critical pedagogical practice. The first of these is ESP's focus on
the concrete aspects of the language needs of specific subject areas, occupa-
tions, and social groups. This is a characteristic that makes ESP distinct
from other forms of second language education (Master, 2005). The second
aspect is that of the emerging strength of critical perspectives within ESP
that have critiqued exclusively pragmatic and instrumental concerns within
the field (Benesch, 1994; Pennycook, 1997).

The intention is to contribute to an emerging awareness of complementary
research interests developing between ESP and critical pedagogies in second language education (see e.g., Belcher, 2006, pp. 142–144). Through its
occupational, institutional, and subject-specific rigor, ESP potentially offers
grounded micro-perspectives on language, power, and identity that have, at
times, been found lacking in the theoretical adventurism often prevalent in
critical texts. Conversely, for ESP, critical theories and pedagogies enhance
contextual understanding and potentially expand the linguistic means by
which goal-directed ends can be effectively achieved in this context and
enhance the possibilities for transformative pedagogies that are invigorated
through a fusion of pragmatic and politicized strategies. In a sense the onion
is peeled back in this context through a focus on how ESP can be used to
illuminate inequalities based on categories of identity.

A discussion of national and/or regional policies regarding citizenship
education lacks credibility unless it is articulated in terms of globalization
processes and the threats and opportunities they pose for nation-states. On

the one hand, the unprecedented transnational migrations in today's world have given rise to citizenship allegiances that are multiple and global, and sometimes fundamentalist in ways inimical to the cohesion of pluralistic societies. On the other, the withering capacity or willingness of national governments to mitigate the inequities of global capitalism on behalf of its most vulnerable citizens has resulted in increased poverty and marginalization of transnational workers (Stasiulis & Bakan, 2005). Such global-national tensions have given rise to contested and competing notions of citizenship in ESP settings but also to creative and transformational pedagogies (see Westheimer & Kahne, 2004) in which second language learners can be oriented toward social justice issues of local, national, and international consequence.

Tensions within the Citizenship Literature: Passivity or Participation

Citizenship has been a deeply problematic notion within academic discourse since its inception as a separate field of study. Marshall (1950) noted that even though national citizenship formally confers equal status to all members of particular societies, inequalities of class will prevent poorer members of society from participating as fully as those who are richer. In effect, "modern citizenship conferred the legal capacity to strive for the things one would like to possess but did not guarantee the possession of any of them" (Isin & Wood, 1999, p. 28).

As Crick (2007) makes clear, debates about how to define what citizenship is are still central to concerns evident in the academic literature. This concern, fueled by declining youth participation in electoral processes in Western countries (Print, 2007), is marked by increasingly nuanced discussions as to how being a citizen can be actively taken up as a participatory role, rather than as a passive status simply conferred by a nation state (Kennedy, 2007). These debates have long been central to the research literature pertaining to Canadian ESL provision (Derwing, 1992; Joshee & Derwing, 2005).

However, this literature does not examine the notion of subjectivity in ways that are specific to the immigrant experience. Coming to a new country, to a very large extent, means that one's self-perception is disrupted and reconstructed. This process of *deterritorialisation*, as Deleuze and Guattari (1994) termed it, problematizes unitary models of personality development such as those of Cooley, Mead, Dewey or even Freud. The post-structuralist concept of *identity* is a more useful model in explaining how immigrants reconstruct the multiplicity of elements that make up the individual in the context of adopting a new citizenship.

Conceptualizing the Citizen-Subject

Notions of "being" and/or "becoming" a citizen of any nation-state require consideration of how identities or, more specifically, political subjectivities are formed and prepared for civic life and continuity. The terms *subject* and *subjectivity*, themselves, offer particular perspectives on identity, particularly as illuminated by way of Norton's (2000) innovative introduction of feminist post-structural theory into TESOL. The citizen-subject, conceptualized via Norton, is not the autonomous, free-reasoning individual of Enlightenment lore, nor is he or she the passive recipient of values ascribed through membership in timeless and rigid social categories. Instead, the citizen-subject is conceptualized as both shaped by the dominant discourses of nationhood but also enabled as a potential agent of change, a source of counter-discursive readings that cumulatively and over time serve to transform and/or hybridize the socio-political spaces into which he or she is ostensibly integrated/assimilated. Yet, to reiterate post-structural precepts, it would be unwise to exaggerate the coherence and calculation that might appear to underpin oppositional practices in the public sphere. Identities, both of the individuals, communities, and nation-states, in this respect, are seen as sites of conflict, contradiction, and change, particularly in light of the threats and opportunities posed by globalization (see Block & Cameron, 2002; Kumaravadivelu, 2008).

Foreigners, Globalization, and Constructions of Citizenship

Globalization processes shape both material realities and imagined possibilities for citizens. Material effects abound in the growing disparities created through the intensification of economic interdependencies and the aggressive promotion of Western-based cultural commodities and values that undermine local communities. Aligned with this promotion is the emergence of English as the default lingua franca of prosperity and mobility and the subsequent pressures placed on the long-term vitality of local vernaculars.

Regarding the imagination, the expansion and accessibility of global media systems—mainstream and alternative—has profound and often unpredictable effects on citizenship practices. A media window onto far away places, for example, can set into motion local and regional aspirations that national governments may lack the capacity to fulfill. Globalized media, similarly, act on our desires in often unconscious and surreptitious ways, a popular sitcom from abroad, for example, serving to valorize the rights of women, youth, and religious and ethno-linguistic minorities in ways that threaten rigid social hierarchies and nation-state identities founded on strong mono-cultural and monolingual ideologies. Through the growing democratization of information via digital networks, the voices of distant liberatory movements can be heard, previously censored images of political and economic oppression can be circulated, and the citizens of liberal democratic societies thus potentially guilted into demanding action and accountability from their corporate and elected leaders (see e.g., Dartnell, 2006, Rodowick, 2002).

While the multidirectional capacities of new media may foster global consciousness-raising and effective transnational movements, they also complicate the integration/assimilation of immigrants into nation-states and their existing participatory structures. In English-dominant, immigrant-receiving countries, for example, most newcomers gravitate toward cosmopolitan centers such as New York, London, Sydney, Toronto, or Vancouver, creating for themselves transnational, juxtaposed lives in which geographical distances are instantaneously bridged through various communications technologies (i.e., the Internet, movies, newspapers) and life "abroad" is eased by an abundance of social services, consumer products, and employment possibilities through the home language. This growing prevalence of deterritorialized, expatriate cosmopolitanism challenges conventional approaches to citizenship training in the ESL/ESP classrooms, requiring creative and situated strategies on the part of teachers.

Recognizing these assimilative tensions exacerbated by globalization, it would be useful to consider why immigrant-receiving nations continue to promote the kinds of immigration patterns that they do, especially of the highly skilled, educated, and affluent, those most likely to embrace transnational and cosmopolitan values over nationalistic ones. Altruism and pure humanitarianism rarely motivate policy. In Canada, as in most center-based societies, demographic realities indicate aging and declining populations, and the concomitant dangers this poses for long-term economic prosperity and the provision of cherished social programs (e.g., publicly funded health care).

While addressing such developments shows clear prudence and pragmatism, an intriguing supplementary explanation, as conceptualized by Bonny Honig (2001), is also worth consideration. Following Honig, we might reverse a central underlying question that frames this chapter. Instead of asking exclusively how best to confer citizenship values onto newcomers, we should also ask how the newcomer confers citizenship upon those whose roots in the nation are long and deep. In other words, what additional ideological and identity-forming functions does the presence of the "foreigner" serve in the stabilization of the status quo? Honig argues that one of the primary functions served is that of legitimation. Among us, and "here" of their apparent volition, the presence of immigrants adds legitimacy to the central organizing myths of the nation—its meritocratic, progressive, and egalitarian ideals—especially during times of tarnished reputation, when solidarity diminishes and the exceptionality of the nation-state and its dominant elites is increasingly held up to critical scrutiny. On the world stage as well, the presence of newcomers serves as a kind of vindication for the nation's values as it competes in the global marketplace of ideas, aggressively promoting its brand of citizenship in the pursuit of needed foreign capital and expertise. Still, as Honig astutely observes, this legitimizing function is a double-edged sword in that the newcomers we encounter often resist or exceed their stereotype; that is, some may not conform to assigned roles as "model minorities" who, for the sake of future generations, passively toil in jobs for which they are over-qualified. As they voice their resentment, questioning the nation-state's meritocratic and egalitarian ideals, they draw attention to the very contradictions and embedded inequalities that their presence is intended to conceal.

Honig's thesis is insightful for two reasons in the key issues being raised in this chapter. On the one hand, it suggests credible discursive and ideological reasons for the pervasiveness and normalization of passive citizenship practices in ESP and ESL. It helps explain, for example, why L2 writing instructors deem "inauthentic" ESL/EAP student narratives that fail to reiterate and celebrate cherished national narratives and originary myths (for an "Ellis Island" representation, see Harklau, 2003). It also explains the commonsensical propensity to favor memorization—of facts, dates, and founding fathers *(sic)*—over critical investigation that illuminates past injustices and collective efforts toward their amelioration. Treated in this static, positivistic manner—what Derwing (1992, p. 193) aptly describes as a "test mentality"—acquiescence to existing arrangements is enhanced for both the foreigner and the native born.

Still, as Honig suggests, the "foreigner" in our midst offers a voice no longer available to the habituated. Conceptualized this way, ESP/ESL students are seen as sources of critical, participatory insights and texts, revealing complexities that problematize the rigid categories (e.g., as partially formed citizens based on their perceived L2 limitations) imposed on them by discourse and manifest in policy and curricula. To reiterate, Honig's thesis is a provocative one with clear implications for the preparation of citizens in any liberal democratic society. One such society is Canada.

Canadian ESL Programming, Tasks, and the Hidden Curriculum

As Benesch (1994) notes, citizenship preparation is an integral aspect of second language education where large numbers of immigrants are being integrated into modern nation states. Within the Canadian context, federal policy documents (Citizenship and Immigration Canada, 2006) make it plain that ESL programming is for the dual purposes of teaching the second language and integrating newcomers. The crucial importance of adult English as a Second Language programming for the integration of newcomers has also been acknowledged in a plethora of teaching materials and curriculum guidelines (Ilieva, 2000), and in the academic literature (Wong, Duff & Early, 2001).

For nation-states such as Canada, the integration of newcomers is a pressing problem in light of globalization and the unprecedented number of migrants on the move world-wide. To reiterate, developed countries are increasingly competing with one another to attract skilled immigrants and take advantage of these vast diasporas in ways that preserve and strengthen democratic institutions, social cohesion, and economic vitality (Citizenship and Immigration Canada, 2008).

The string of events that led to the creation of the current structure of adult ESL programming in Canada started in 1990, when the federal government initiated a major policy shift in response to changing demographic and economic forces. In response to the perception that high levels of immigration were vital to Canada's long-term economic and political interests, priority was given to second language education on a centralized and consistent basis for the first time. ESL programming was seen as central to the removal of barriers to newcomer integration and the ability of the nation-state to reap the full financial benefits of immigration (for a fuller description of the history of ESL programming in Canada, see Fleming, 2007).

LINC (Language Instruction for Newcomers to Canada program) assessment and curriculum procedures are framed by the Canadian Language Benchmarks (CLB). The CLB covers the full range of English proficiency (from beginning to full fluency), incorporates literacy and numeracy, emphasizes tasks and situations, features stand-alone descriptors per level, encourages local curriculum development, and includes proficiencies related to learning strategies and sociocultural and strategic competencies.

CLB development is overseen by the Centre for Canadian Language Benchmarks (CCLB), a non-profit organization founded in 1998 and funded by the federal government. It is "governed by a nationally representative, multi-stakeholder board of directors including representation from government, English as a Second Language and French as a Second Language experts and language assessors" (CCLB). The official character of the CLB is attested to by government support for the CCLB and the fact that the CLB was painstakingly developed in a long series of consultations and draft formulations facilitated by federal agencies (Norton Pierce & Stewart, 1997).

However, before proceeding to a detailed examination of the CLB and its related documents, some issues related to the nature of task-based assessment and hidden curricula will be reviewed. These issues pertain closely to the part content plays in a document of this sort and to the relationship between assessment instruments and curricula. It is contended that the CLB is a hidden curriculum (Jackson, 1968) in the sense that it encapsulates a privileged body of content and methods meant to socialize learners (and teachers).

Tasks have been commonly employed, as both criteria for assessment and as ways to organize pedagogical activities, since the broad currency of *experiential learning* was established in general education. This form of education, which is generally taken to mean "learning by doing," had its early roots in the mid-nineteenth-century shift from formal, abstract education in schools to practice-based education, elements of which are foundational in the pedagogy of both Dewey and Freire (Lewis & Williams, 1994).

Although the term *task* has had a long history in general education theory, it is important to note that it was not common to use the term in describing SLE classroom objectives and activities prior to the late 1980s (Long & Crookes, 1992). In second language education (SLE), the use of the term *task*, in fact, has been closely associated with assessment since the advent of the communicative approach. In one of the first discussions of the communicative approach in curriculum design, for example, Johnson (1979) makes the links between curriculum development, tasks, and assessment very clear:

> Fluency in the communicative process can only develop within a 'task-orientated teaching'—one which provides 'actual meaning' by focusing on tasks to be mediated through language, and where success or failure is seen to be judged in terms of whether or not these tasks are performed. (p. 200)

Thus, within the communicative approach, the choices an SLE teacher makes about what to teach are made in light of the outcomes and objectives their pedagogy is meant to achieve. In other words, one first sets one's learning goals and then determines what sequence of tasks best achieves them. Achieving these tasks is the criterion used by teachers to determine whether or not their learners have successfully mastered the material and can thus proceed to the next level of instruction. What is important to our argument here is that content is integral to task design within the communicative approach to second language education.

Today, tasks are prominent in many popular ESL teacher education manuals and course texts (e.g., Brown, 2000). Many SLE scholars have elaborated task-based curriculum models (Skeehan, 2002) and tasks have long been significant elements developed within many curriculum and assessment benchmark projects undertaken by national governments (Brindley, 1995).

As is often the case with national language policy implementation (Shohamy, 2007), the absence of a federally mandated curriculum has meant that the assessment and placement instrument, in this case the CLB, has become the de facto guideline for instructional content in most jurisdictions and not a set of randomly chosen assessment criteria. It is no wonder, under these circumstances, that some scholars and curriculum resources centers have referred to it unambiguously as a curriculum document (Pennsylvania Department of Education, 2006).

As the document recommends, teachers and assessment officers might very well feel free to extract the language embedded within the sample tasks and to add other content as they see fit. However, the content already found within the document is, as shall be demonstrated, the starting point for those educators who use it. Thus, the content is privileged, in the sense that its importance is stressed by its inclusion. Absent content is not privileged and reveals serious shortcomings within CLB. Because of the CLB's nature as a national curriculum document, the content found within it (and excluded from it) takes on an official character.

These contradictory views on whether the document is an instrument for assessment or task/curriculum development are found within the CLB itself. Even though the author states in its introduction that the CLB is "not a curriculum guide" (Pawlikowska-Smith, 2000, p. viii), she does say, in the very next paragraph, that the CLB does describe "what adult ESL instruction should prepare adult ESL learner to do." Thus, the CLB quite clearly sets up tasks that learners are meant to perform in order to advance to the next level of instruction. Teachers, as the document plainly states, are expected to organize learning opportunities for the successful completion of these tasks. The claim that the CLB is not meant to inform curriculum development is rather dubious. As Fox and Courchêne (2005) point out,

> although the *CLB* is neither a curriculum nor test according to its develop-
> ers, providing details regarding text length and sample tasks leads anyone
> using the document to use these as guidelines for task development.
> (p. 13)

This point is reinforced by a study of LINC teachers recently conducted by Haque and Cray (2007), in which their respondents confirmed that the CLB was something they could not ignore as a set of reference points for curriculum development.

It is important to note that making pedagogical decisions in reference to curriculum guidelines requires a fair degree of professional autonomy (Fleming, 1998). Unfortunately, the insecurity inflicted on ESL program-ming within Canada through various funding strategies and conditions has served to deprofessionalize the field (Burnaby, 2002; Haque & Cray, 2007). In comparison to other educational sectors, ESL teachers are often paid far less and have limited access to professional development in workplaces that are transitory and poorly supported in terms of resources. As a result, few ESL teachers have time to focus on developing context-sensitive pedagogies related to critical citizenship and subsequently develop an overreliance on materials that are superficially Canadian. In sum, the CLB performs the function of institutionalizing ESL instructors by providing them with a tem-plate for their classroom practices and framing their assessment procedures. Under these circumstances, privileged content, in the sense we have talked about above, is difficult to augment or resist.

The Canadian Language Benchmarks: Promoting Hierarchies of Citizenship

The Canadian Language Benchmarks 2000: ESL for Adults (Pawlikowska-Smith, 2000) is made up of more than 200 compact pages. The bulk of the document consists of the actual benchmarks, arranged in 12 levels, from basic English language proficiency to full fluency.

The preface and introductory chapters provide an interesting segue into the rest of the text. In an obvious reference to the original policy initiatives that gave rise to the CLB, the Board of Directors for the CCLB make use of the preface to tell the fictional story of a 25-year-old immigrant from Indonesia who is confused about how his English level had been assessed by his previous school when he changes institutions. According to the preface, this situation is occurring less and less frequently. In addition, so the preface emphasizes, immigrants are now able to refer to the CLB in such high-stakes situations as demonstrating their English language ability to employers and to gain entrance to educational institutions. This shift is described by the authors of the preface as no less than a "revolution."

Even more tellingly, the preface also states that, thanks to the CLB, learners will be able to "plot out for themselves, in advance, their own paths of language learning to attain their goals" (p. v). This is an important point. If learners can predict how their learning will progress upon entrance into the "CLB movement" (as the preface characterizes programs that have adopted the *Benchmarks*), then is this document not more than simply a description of the English language at a particular level of proficiency? Leaving aside the problem of whether "one size fits all," does this document not now become a set of learning objectives meant to inform curriculum development?

This ambiguity continues into the text's introduction, which says that the *Benchmarks* are "a national standard for planning second language curricula for a variety of contexts" (p. viii), while stating categorically that it is "not a curriculum guide: they do not dictate local curricula and syllabuses" (p. viii). The document even attempts to "have its cake and eat it too" in terms of methodology. Even though the author states that the CLB is "not tied to any specific instructional method" (p. viii), the introduction emphasizes the need for instructors to adhere to common hallmarks of the communicative approach (Brown, 2000): learner-centered instruction, task-based proficiency, and communicative competency.

As a close examination of the CLB and seven closely related official documents reveals, short shrift is given to "being Canadian." There are only three vague references that pertain to citizenship: "understand rights and responsibilities of client, customer, patient and student" (p. 95); "indicate knowledge of laws, rights, etc." (p. 116); and "write a letter to express an opinion as a citizen" (p. 176). It is also very revealing that the word *vote*, for example, does not appear in this or in any of the other seven major documents associated with the CLB. At the very highest levels of English language proficiency (at the point at which one is writing research papers at universities), there are only vague and general references to developing opinions about current events, writing letters to the editors of newspapers, and participating in meetings.

The document seems to view English language learners as having rights and responsibilities that pertain almost exclusively to being good consumers. The content includes the need for learners to understand their rights and responsibilities as a "client, customer, patient and student" (p. 95), but not as workers, family members, participants in community activities, or advocates.

In addition, issues related to trade unions and collective agreements are only mentioned twice (again, at the stage at which one is able to write research papers). Labor rights, such as filing grievances, recognizing and reporting dangerous working conditions, and the enforcement of legislated standards of employment are non-existent.

The content found within the CLB was in great contrast to the conceptions of citizenship described by immigrants in a recent study Fleming (2008) conducted of learners enrolled in a LINC program. In a series of 25 in-depth interviews, a group of Punjabi-speaking learners made it clear that they predominantly thought of "being Canadian" in legalistic terms. Their conceptions centered on rights, adherence to law, and respect for national multicultural policy. These learners, many of whom worked as agricultural laborers or semi-skilled construction workers, provided concrete examples of their struggles to obtain safe working conditions and access to basic standards of employment such as overtime or statutory holiday pay. Consumer rights, such as the few cited in the CLB, did form a part of their concerns. However, an overriding aspect of their conceptualizations of citizenship was in reference to employment rights and voting, both of which, as we noted above, were virtually non-existent in the CLB.

As noted, ESP's focus on concrete aspects of the language needs of specific social groups is a characteristic that makes the field distinct from other forms of second language education. Examination of the citizenship education needs in the Canadian ESL context makes it apparent that a fundamental question in this regard is how (or by whom) these needs are defined. The CLB tended to approach "Canadian-ness" in terms of normative standards, including various forms of social behavior, which could be taken to imply the existence of a dominant and singular culture to which second language learners have to conform. Citizenship rights at the basic level of English language proficiency had no place in the document. Rights related to voting, employment, or group membership were virtually non-existent. The participants in the 2008 study, however, spoke of being Canadian predominantly in terms of citizenship rights, multicultural policy, and the obligations of being citizens. Any curriculum based on the concerns of the learners themselves would look very different from one based on the official assessment/ curriculum document in this context.

A parallel here can be made with the way in which needs analyses have been problematized in the ESP literature. As Jasso-Aguilar (1999) points out, unbalanced distributions of power have rarely been questioned by researchers examining how goals and objectives are determined in vocational training contexts. All too often, the opinions of employers and other powerful outsiders are privileged over those expressed by workers and less powerful insiders. As a result, ESP programming goals are skewed toward the needs of managers and not those workers actually taking the training.

Similarly, in the case of citizenship education, programming goals are overwhelmingly set by the state, through the expertise of outsiders such as policy advisors, curriculum developers, program managers, and (dare we say it) academics. Even though learners are consulted through their settlement organizations or in occasional venues like TESL Canada Learners Conferences, there have been very limited opportunities for insiders (i.e., the learners) to influence the goals of citizenship education. Certainly, the voices of outsiders in this context are privileged over those of insiders.

The CLB Document: Complicating Frames of Reference

As a stand-alone text, content analyses of the CLB—of tasks and themes stated, implied, and concealed—provide numerous examples to support its depiction as a "hidden curriculum," one that promotes a dutiful, obedient, and passive engagement with the politics of the nation-state. Analyses on these terms alone, however, might not provide a complete understanding of the complex discursive processes involved, or the whole array of techniques through which institutional power is exercised in liberal democratic societies. That is, while it is important to critique the propositional content of a document such as CLB, such critiques are easily allayed through the strategic expansion and inclusion of items identified as necessary for participatory citizenship practices. Indeed, evidence of this occurrence can be found in subsequent LINC 4–6 and LINC 5–7 curriculum documents, both of which include explicit themes and related tasks that are critical-analytic and participatory in relation to Canadian society.

As to whether such themes are merely ornamental—window-dressing to placate academics and community activists concerned with immigrant settlement—is a complex question worth considering. For example, Pinet's (2006) study of the production, interpretation, and implementation of a LINC document arising from the CLB describes how one teacher created her own transformative syllabus, exploring issues of racism and sexism in Canadian society based on the presence of "human rights" and "workers' rights" as thematic inclusions in the LINC 4–6 guidelines. Though this utilization of the guidelines was perceived as too ideological and/or marginal to students' needs by some colleagues, the fact that she was able to correlate her syllabus to explicit themes in the guidelines served to legitimize her more critical approach. Still, as Pinet shows, she is only one of six informants to interpret the document in a transformative way, the other five using relatively more passive, transmission-based approaches in implementing ESL citizenship material. Choices present do not necessarily translate into choices taken. Clearly, there exists a whole array of identity-forming discourses that condition the range of meanings practitioners generate in their interactions with curricula. Nation-state power, in this respect, is deployed not only in the content on display in an official document but also in the local strategies that manage the document's reception, the intertextual and contextual conditions through which preferred meanings are validated and particular social practices legitimized. Through this articulation—whereby curricular documents, funding policies, and prevailing attitudes around language education work in concert—the passivity of a "hidden curriculum" may persist in spite of cosmetic changes made to its appearance. In this articulated sense, Canadian ESL policy structures can be seen as mitigating against critical practices that address social inequalities, hence reinforcing a hierarchical structure to Canadian citizenship that exists both within the nation-state (Bannerji, 2000) and within a globalized frame (Stasiulis & Bakan, 2005).

Exploring Critical Citizenship in ESP: Practices and Principles

The Canadian context would suggest an additional, critical sub-field of language specialization within ESP, for lack of a better acronym, one that might be called ESD: *English for Self-Defense*, the rationale for which can be gleaned from Morgan and Ramanathan's (2005) survey of critical literacies in language education:

> Arguably, such skills [i.e., critical literacies] are not just options but necessities, if not forms of self-defense against the intrusiveness of corporate advertising, the growing sameness of cultural products and information from global media empires, and the expansion of sophisticated forms of surveillance and data sharing employed in the name of security. . . .

[O]ur job as educators partially entails cultivating a citizenry that is able to negotiate and critically engage with the numerous texts, modalities and technologies coming at learners, and because we now collectively occupy globalized, interconnected spaces that insist on such critical engagement. (p. 152)

In their survey, the authors suggest a number of key principles and exemplary practices (e.g., a "tool-kit" for action, pp. 156–159) by which such an ESD orientation might be realized and integrated into syllabus design with the intended effect of critically invigorating conventional ESP/EAP curricula. Through critical narrative inquiry, textual juxtapositions, teacher talk, and the use of multimodal resources, student awareness of the "personformative" nature of texts and discourse is heightened, in turn facilitating oppositional readings and practices around dominant constructions of nation-state citizenship and its attendant privileges and responsibilities.

Commercially published books and materials that address critical or active citizenship are uncommon given the ELT industry's propensity toward global distribution and generic course books whose concomitant profitability is enhanced through the maintenance of the ideological status quo in print (see e.g., Gray, 2002). Still, there are a few notable exceptions from smaller publishers and/or non-profit organizations, some of which are cited here. One highly regarded publication is *The Change Agent: An Adult Education Newspaper for Social Justice*, published by the New England Literacy Resource Center (www.nelrc.org/changeagent). Many of its theme-based issues take up concerns relevant to ESP and ESL contexts and are available as downloadable pdf files. Two issues relate directly to citizenship practices (Issue 18, March 2004—Voting in the 2004 Elections; Issue 6, February 1998—Civic Participation) and are full of excellent readings and activities that are interculturally informative and critically analytic in relation to civic concerns. One 2008 issue addressed the theme of voting and advocacy.

The World around Us: Canadian Social Issues for ESL Students, co-authored by Christine Hoppenrath and Wendy Royal (1997), explores controversial family, community, and social justice issues from a Canadian perspective, a somewhat rare occurrence. A chapter on critical media literacy is particularly useful for citizenship pedagogies in that it encourages analyses of media bias and particular class interests reflected in the selection and representation of current issues in the news. The chapter's multiliteracies/multimodality perspective, in which both visual (e.g., advertising) and print media are analyzed, raises awareness of how mainstream media influence individual and collective identity negotiation.

An ESD "tool kit," one in which participatory citizenship is modeled and promoted for teachers and students, would seem incomplete without the imprint of Paolo Freire and his notions of problem-posing and critical consciencization. Wallerstein and Auerbach's (2004) *Problem-Posing at Work: Popular Educator's Guide* is an outstanding classroom resource, integrating Freirien concepts and strategies in inspiring and accessible ways. As well, the notion of global citizenship, raised here, is expertly developed in a chapter titled "Connecting Local and Global Action: The Role of Pedagogy in Social Change." Substantial chapter references and supplementary references make this an essential text for the development of critical practitioners. The influence of Freire is also strongly evident in Arnold, Burke, James, Martin, and Thomas's (1991) *Educating for a Change*, a book that is similarly useful for developing social advocacy skills and community organizing strategies.

In addition to these materials, two case studies developed notions of critical citizenship through context-sensitive pedagogies in ESL and ESP settings. The first (Morgan, 2002) took place in a Chinese settlement agency in Toronto that co-sponsors several LINC and provincially funded adult ESL classes. Notably, many of the students in Morgan's class had recently immigrated to Canada from Hong Kong in advance of China's 1997 reacquisition. The political stability they sought, however, was undermined by an imminent referendum on the province of Quebec's separation from the Canadian federation, a development frequently raised and questioned in the mixed-level (intermediate to advanced) ESL class Morgan taught: "Would Canadians go to war to prevent Quebec's separation? What would happen to the Canadian dollar?" And similar to most Canadians, students were unsure of what the actual referendum question meant.[1] Similarly, the meaning and implications of words such as *sovereign* and *sovereignty* in comparison to *independence* or *separation* were particularly confusing, as witnessed by the number of students searching in their bilingual Chinese-English dictionaries for explanations.

---

[1]The 1995 Quebec Referendum question: "Do you agree that Quebec should become sovereign, after having made a formal offer to Canada for a new economic and political partnership, within the scope of the bill respecting the future of Quebec and of the agreement signed on June 12, 1995?" (*Toronto Star,* Sept. 8, p. A1)

Morgan made this the focus of a lesson, drawing on students' L1 literacy strategy of "bottom-up" or "lexis-centred" reading (Bell, 1995; Parry, 1996).[2] Through their use of bilingual dictionaries and the application of decompositional strategies based on L1 word formation (see e.g., Zhou & Marslen-Wilson, 1994), several students discovered and debated intrinsic word properties that they saw as contributing to the political controversy surrounding the referendum question. The class discussion soon shifted toward broader concerns—debates over how Canada should respond to the outcome of a yes vote, and to comparisons with Hong Kong post-1997. These discussions were remarkable for their unprecedented level of engagement with social issues and the complex and often contradictory negotiations of transnational identities taking place (i.e., to what extent are we now Chinese *and* Canadian?). Much of the dictionary work and small group conversations took place in L1, but as a foundation for whole class, L2 discussions, in which stronger English speakers helped out weaker ones in expressing their views in the target language.

In sum, participatory citizenship in an L2 was enabled by L1 use and traditional L1 literacy strategies, a classroom approach notably absent in the CLB document. What might be observed—indeed stigmatized—as methodologically and acquisitionally remedial (i.e., bilingual dictionary translation), or indicative of a lower-order cognitive task (i.e., decoding) through a CLB framework, was recontextualized in ways that enhanced critical engagement and an understanding of language and power around the Quebec referendum that would exceed the ideological awareness of many so-called native speakers and longstanding citizens.

Our second pedagogical example takes place in Australia and describes a workshop on teaching critical thinking in EAP (Thompson, 2002). Several aspects of this workshop are exemplary. First, it effectively integrates a

---

[2]The prodigious demands of learning thousands of characters in becoming literate in Chinese have, for most Chinese students, placed vocabulary learning at the center of learning a foreign language. In a bottom-up or lexis-centered approach, students' process of reading is one in which denotative meaning of individual lexical items is first deduced, after which existing knowledge of L2 syntax is employed to work out how they might fit together. Following this, descriptive and generalized meanings are formulated. Finally, as Parry (1996) notes, "only as they advanced towards a translation of the text did they feel able to relate it in any meaningful way to their experience" (p. 680). Of course, not all Chinese students in Morgan's class rigidly followed this process, but most did view the mastering of L2 vocabulary as essential and preferably through bilingual dictionary use and memorization of word lists rather than through incidental learning and/or inferential reading strategies.

critical-ideological component within a set of pragmatic ESP language tasks (e.g., assessing and integrating research material in academic essay writing). Second, it engages with identity negotiation by drawing students' attention to the person-formative nature of texts and genres and their effects on judgments regarding truth claims. Third, future citizens of Australia are introduced to one of the nation-state's most pressing and controversial issues: the land claims and rights provisions of Australian aboriginals. Given this topic and the students involved, this workshop should also be seen as relevant to notions of global citizenship and the emergence of aboriginal land claims and the revitalization of indigenous languages and cultures as universal rights and moral imperatives requiring governmental intervention.

In the workshop, four short texts on the origins of aboriginals—of distinctive historical genres, and two by indigenous authors—were closely analyzed in ways that support critical evaluation of academic research in support of essay writing. At the same time, these analyses and the overall workshop format, including the teacher's strategic questions and interventions, had a kind of cumulative, problem-posing (cf. Freire) effect whereby participants were made aware of their own cultural biases and the politics of representation—how textual choices mediate our perceptions of historical "truth" and, consequently, our capacity to recognize and subsequently redress past injustices. Of course, not all students follow similar pathways of meaning-making or arrive at the same level of sociopolitical understanding. Still, what makes this approach so impressive is the critical *potential* built into the overall structure of the activity. As with the lesson on the Quebec Referendum, critical language awareness of texts, genres, or key vocabulary complement—rather than displace—more conventional language learning tasks in an EAP or ESL context. Through active engagement students learn that language is never neutral in debates and struggles over social futures. And they also become more effective users and producers of texts in schools and public life.

Current Issues/Future Directions

A focus on exemplary materials and practices draws attention to current challenges and gaps in the field. For one, it seems paradoxical to be promoting participatory citizenship in ESP/ESL within societies notable for their declining participation in conventional public practices of democracy (i.e., voting, membership in formal political parties). This appearance of paradox, however, is somewhat misleading if Honig's (2001) provocative thesis is revisited to reiterate the ideological or discursive work achieved when official citizenship resources in the form of curricula and materials are created and publicly promoted. While such resources might first appear as exclusively serving the integration needs of newcomers, they should also be seen as reminding the native-born of the privilege of being Canadian or American, as examples. In this respect, "participatory" practices in ESP/ESL—and the lavish public display of flag-waving citizenship ceremonies—serve the additional function of countering political cynicism and indifference in the general populace by suggesting the intrinsic value of citizenship conferred.

At the same time, policy and curricula should not be evaluated in textual isolation. Policy makers may appear to respond constructively to stakeholder criticism and address existing gaps through the inclusion of more participatory content (e.g., LINC 4–6 and 5–7 curricula), yet deny the material resources necessary for the development and realization of such content in classroom settings. The Canadian research cited in this chapter strongly corroborates this type of situation and its pedagogical effects (Burnaby, 2002; Haque & Cray, 2007). Professional insecurity and poor working conditions are the norm for non-credit adult ESL programming. As noted, scarcity of Canadian-specific resources (Thomson & Derwing, 2004) and the lack of paid professional development opportunities also mean that critical citizenship materials and locally relevant lesson plans are less likely to be generated. In the Canadian context, as well, existing funding models in which minimum attendance numbers must be maintained serve to prioritize lower-level ESL and LINC programs, where survival English skills and the most basic and passive forms of task-based citizenship instruction in L2 are likely to occur. More advanced ESL/ESP students—those most capable of critical inquiry and active citizenship in an L2—are also the most likely to leave a LINC class on short notice when job opportunities arise. For those who remain in lower-level classes, an additional obstacle may arise through interactions with teachers whose ESL/ESP preparation has been informed by dominant monolingual ideologies, English-only approaches, and subtractive bilingual models in the TESOL field, all of which serve to infantilize L2 students and devalue their political experiences and insights as might be expressed through their L1. In short, awareness of this "bigger picture"—of how textual and extra-textual factors articulate in both productive and restrictive ways—is crucial for those interested in promoting critical citizenship in their programs and classrooms.

Another crucial issue for the ESP classroom involves our response to students' own expressions of indifference or resistance when presented with critical citizenship resources that we have created or endorsed. Not all L2 students value time spent on civic or public concerns. The notion of politics can invoke painful memories for some or a sense of inadequacy in others based on prior identity experiences (e.g., gender, race) and/or ascribed roles in which public participation is discouraged or prohibited. Still, the student who at one moment claims "I am not interested in politics" will show a remarkable propensity to debate so-called domestic affairs at the next. Lankshear and Knobel (1997) address this issue by recommending a more "holistic" approach, in which the personal and the political are more closely and deliberately aligned in the promotion of critical literacies and active citizenship:

> Struggles within the private sphere to win a more equitable distribution of domestic work and decision-making power inside the family, and struggle by migrants to negotiate a viable and satisfying identity within their new life situation, become facets of actively constructing and practicing citizenship. (p. 101)

This conflation of the personal and political is an area of particular strength within critical ESL pedagogies, especially through the work of feminist scholars whose perspectives on critical narrative and L2 autobiography have illuminated social inequities in unique ways unmet through conventional modes of inquiry (e.g., Pavlenko, 2007; Steinman, 2005; Vandrick, 1999). The challenge for teachers, as this research indicates, is to find ways of building upon the private, everyday concerns of students and connecting them to issues of equity and social justice in the broader community.

It is in respect to this last issue that this chapter comes full circle in its focus on complementarity between ESP's instrumental and pragmatic orientations and critical pedagogy's concerns with power and identity. To act on the world *purposively* through language—a central theme of ESP and this collection—often requires reconnecting the "non-purposive" elements of everyday life, work, and schooling in ways that foreground the complex micro-operations of power and discourse in the positioning of citizen-subjects. Critical pedagogies are particularly suited for such a task. Yet the critical has often eclipsed the pedagogical as seen through the generous excess of theoretical insights proffered in published form. The real-world purposiveness of ESP suggests important second language tools with which to enhance the pedagogical dimensions of critical work. Toward this end, and the promotion of critical citizenship, it is worth revisiting Marx's (1888/1983) famous pronouncement in his "Theses on Feuerbach": "Philosophers have only *interpreted* the world in various ways; the point is to *change* it" (p. 158, italics in original). Through collaboration and the bridging of vision with action, ESP and Critical Pedagogy in tandem have much to offer in the service of both academic and social advancement.

*   *   *

BRIAN MORGAN is an associate professor in the Department of English at Glendon College/York University in Toronto. His research interests include research and theory on language and identity, critical EAP pedagogies, and language teacher education. He is a co-author and consultant of several curricula based on the Canadian Language Benchmarks and the recent co-editor (with Vaidehi Ramanathan) of the 2007 *TESOL Quarterly* special issue on *Language Policies and TESOL: Perspectives from Practice.*

DOUGLAS FLEMING is an assistant professor in the Faculty of Education at the University of Ottawa. His research interests include critical citizenship theory, second language policy, and teacher agency in ESL curriculum decision making. He has been a program supervisor and curriculum writer for a variety of institutions, including Language Instruction for Newcomers to Canada, Citizenship and Immigration Canada, the Toronto and Surrey School Districts, and several agencies serving immigrants. He has also been a teacher since 1984.

REFERENCES

Anderson, B. (1983). *Imagined communities: Reflections on the origin and spread of nationalism.* London: Verso Editions/NLB.

Arnold, R., Burke, B., James, C., Martin, D., & Thomas, B. (1991). *Educating for a change.* Toronto: Between the Lines Press.

Bannerji, H. (2000). *The dark side of the nation: Essays on multiculturalism, nationalism and gender.* Toronto: Canadian Scholars' Press.

Belcher, D. D. (2006). English for specific purposes: Teaching to perceived needs and imagined futures in worlds of work, study and everyday life. *TESOL Quarterly, 40,* 133–156.

Bell, J. (1995). The relationship between L1 and L2 literacy: Some complicating factors. *TESOL Quarterly, 29*, 687–704.

Benesch, S. (1994). ESL, ideology, and the politics of pragmatics. *TESOL Quarterly, 27*, 705–716.

Block, D., & Cameron, D. (Eds.). (2002). *Globalization and language teaching.* London: Routledge.

Brindley, G. (1995). *Assessment and reporting in language learning programs: Purposes, problems and pitfalls.* Paper presented at International Conference on Testing and Evaluation in Second Language Education, Hong Kong University of Science and Technology.

Brown, H. D. (2000). *Teaching by principles.* New York: Barnes and Noble.

Burnaby, B. (2002). Reflections on language policies in Canada: Three examples. In J. W. Tollefson (Ed.), *Language policies in education* (pp. 65–86). Mahwah, NJ: Lawrence Erlbaum.

Citizenship and Immigration Canada. (2006). *Report to Parliament.* Ottawa, Canada: Communications Branch, Citizenship and Immigration.

———. (2008). *Annual report to Parliament on immigration, 2008.* Retrieved May 8, 2009, from www.cic.gc.ca/english/resources/publications/annual-report2008/message.asp

Crick, B. (2007). Citizenship: The political and the democratic. *British Journal of Educational Studies, 55*(3), 235–248.

Dartnell, M. (2006). *Insurgency online: Web activism and global conflict.* Toronto: University of Toronto Press.

Deleuze, G., & Guattari, F. (1994). *What is philosophy?* London: Verso.

Derwing, T. (1992). Instilling a passive voice: Citizenship instruction in Canada. In B. Burnaby & A. Cumming (Eds.), *Socio-political aspects of ESL* (pp. 193–202). Toronto: OISE Press.

Fleming, D. (1998). Autonomy and agency in curriculum decision-making: A study of instructors in a Canadian adult settlement ESL program. *TESL Canada Journal, 16* (1), 19–35.

———. (2007). Adult immigrant ESL programs in Canada: Emerging trends in the contexts of history, economics and identity. In J. Cummins & C. Davison (Eds.), *The international handbook of English language teaching* (pp. 185–198). New York: Springer.

———. (2008). *Becoming Canadian: Racialized citizenship, ESL learners, national second language policy and the Canadian Language Benchmarks.* Berlin: VDM.

Fox, J., & Courchêne, R. (2005). The Canadian Language Benchmarks (CLB): A critical appraisal. *Contact, 31*(2), 7–28.

Gray, J. (2002). The global coursebook in English language teaching. In D. Block & D. Cameron (Eds.), *Globalization and language teaching* (pp. 151–167). London: Routledge.

Haque, E., & Cray, E. (2007). Constraining teachers: Adult ESL settlement language training policy and implementation. *TESOL Quarterly, 41,* 634–642.

Harklau, L. (2003). Representational practices and multi-modal communication in US high schools: Implications for adolescent immigrants. In R. Bayley & S. R. Schecter (Eds.), *Language socialization in bilingual and multilingual societies* (pp. 83–97). Clevedon, UK: Multilingual Matters.

Honig, B. (2001). *Democracy and the foreigner.* Princeton, NJ: Princeton University Press.

Hoppenrath, C., & Royal, W. (1997). *The world around us: Canadian social issues for ESL students.* Toronto: Harcourt Canada.

Ilieva, R. (2000). Exploring culture in texts designed for use in adult ESL classrooms. *TESL Canada Journal, 17*(2), 50–63.

Isin, E. F., & Wood, P. K. (1999). *Citizenship and identity.* London: Sage.

Jackson, P. (1968). *Life in classrooms.* New York: Holt, Rinehart & Winston.

Jasso-Aguilar, R. (1999). Sources, methods and triangulation in needs analysis: A critical perspective in a case study of Waikiki hotel maids. *English for Specific Purposes, 18*(1), 27–46.

Johnson, K. (1979). Communicative approaches and communicative processes. In C. Brumfit & K. Johnson (Eds.), *The communicative approach to language teaching* (pp. 192–205). New York: Oxford University Press.

Joshee, R., & Derwing, T. M. (2005). The unmaking of citizenship education for adult immigrants in Canada. *Journal of International Migration and Integration, 6,* 61–80.

Kennedy, K. (2007). Student constructions of active citizenship: What does participation mean to students? *British Journal of Educational Studies, 55*(3), 304–324.

Kumaravadivelu, B. (2008). *Cultural globalization and language education.* New Haven, CT: Yale University Press.

Lankshear, C., & Knobel, M. (1997). Critical literacy and active citizenship. In S. Muspratt, A. Luke, & P. Freebody (Eds.), *Constructing critical literacies: Teaching and learning textual practice* (pp. 95–124). Cresskill, NJ: Hampton Press.

Lewis, L. H., & Williams, C. J. (1994). Experiential learning: Past and present. *New Directions for Adult and Continuing Education 62* (Summer 1994), 5–16.

Long, M. H., & Crookes, G. (1992). Three approaches to task-based syllabus design. *TESOL Quarterly, 26*(1), 27–55.

Marshall, T. H. (1950). *Citizenship and social class and other essays*. Cambridge, UK: Cambridge University Press.

Marx, K. (1983). Theses on Feuerbach. In E. Kamenka (Ed.), *The portable Karl Marx* (pp. 155–158). New York: Penguin Books. (Original work published 1888)

Master, P. (2005). Research in English for specific purposes. In. E. Hinkel (Ed.), *Handbook of research in second language teaching and learning* (pp. 99–115). Mahwah, NJ: Lawrence Erlbaum.

Morgan, B. (2002). Critical practice in community-based ESL programs: A Canadian perspective. *Journal of Language, Identity, and Education, 1,* 141–162.

Morgan, B., & Ramanathan, V. (2005). Critical literacies and language education: Global and local perspectives. *Annual Review of Applied Linguistics, 25,* 151–169.

Norton, B. (2000). *Identity and language learning*. Harlow: Pearson.

Norton Pierce, B., & Stewart, G. (1997). The development of the Canadian Language Benchmark Assessment. *TESL Canada Journal, 8*(2), 17–31.

Parry, K. (1996). Culture, literacy, reading. *TESOL Quarterly, 30,* 665–692.

Pavlenko, A. (2007). Autobiographic narratives as data in applied linguistics. *Applied Linguistics, 28*(2), 163–188.

Pawlikowska-Smith, G. (2000). *Canadian language benchmarks 2000*. Ottawa, Canada: Centre for Canadian Language Benchmarks.

Pennsylvania Department of Education (2006). *ESL resources*. Retrieved February 12, 2007, from www.pde.state.pa.us/able/lib/able/ pubs/focus0503.pdf

Pennycook, A. (1997). Vulgar pragmatism, critical pragmatism, and EAP. *English for Specific Purposes, 16,* 253–269.

Pinet, R. (2006). The contestation of citizenship education at three stages of the LINC 4 & 5 curriculum guidelines: Production, reception, and implementation. *TESL Canada Journal, 24*(1), 1–21.

Print, M. (2007). Citizenship education and youth participation in democracy. *British Journal of Educational Studies, 55*(3), 325–345.

Rodowick, D. N. (2002). Introduction: Mobile citizens, media states. *PMLA, 117*(1), 13–23.

Shohamy, E. (2007). The power of English tests, the power of the English language and the role of ELT. In J. Cummins & C. Davison (Eds.), *The international handbook of English language teaching* (pp. 521–532). New York: Springer.

Skehan, P. (2002). A non-marginal role for tasks. *ELT Journal 56*(3), 289–295.

Stasiulis, D., & Bakan, A. (2005). *Negotiating citizenship: Migrant women in Canada and the global system*. Toronto: Toronto University Press.

Steinman, L. (2005). Writing life 1 in language 2. *McGill Journal of Education, (40)*1, 65–79.

Thompson, C. (2002). Teaching critical thinking in EAP courses in Australia. *TESOL Journal, 11(4),* 15–20.

Thomson, R. I., & Derwing, T. M. (2004). Presenting Canadian values in LINC: The roles of textbooks and teachers. *TESL Canada Journal, 21(2),* 17–33.

Vandrick, S. (1999). ESL and the colonial legacy: A teacher faces her "missionary kid" past. In G. Haroian-Guerin (Ed.), *The personal narrative: Writing ourselves as teachers and scholars* (pp. 63–74). Portland, ME: Calendar Islands Publishers.

Wallerstein, N., & Auerbach, E. (2004). *Problem-posing at work: Popular educator's guide.* Edmonton: Grass Roots Press.

Westheimer, J., & Kahne, J. (2004, February). Teaching citizenship: Preparing students to become effective, active participants in our democracy. *Virginia Journal of Education, 97(5).*

Wong, P., Duff, P., & Early, M. (2001). The impact of language and skills training on immigrants' lives. *TESL Canada Journal, 18(2),* 1–31.

Zhou, X., & Marslen-Wilson, W. (1994). Words, morphemes and syllables in the Chinese mental lexicon. *Language and Cognitive Processes, 9,* 393–422.

Afterword:
Where Have We Come From
and Where Are We Now?

BRIAN PALTRIDGE
University of Sydney

As this book clearly shows, the area of English for Specific Purposes has come a long way from its earliest days when it was seen mostly as a matter of teaching the grammar and vocabulary of specialist registers such as scientific and technical English. We have seen changes in how language is analyzed, how it is described and how it is taught, what it means to use language in specific purpose settings, and how we think about this in both theoretical and practical terms. We have also moved in how we go about understanding the nature of learners' needs as well as the nature of specific purpose settings.

The view of language in the area of English for Specific Purposes has shifted, in some ways, quite dramatically. In 1987 Hutchinson and Waters, for example, said "the fact that language is used for a specific purpose does not imply that it is a special form of the language, different in kind from other forms" (Hutchinson & Waters, 1987, p. 18). English for Specific Purposes, they argued, is "*not* a matter of Science words and grammar for

Scientists, Hotel words and grammar for Hotel staff and so on" (their emphasis). Indeed, in their view:

> There is no grammatical structure, function or discourse structure that can be identified with Biology or any particular subject. Such things are the product of the communication situation (lecture, conversation, experiment, instructions etc.) and the level (engineer, technician, manager, mechanic, university etc.). (p. 165)

Hutchinson and Waters argued that there are "only two ways in which the subject has any kind of influence on the language content" (Hutchinson & Waters, 1987, p. 165). These are in the vocabulary of the text and in the proportion of some grammatical and structural forms in certain subject areas. Hutchinson and Waters' view was that grammatical forms found in scientific texts are also found elsewhere in English and that "the rules for their creation and use do not vary with subject" (Hutchinson & Waters, 1987, p. 166). In their view, the main reasons for teaching ESP were face validity, familiarity, and motivation. Students will respond better, they argued, to material that looks relevant, and if students have become familiar with a certain kind of text in the classroom, they will then be less anxious, and in turn more motivated, to tackle the text in the real word. ESP teachers should, they argued, "make learners aware of the lack of specificity of their needs" (Hutchinson & Waters, 1987, p. 167) saying that, in their view, there is little justification for subject-specific ESP.

Both corpus-based and genre studies have, however, changed our view of this. Biber (1988), for example, in a large-scale study made up of nearly one million words and 23 different genres, found a wide range of linguistic variation within the genres he examined, some of which he describes as "surprising and contrary to popular expectation" (Biber, 1988, p. 178). In order to more accurately account for the "complexity of discourse complexity" (Biber, 1992, p. 133), Biber proposed a framework for text analysis based on an analysis of linguistic features of texts combined with an examination of patterns of underlying dimensions of variation in complexity. Biber's conclusion was that "different kinds of texts are complex in different ways (in addition to being more or less complex)" (Biber, 1992, p. 133) and that many earlier conclusions that have been reached about specific purposes language use "reflect our incomplete understanding of the linguistic characteristics of discourse complexity" (Biber, 1992, p. 135).

Genre studies have also shown that there are significant differences between genres in terms of typical language features, rhetorical structures, as well as the extent to which these may vary and still be an example of the particular genre. Systemic functional genre analysts, for example, argue that descriptions of genre-specific language need to be probabilistic, rather than deterministic (Halliday, 1991). That is, they need to be based on a "more likely/less likely," rather than an "either/or" position of occurrence in the particular kinds of texts. We have also moved from the view of genre as form alone to discussions of issues such as what it is that someone needs to know in order to successfully use a genre (genre knowledge), how we can raise students' awareness of this (genre awareness) and how we might help learners become more rhetorically aware (Hyland, this volume; Johns, this volume; Johns, 2008; Johns, 2009) as we deal with different genres in the classroom. Discussions have also turned to new and emerging genres (Planken & Nickerson, this volume) and how we might deal with these in ESP classrooms. There have also been discussions of the relationships between genres, inspired first of all by the work of Bazerman (1994) and his notion of systems of genres, and taken up by writers such as Devitt (2004), Swales (2004), and Tardy (2003) in their discussions of genre networks, genre sets, genre chains, and repertoires of genres. The multimodal nature of the texts our students need to use is gaining increasing attention as is the whole issue of varieties of English in ESP settings and whether, indeed, the goal in ESP teaching should be native-like competence (Nickerson, 2005; Planken and Nickerson, this volume). The increasing use of English by non-native speakers as a lingua franca in business communications has brought this to the fore and will clearly continue to do so.

Even where students are expected to exhibit more native-like use of English, the picture has become more complicated. Looking at academic writing, for example, there are different views as to what is expected and appropriate in different academic settings. As Lea, and many others, have pointed out:

> Each discipline and each subject within each discipline has specific ways of ordering and presenting knowledge. What is regarded as appropriate in one subject may be regarded as inappropriate in another (Lea, 1994, p. 218).

The work of Hyland (2004, 2002; Hyland & Bondi, 2006), in particular, has shown us how the use of language varies in terms of rhetorical patterns and linguistic features across disciplines, especially in their written genres, and that these cannot be divorced from the teaching of the subject itself (Hyland, 2002). What this leads us to, then, is a very situated (Lave & Wenger, 1991) view of the use of language for specific purposes and one that is tightly bound up with the community of practice (Barton & Tusting, 2005; Wenger, 1998) in which the language is used. Learning to become a member of a community of practice (which many of our learners aim to do) is, however, a complex issue. Membership of communities of practice, as Rock (2005, p. 79) argues, "is both accomplished and ratified" (or not) through our use of language and our participation in these genres. We learn how to participate *at the same time* as we participate in specific genres. As we do this we learn not only specialized ways of using language (Casanave, 2008) but also what this use of language says about who we are or, rather, how we wish to be seen. In Butler's (1990, 2004) terms, we learn how *to do* (or as she would say, *perform*) the various roles and identities that we take on as, through the use of language (and other means), we present ourselves to others. In *saying* something, then, we both *do*, or become it (Cameron & Kulick, 2003). Thus, as we learn *to do* biology, or *to do* sociology, we, at the same time, begin to participate in and become part of that community (Hyland & Bondi, 2006).

Views of context in ESP have extended well beyond the early days of ESP. As this volume shows, sites of ESP teaching have extended to schools (Cruickshank), university classrooms (Feak; Hyland; Johns), the workplace (Lockwood, Forey, & Elias), professional education (Belcher; Bhatia; Northcott; Planken & Nickerson; Shi), immigrant settings (de Silva Joyce & Hood; Morgan & Fleming), and many other contexts of teaching and learning. Within these settings issues of audience (Hyland, this volume; Johns, 1990, 1997) and many other issues such as gender, class, and race (Bedford, 2009; Belcher, 1997, 2001; Kubota, 2003) are being brought to our attention. One of the ways in which these issues are being explored is through the use of critical ethnographies (Starfield, 2009; Talmy, 2009). Critical ethnography has enormous potential in ESP research to help us understand the "what could be" (Madison, 2005, p. 5; Thomas, 1993, p. 5) of our students' goals that will help them become central, rather than peripheral (Lave & Wenger, 1991) members of their desired academic, professional, or other communities. Thus, together with our extended view of genre (Belcher, 2004, 2006; Johns, 2008; Paltridge, 2007), the notion of situated learning and communities of practice has important implications for how we think about what we do in ESP classrooms as well as how we go about doing it.

And, finally, we have the issue of needs which, as Northcott and Shi (this volume) point out, is still a central issue in ESP teaching and research. Here too, ethnographies are playing an important part in helping us understand what it is that our learners need to do with language in order to achieve their particular goals. Flowerdew (2008), for example, through his use of corpus analytic and ethnographic techniques, has aimed to get an inside view of professional writers' expertise by exploring not only what professional writers do, but also why they do it. In his study, Flowerdew found the genres he was exploring were being written within particular constraints, with the writers using genre templates to write their texts, something that is often seen negatively in the genre literature. This reminds us of Devitt's (2004) discussion of genre where she says both choice and constraint are features of genres and that it is not the case that choice is good and constraint is always bad. Nor, as she says, is it a case of "anything goes." Indeed, sometimes there are reasons for being less creative in the use of particular genres. Our learners need to know, then, how far they can go and still be successful users of a genre. These kinds of analysis can help us understand how people, in Austin's (1975) terms, "do things with words" in order to get things done; that is, how they use words in repeated communicative events and as repeated social practices in order to achieve particular goals. Hyland (2002) has made the case for increased specificity of this kind in ESP research and teaching. What he has shown is how far we have come in understanding how people "do things with words" (and do them differently) in different disciplinary settings. He also, importantly, argues that we need to explore *why* people do things in the ways that they do. As he points out, people may do the same thing—for example establish credibility, argue, or persuade— but do it very differently in different situations. Research in ESP, then, can be critical, it can be ethnographic, and it can be specific. Research of this kind can give us an inside view of the worlds in which our learners are wishing to participate. It can, at the same time, ask "what if" and "what could be" in terms of what their participation in these worlds might mean.

Each of the chapters in this book has shown us, in different ways, how far we have come as well as given us direction for where we might go in ESP theory and practice and how we might get there. To paraphrase the work of Johns (1997), different texts, roles, and contexts lead to different ways of doing things with words, different ways of joining in on disciplinary and professional conversations, and different "ways of belonging." As Costly (2008, p. 85) has argued, all of this is not innate. It is something people learn and something they learn to do. This book has shown, in different ways, what this learning might entail, and moves us forward in our thinking about how we might help ESP learners do this.

*   *   *

BRIAN PALTRIDGE is professor of TESOL at the University of Sydney. He is author of *Genre, Frames and Writing in Research Settings* (1997), *Making Sense of Discourse Analysis* (2000), *Genre and the Language Learning Classroom* (2001), *Discourse Analysis* (2006), *Thesis and Dissertation Writing in a Second Language* (with Sue Starfield, 2007), and with his TESOL colleagues at the University of Sydney, *Teaching Academic Writing* (2009). With Sue Starfield, he co-edits the journal *English for Specific Purposes*.

REFERENCES

Austin, J. L., (1975). *How to do things with words*. Cambridge, UK: Cambridge University Press.

Barton, D., & Tusting, K. (Eds.). (2005). *Beyond communities of practice: Language power and social context*. Cambridge, UK: Cambridge University Press.

Bazerman, C. (1994). Systems of genres and the enactment of social intentions. In A. Freedman & P. Medway (Eds.), *Genre and the new rhetoric* (pp. 79–101). London: Taylor & Francis.

Bedford, S. L. (2009). *A critical ethnography of race in business English education*. Unpublished doctoral dissertation, University of Sydney.

Belcher, D. (1997). An argument for nonadversarial argumentation: On the relevance of the feminist critique of academic discourse to L2 writing pedagogy. *Journal of Second Language Writing, 6*, 1–21.

———. (2001). Does L2 writing theory have gender? In T. Silva & P. K. Matsuda (Eds.), *On second language writing* (pp. 59–71). Mahwah, NJ: Lawrence Erlbaum.

———. (2004). Trends in teaching English for specific purposes. *Annual Review of Applied Linguistics, 24*, 165–186.

———. (2006). English for specific purposes: Teaching to perceived needs and imagined futures in worlds of work, study, and everyday life. *TESOL Quarterly, 40*, 133–156.

Biber, D. (1988). *Variation across speech and writing*. Cambridge, UK: Cambridge University Press.

————. (1992). On the complexity of discourse complexity: A multidimensional analysis. *Discourse Processes, 15,* 133–163.

Butler, J. (1990). *Gender trouble: Feminism and the subversion of identity.* New York: Routledge.

————. (2004). *Undoing gender.* London: Routledge.

Cameron, D., & Kulick, D. (2003). *Language and sexuality.* Cambridge, UK: Cambridge University Press.

Casanave, C. P. (2008). Learning participatory practices in graduate school: Some perspective-taking by a mainstream educator. In C. P. Casanave & X. Li (Eds.), *Learning the literacy practices of graduate school: Insiders' reflections on academic enculturation* (pp. 14–31). Ann Arbor: University of Michigan Press.

Costly, T. (2008). "You are beginning to sound like an academic": Finding and owning your academic voice. In C. P. Casanave & X. Li (Eds.), *Learning the literacy practices of graduate school: Insiders' reflections on academic enculturation* (pp. 74–87). Ann Arbor: University of Michigan Press.

Devitt, A. (2004). *Writing genres.* Carbondale: Southern Illinois University Press.

Flowerdew, J. (2008). *The textual and the ethnographic in genre analysis for ESP.* Colloquium presentation, American Association of Applied Linguistics Conference, Washington, DC.

Halliday, M. A. K. (1991). Towards probabilistic interpretations. In E. Ventola (Ed.), *Functional and systemic linguistics: Approaches and uses* (pp. 39–61). Berlin: Mouton de Gruyter.

Hutchinson, T., & Waters, A. (1987). *English for specific purposes: A learning centred approach.* Cambridge, UK: Cambridge University Press.

Hyland, K. (2002). Specificity revisited: How far should we go? *English for Specific Purposes, 21,* 385–395.

————. (2004). *Disciplinary discourses: Social interactions in academic writing.* Ann Arbor: University of Michigan Press.

Hyland, K., & Bondi, M. (Eds.). (2006). *Academic discourse across disciplines.* Bern, Switzerland: Peter Lang.

Johns, A. M. (1990). L1 composition theories: Implications for developing theories of L2 composition. In B. Kroll (Ed.), *Second language writing: Research insights for the classroom* (pp. 24–36). Cambridge, UK: Cambridge University Press.

————. (1997). *Text, role and context: Developing academic literacies.* Cambridge, UK: Cambridge University Press.

————. (2008). Genre awareness for the novice student: An on-going quest. *Language Teaching, 41,* 237–252.

————. (2009). Situated invention and genres: Assisting Generation 1.5 students in developing rhetorical flexibility. In M. Roberge, M. Siegal, & L. Harklau (Eds.), *Generation 1.5 in college composition: Teaching academic writing to U.S.-educated learners of ESL*. Mahwah, NJ: Lawrence Erlbaum.

Kubota, R. (2003). New approaches to gender, class, and race in second language writing. *Journal of Second Language Writing, 12*, 31–47.

Lave, J., & Wenger, E. (1991). *Situated learning: Legitimate peripheral participation*. Cambridge, UK: Cambridge University Press.

Lea, M. (1994). 'I thought I could write until I came here': Student writing in higher education. In G. Gibbs (Ed.), *Improving student learning: Theory and practice* (pp. 216–226). Oxford, UK: Oxford Centre for Staff Development.

Madison, D. S. (2005). *Critical ethnography: Method, ethics, and performance*. Thousand Oaks, CA: Sage.

Nickerson, C. (2005). English as a lingua franca in international business contexts. *English for Specific Purposes, 24*, 367–380.

Paltridge, B. (2007). Approaches to genre in ELT. In J. Cummins & C. Davison (Eds.), *The international handbook of English language teaching* (Vol. 2, pp. 849–861). Norwell, MA: Springer Publications.

Rock, F. (2005). "I've picked some up from a colleague": Language, sharing and communities of practice in an institutional setting. In D. Barton & K. Tusting (Eds.), *Beyond communities of practice: Language, power and social context* (pp. 77–104). Cambridge, UK: Cambridge University Press.

Starfield, S. (2009). Ethnographies. In B. Paltridge & A. Phakiti (Eds.), *Research Methods in Applied Linguistics*. London: Continuum.

Swales, J. M. (2004). *Research genres: Explorations and applications*. Cambridge, UK: Cambridge University Press.

Talmy, S. (2009). Critical research in applied linguistics. In B. Paltridge & A. Phakiti (Eds.), *Research methods in applied linguistics*. London: Continuum.

Tardy, C. (2003). A genre system view of the funding of academic research. *Written Communication, 20*, 7–36.

Thomas, J. (1993) *Doing critical ethnography*. Newbury Park, CA: Sage.

Wenger, E. (1998), *Communities of practice: Learning, meaning and identity*. Cambridge, UK: Cambridge University Press.

Index

Academically bilingual, 85
Academic knowledge, negotiating, 29–31
Academic literacy instruction in North American tertiary education, history of, 42–43
Academic writing, 61
Accelerated Schools movement, 29
Aims and Scope statements in journals, 92
Alderson, J. C., 151, 158
American education, reforms in, 29
Annual Review of Applied Linguistics, 70
Annual Review of Information Science and Technology, 70
Anstrom, K., 22–23
Antecedent genres, 9
Applied linguistics, 108, 109
Atkinson, D., 63
Auerbach, E., 279
Austin, J. L., 293
Australian Government Publishing Service, 245
Australian Sydney School, 208
Authentic materials
  as models for teaching, 258
  presence of, in classroom, 9
Authentic pedagogy, 29, 30

Bachman, L., 27, 149, 150, 151, 158
Backward mapping, 31–32
Badger, R., 171, 172
Bakan, A., 266, 277
Bakhtin, M. M., 44, 187, 212

BALEAP (British Association of Lecturers in English for Academic Purposes), 12
Banerjee, J., 151, 158
Bank of English, 4, 5
Bargiela-Chiappini, F., 108, 109, 110, 112, 122, 128, 129
Barron, C., 236, 237
Bartholomae, D., 42
Bazerman, C., 44, 187, 208, 291
Beardsley, R. S., 216, 217, 222
Belcher, Diane D., 1, 2, 3, 9, 63, 67, 68, 69–70, 76, 108, 109, 111, 215, 229, 239, 240, 265, 292
BELF (Business English as a Lingua Franca), 5, 15, 129
  comparing professional and aspiring negotiators, 117–20
  consequences of choosing, as corporate language, 114–17
  in multiparty, multicultural business meetings, 120–24
Bell, J., 26, 280
Benesch, S., 6, 7, 13, 42, 43, 46, 219, 265, 270
Bhatia, Vijay K., 4, 15, 45, 127, 167, 171, 172, 173, 178, 180, 186, 187, 189, 203, 292
Biber, D., 290
Biley, F., 235, 236
Bilingual English content classes, 25
Blicq's Summary-Background-Facts-Outcome model, 133
Bloch, J., 72–73
Blogs, 4

297